D0983713

The Men
I Have Chosen
for Fathers

The Men
I Have Chosen
for Fathers

Literary and Philosophical
Passages

Marion
Montgomery

University of Missouri Press
Columbia and London

Copyright © 1990 by
The Curators of the University of Missouri
University of Missouri Press, Columbia, Missouri 65201
Printed and bound in the United States of America
All rights reserved

5 4 3 2 1   94 93 92 91 90

Library of Congress Cataloging-in-Publication Data

Montgomery, Marion.
    The men I have chosen for fathers : literary and philosophical
passages / Marion Montgomery.
        p.   cm.
    ISBN 0–8262–0740–5 (alk. paper)
    I. Title
PS3525.04623M46   1990
813'.54—dc20   90–10854
                                                              CIP

∞™ This paper meets the requirements of the
American National Standard for Permanence of Paper
for Printed Library Materials, Z39.48, 1984.

Designer: Darin M. Powell
Typesetter: Connell-Zeko Type & Graphics
Printer: Thomson-Shore, Inc.
Binder: Thomson-Shore, Inc.
Type face: Sabon

Beyond this quiet valley, the men I have chosen for fathers
    release me. I think they are dying, but with words as firm
    as white stones that whisper the water here by me,
Saying smoothly: what matter—the rain has several virtues.

—"On Fishing Creek, November,
While Waiting Rain after Drought,"
in *Stones from the Rubble*

Contents

Preface   ix

Acknowledgments   xi

Introduction: Ceremony and the Regional Spirit   1

I. In Defense of Evil   9

II. Flannery O'Connor's Sacramental Vision   28

III. Cleanth Brooks and the Life in Art   39

IV. Robert Frost: One Who Shrewdly Pretends   52

V. Ezra Pound: The Quest for Paradise   62

VI. Richard Weaver against the Establishment   103

VII. Solzhenitsyn at Harvard   128

VIII. Solzhenitsyn as Southerner   146

IX. Eric Voegelin and the End of Our Exploring   172

X. Eric Voegelin as Prophetic Philosopher   194

Eric Voegelin as Prophetic Philosopher: Afterthoughts   213

Afterword: Looking Before and After   232

Index   239

Preface

The end is where we start from. . . .
Every phrase and every sentence is an end and a beginning,
Every poem an epitaph.

—T. S. Eliot, "Little Gidding"

I have selected these pieces from essays published over the past twenty-five years. In editing them, I have also revised them somewhat, so that most of them differ from the original publication. I have not ordered this selection according to dates of publication, intending to enhance thematic elements. There is a development in the essays, though not a rigid pursuit. In general, the first essays move from a concern with the literature of the Southern Renaissance to a consideration of that New England "regionalist" Robert Frost, who is more closely allied in his vision to Poe than to his longtime friend and summer neighbor Donald Davidson. The center piece considers Ezra Pound, who was (one might say) haunted by the influence of the regional on art, even as he fled one place for another, ending up in a very limited region, a cage at Pisa. This is a turning point in the collection, structurally and thematically, Pound serving as counterpoint to my concerns. From what is said of Pound we may perhaps better appreciate a regionalist like Richard Weaver, who is as severe as Pound in his own attacks upon the intellectual establishment.

From Weaver, we turn to Solzhenitsyn and Voegelin. As Pound fled east to England, France, Italy, they in their own due season reversed the flight. And though they may be at first thought rather widely removed from Donald Davidson and Allen Tate and William Faulkner, what we discover in them is an affinity: a common concern about Western civilization, out of their understanding of man's nature in society. As Pound is a counterpoint, Solzhenitsyn and Voegelin are complements, with the advantage that, widely removed from each other and from those principals in the Southern Renaissance, their concerns help make clear that the "southern" vision is universal, out of the local. What is thus emphasized is the importance of a central theme running throughout this selection: the difference between the provincial mind and the regional mind. One might say that the principle holding these pieces together is my own belief, made firmer over the years, that we are each born provincial, but with gifts of being sufficient to become regional. I intend to suggest that, whether we realize this truth about ourselves as discrete persons or not, we are moved in our intellectual actions by the tensional pulls to be either provincial or regional, in a battle whose locus is our individual will. Such a dilemma of intellect, I hold, is a consequence of our given nature as intellectual creatures. If I have been sufficiently persuasive in supporting the point, perhaps this book will prove helpful in the recovery of that regional vision I believe necessary to the order of the person, the family, and the community. Such is a condition that may make one more comfortably at home, wherever home happens to be in respect to geography. I myself come at last back to my own place, in the "Afterword," trusting that at least I have become a sounder regionalist for the journey here made.

Acknowledgments

Versions of these essays first appeared in periodicals and in edited collections, and I acknowledge with gratitude those first showings: *Chronicles of Culture*; *Crisis*; *Denver Quarterly*; *Frost Centennial Essays II*, edited by Jac Tharpe (University Press of Mississippi); *Georgia Review*; *Journal of Popular Culture*; *Modern Age*; *Southern Humanities Review*; *Southern Review*; *This World*; *Why the South Will Survive*, edited by Clyde Wilson (University of Georgia Press). I wish especially to express gratitude to the Earhart Foundation for support in the preparation of this manuscript.

The Men
I Have Chosen
for Fathers

Introduction
Ceremony and the Regional Spirit

We come into the sun out of the mystery of silence and move toward the dark wisdom of silence; we manage to make an amazing deal of noise by the way.

Let me cite two texts as background to the words that are to follow, words that must attempt a just correspondence to the reality of our existence as intellectual creatures. The first is an epigraph that Ezra Pound cites approvingly: "Intelligence is international; stupidity is national; art is local." The second is from an essay by Allen Tate called "The New Provincialism," in which he expresses alarm over our civilization's general decay from the local: "Regionalism is . . . limited in space but not in time. The provincial attitude is limited in time but not in space. . . . [P]rovincialism is that state of mind in which regional men lose their origin in the past and its continuity into the present, and begin every day as if there had been no yesterday."

With Pound, I take poetry or any making by intellect as necessarily local. For intellect uses the world immediately adjacent to the poet's mind and senses, whatever modifications his mind may give it in an attempt upon the universal. It uses the language the poet hears, or thinks he hears, however he may adapt that language to his sense of form. Time and place nevertheless are always threats to language, as they are to man, who is by his soundest differentiation the user of signs, of "language." Time and space limit language's spirit, even as they also threaten to overcome that spirit that announces itself through language. The world's threat, the dangers of time and place, is inevitable, given the soul's anxiety for autonomy. That is, time and place burden soul with insistences upon its finiteness. The world that particularizes finite soul, let us say, is a tyrannical host to any person, and so of necessity to the poet. There are two senses of *tyrannical host* here, the juxtaposition of which suggests the world's threatening sustenance: *tyrannical* on the one hand as we speak it of Pisistratus at Greece's high point, or on the other of Stalin; *host* as we speak it of Chaucer's Franklin, or of the oak's relation to mistletoe.

The local—the world adjacent, as revealed to the poet's mind—is consequently the poet's relevant concern insofar as he hopes to transcend time and place by his poetry. The greatest of our poets know this; and so do we teachers

1

or readers, in consequence of which those burdens to poetry signified by time and place are concerns we must address in our attempt to understand the effect of great poetry upon us. After the profound effect of *Oedipus the King* upon us, who does not become fascinated with fifth-century Athens? And so on down the line—you supply the poems and poets of thirteenth-century Florence, fourteenth- and sixteenth-century London, nineteenth-century Paris, twentieth-century Nashville. For the poet's reader no less than for himself, the local—the coincidence of event with time and place—threatens the larger resonances of that event called poetry, whose proper arena is a timeless placelessness. The danger of time and place to poetry is the possible entrapment of poetry by history.

Now the problem the poet has in achieving a transcendence of the local in his art—in moving his art beyond the jealous intrusions of the local—does not lie in his struggle with time and place so that he may escape them, as if escape were the primary end, though this has been the poet's general inclination in my lifetime. As if one might by going to New York or London or Paris thereby throw off all the iron weights upon the wings of his song. Such is an enduring temptation to the poet, one that Dante rejects dramatically at the outset of his great poem: his pilgrim may not climb the Mountain of Hope before he goes into and through the dark world so palpably local. The first necessity is to address time and place, engage the realities of finite existence as directly experienced. And so Dante performs that symbolic drama by descending where hope is all but abandoned, into Hell, as prelude to an awakening on Purgatory. Throughout, his poem is freighted most marvelously with the local, but most especially in his Hell. And through the bearing of that weight of the local, he arrives at last at a moment of vision, a resolution of his journey. After which, however, he must return to the presence of time and place, back into this present moment in this discrete place to sing his journey.

If great poetry is of necessity local, we may I believe distinguish it from a lesser poetry that also uses the local. That is, some poetry may be said to be *provincial* rather than *regional*, in Tate's senses of those terms. It is a regional deportment toward the world of the local, I believe, that leads to a transcendence of the local, for the poet no less than for those of separate callings, since by nature all are intellectual creatures. Dante's election of vulgar Italian is evidence of a stirring regional spirit put in operation against a provincial attitude toward Latin as the necessary instrument of any high poetry, an attitude incidentally that brought Latin's death at last. And Shakespeare's address to Plutarch might exasperate a Ben Jonson, but it leads to that sort of "regionalizing," that, as E. A. Robinson puts it (into Ben Jonson's mouth), allows Shakespeare to fill

> . . . out of his
> Miraculous inviolable increase
> . . . Ilion, Rome, or any town you like
> Of olden time with timeless Englishmen.

Whether a poet turn out to be provincial or regional in his bearing toward the local is determined, I would have it, by a piety that is almost presumptuous. Piety here is the discriminating reverence through which the poet takes and uses the local, and the threat of presumption lies in his *taking*. Piety is the mode of his ceremonial awareness of time and place. (I define ceremonial awareness as an action, whether or not words are said aloud.) The poet *must* use the local, that which is mediate through his senses to mind of the transcendent. But as we have been saying, he may use the local in a provincial or regional way. The difference is revealed by his deportment in relation to his origins and in relation to the immediacy of the time and place that impinge upon his discrete being. In respect to provincialism, consider that the terms *academic* and *beat*, as applied to poets, have been about equally terms of derision. When either term is used in derogation, it is intended to carry some of the onus in our term *provincial*. *Academic* poetry means poetry that takes form to be a mechanical relating of metrics to metaphor by wit, sanctioned primarily by history, the whole activity of this poetry at last divorced of the poet's commitment to *what* he is saying or to *that* of which he speaks. On the other hand, *beat* poetry means those ceremonies of naive innocence "full of passionate intensity," whose origins the beat poet takes to be at least no more remote than that last great "happening" for his benefit, whether World War II, or the Korean War, or the Vietnam War, or, in dull times, Irangate.

But whether regionally or provincially academic or beat, all poetry has one aspect in common—some degree of the ceremonial. From Homer's invocation of the muse to Allen Ginsberg's mad incantation of his own spirit through a catalog of epithets. Whatever the use or abuse, it is through the ceremonial that one may recover that regional state of awareness of existence that I hold desirable. Indeed, *regional* as I mean it is that state of mind in which one is most acutely aware of the necessity of those ceremonies of innocence that Yeats announces our age to have lost. His lines are desperate ones, perhaps the most often quoted from his vast work, though honored more for their apparent topical (*provincial*) cogency than for their timeless virtues. They do touch a sore spot in decaying community, but the symptom of soreness—even of acute pain—if taken to be merely topical loses recognition that community is always in decay. Yeats remarked, between wars, that

> Turning and turning in the widening gyre
> The falcon cannot hear the falconer;

Things fall apart; the center cannot hold;
Mere anarchy is loosed upon the world,
The blood-dimmed tide is loosed, and everywhere
The ceremony of innocence is drowned;
The best lack all conviction, while the worst
Are full of passionate intensity.

Spiritual and intellectual maturity, which I assume as desirable, is a growth in which the blood-dimmed tide of the self is reduced from that anarchy bred always in any time or place by the phantom desire of individual autonomy. A poet might put it that, through ceremony, the blood of the self and the bread of the local become transformed beyond the mere provincialities of self or of place. Maturity in the soul is a growth from that provincialism, into which the individual soul always finds itself born, toward a regionalism which requires of it, for instance, that "brotherly deference" Confucius speaks of or that "charity" Saint Paul extols as making us members one of another. But to arrive at that awareness means we travel a long path, one that T. S. Eliot speaks of, having labored it himself. He says in "Little Gidding," "the end of all our exploring / Will be to arrive where we started / And know the place for the first time." That is, maturity in the discrete person is reached when he returns to the local, himself transformed, as Dante the man must do if he is to be adequate as Dante the poet to the demands of a *Divine Comedy*. That is the burden of the greatest poetry, whether the spectacle of the *Odyssey* or the agony of *Oedipus* or the visionary triumph of the *Divine Comedy*. It would be simplistic, of course, to suppose that I mean here that one must literally return to the geographical point of his origin. That would be to misunderstand *arrive* in Eliot's words as Nicodemus misunderstands Christ's teaching that one must be born again. In neither saying is there the fundamental meaning that one must enter a second time into his mother's womb or into the point of place in time from which he came.

As poet, living in the shadow of these and other great strains built on supreme theme, I have been fortunate in the local. I came to an awareness of ceremonial necessities to our fallen innocence when those ceremonies were still practiced more generally than now, though they were in obvious decay for reasons that my own provincialism prevented me from understanding. (I repeat, each is born into a provincialism of the self, whatever the actualities of his time and place.) I recall now that my grandfather held a position in his family, whether blessing the family meal or presiding at the fall hog-killing, that few of my contemporaries hold as fathers or will as grandfathers. His was a position maintained through forms of ceremony more ancient than he, through which he acknowledged nature's seasons and his own responsibilities, however imperfect and unarticulated his acknowledgment. An important inheritance colored our family activities, though it was not valued always as warranted. But nevertheless such gifts always linger for the taking. And there is no statute of limitations on our coming into possession, short of death itself.

But to ceremony. Ceremony is the form of active participation in being, in celebration of the gifts of being. Thus ceremony may move us beyond a merely natural provincialism through an openness to existence itself. Ceremonies are the forms through which we discover ourselves at least higher than vegetable or animal without our depreciation of vegetable or animal; the forms whereby we acknowledge with generosity of spirit the existence of that which is separate from the self. Thus at last we may come to that most difficult generosity of all, that whereby we truly value our own self. Ceremony is necessary to that sanity and health whereby we can say that we are at home in the world, and know thereby that at a higher level we are only acceptable guests of being for a brief duration of time and place. That is the point at which we turn to the local and see it for the first time.

At its most basic, ceremony is orderly awareness toward existence. Its most immediate instrument, given our created nature, is language. Which means that, in high poetry, form is neither mechanical nor arbitrary. It is the ceremonial use of language helping to direct desire so that desire may prove worthy of the desiring soul, a point perhaps neglected by too many poets, academic or beat. Language implies an imperative nature in ceremony, whether one look to the grammar of a sentence or to the meter, rhyme, logic of a sonnet. The major poets of our century—Yeats, Eliot, Pound, the Nashville Fugitives—have felt that at certain points of our history there was a more general respect for the ceremonial nature of language than in our own age. They recognized in history as well periods very like our own in which ceremony was in rapid decay. I cite one indication of such decay; Thucydides says, in the *Peloponnesian Wars* 3.82–84, discussing that growth of provincialism which destroyed the Greek states: "The meaning of words had no longer the same relation to things. . . . An attitude of perfidious antagonism everywhere prevailed; for there was no word binding enough nor oath terrible enough to reconcile enemies." And before Thucydides, Euripides dramatized the point tellingly in *Medea*, when Medea and King Aegeus attempt to discover an oath sufficiently strong to bind themselves in an agreement with mutual benefit. Of course the danger to the prophetic poet, if he underline a provincialism become dominant at a particular time in a particular place, is the wrath of the provincial mind. We remember that Euripides died in exile.

Ours, then, is not the only age plagued by "credibility gaps." And our Thucydides (one of them), Ezra Pound, for fifty years warned us to look to our language, lest we find ourselves overcome by disorderly unawareness. Still, the vestigial manifestations of ceremony have become for us increasingly routine and mechanical, largely under the pressures of technology. We have virtually abandoned intelligence. Government forms to be filled out in quadruplicate, filed alphabetically, then thrown in the trash can; or worse entered into the computer to determine each individual by button pushing. Our traffic rituals involved in getting home through the evening rush hour. Our envelope mailing to the Community Chest at the end of the month when we pay the light bill. Discrimination lost through language abandoned, it is little wonder that one take any piece of music or art or any poem to be as good as any other—so long as none of them breaks too disturbingly into our nervously autonomous awareness. We have become accustomed to, and prefer, only a foggy throbbing of the heart, one still allowed insofar as we are sufficiently isolated in our self from the techniques of technology. Meanwhile, technique, void of ceremony, becomes the Black Mass of the provincial mind. On the point, see Jacques Ellul's *Technological Society*.

Ceremony, let me insist, is an imperative wherever and whenever there is a legitimate necessity of addressing oneself to something or someone other than the self. Impious ceremony, dispirited technique, is the mechanical, though self-conscious, conduct of the self in nature and society, whether we are *On the Road* with Jack Kerouac or caught up in sterilized iambics with the "Cornbelt Metaphysicals," as Kenneth Rexroth characterized the academic poets of his day. As poet, I am disturbed that impious ceremony dominates life as well as art; the symptoms are in the order of precedence in our traffic rituals, whether in freeway competition or doorway competition; whether in the presence of stranger to stranger, teacher to pupil, father to son. The four-way stop on our roads is its parable. We have manner still; and so long as it yields efficiency we defer to manner. But we have lost manners, the rituals of community ceremony, the tradition of community beyond mere history or mechanics.

Consider the ceremonial aspects of this most common experience: we each of us on occasion, and many as a matter of routine (that is, ritual voided of the ceremonial), stop at some Burger Haven for a hamburger, french fries, milk-shake. In a building vaguely reminiscent of the temple, we encounter a hierarchy of servers, each related to the other by technological rank. They are likely to wear robes of office, inscribed shirt and cap at least. They perform a service through the disciplines of technique, vaguely reminiscent of ritual. The immediate priest at the window performs the final act to absolve us of our hunger. From the beginning of the operation we witness gestures of communion, but they are gestures from which the significance of "give us this day our daily bread" has been rather carefully removed through the dictates of technology, the new god of our international provincialism. Any spilled orange juice (or in the new ceremonial language, "O.J.") is hardly a libation. What we witness is mechanism usurping message, technique absorbing any virtues of piety toward the mediating local, most immediately the hamburger in hand.

When I consider my awareness of myself in this blind new world of the Burger Temple and reflect on the lost piety toward existence in its mechanics of ceremony, when I remember at least my grandfather's table, I must conclude that the Burger Temple hardly feeds the body what is required, however fresh the beef or vitamin-added the O.J. One grants an efficiency; the Temple serves a multitude, and the biological body itself may flourish. It is even possible in such deadening routine perhaps to recover living ceremony. But only if we don't develop an ulcer from a nagging spirit in us still ravenous for food raised by proper ceremony to the virtues of daily bread, without which we perish— ourselves merely a sacrificial food to the new god, technology.

I have a rather dark view of the possibilities of our survival as "Western" civilization, of our survival as a particular nation. I have too regularly borne in upon me the evidence that "stupidity is national," evidence that intelligence lusting after provincial internationalism loses the art of the local, so that only by calamity or accident does it seem possible to return to the local and know it in a "regional" way—that is, under the aspect of eternity. My view will seem a dark one to many. But I also see cause for hope, the same cause that has always been present for a recovery from any decline in any epoch. That is why I am most constantly concerned with a particular institution in which the ceremonies of innocence have been traditionally exalted, from Homer's day to our own, though it is an institution in rapid decay in our time, so distressingly rapid the decay that we need reminding often that so it was at Athens in Thucydides' day and at Rome when Petronius wrote his black-humor novel, *The Satyricon*.

I mean, of course, the institution we call the family, now so much a popular concern. What I urge as necessary to community recovery is the restoration of ceremony in the family. Only so may there be any stability possible in this third great wave of Western history now ebbing from us. There is certainly little hope of recovery in those *techniques* for family recovery, considered and argued for and acted upon, that take origin in abstractionism by institute or agency. How- ever empowered, they must fail. For it is only from ceremony recovered at the most local level that one may learn the piety necessary to the recovery of family, a piety such as that which bound Telemachus and Odysseus, Anchises and Aeneas to Ascanius. Otherwise, family must become itself a miniature agency for the operation of technique, a block in the pyramid raised to technology. Family is corporate, but not in a legal sense. More literally, family is a body in nature raised by ceremony in a sacramental way beyond the merely natural, though always permeated by the natural. Out of ceremony—the discipline of body and mind in respect to the self as the self must relate to all that is not itself—out of ceremony eventually is recovered a manner of being larger than the naturally provincial being of the child before he finds his place in the family and in a community of families. A reverence for family, as does the reverence for self, leads to reverence of selves and families of selves. Thus only may be restored the prospect of viable—life-giving—civilization.

It is to the family that we must look for such recovery. And we may with some expectation and hope look to the poet in this struggle for recovery. For his is the gift of words sacramentally transformed through piety, through his "regional" address to being, that may recover to us lost and forgotten ways of our proper being in the world. But lest we be misled by a sentimentally attractive Utopian desire for such recovery, and thus made susceptible to hopelessness, we must remember always Saint Paul's caution to the Hebrews: "Here we have no continuing city." We might remember as well Eliot's imperative words against that despair that always succeeds the collapse of piety: "if the Temple is to be cast down / We must first build the Temple." And always, in any time or place, we build the temple of stones from the rubble. As we turn back to those stones strewn amid history's rubble, back to the local which we must encounter in this very moment in this very place, it is possible we may recover a visionary moment, recognizing that the end of all our exploring has indeed pointed to our returning whence we started to see that place truly for the first time. Always, from that moment, we must move on in time and place, though perhaps with firmer assurance that at last "all manner of thing shall be well."

I. In Defense of Evil

*The ideal embodied in Launcelot . . . offers the only possible escape
from a world divided between wolves who do not understand, and
sheep who cannot defend, the things which make life desirable.*

—C. S. Lewis, "The Necessity of Chivalry"

i

Southern literature, like the South itself, is such a various creature that one is ill-advised to pronounce dogmatically upon it, though that is a temptation difficult to resist—caught up as we have been by that impressive flowering of letters in this century known as the "Southern Renaissance." At risk of some presumption, then, I should like to limit our attention to a particular kind of Southern literature—or rather to a particular kind of Southern writer who may be distinguished from a variety of his brothers, in and out of the South. I feel a special affinity to this writer, and for that reason let me here give warning that my testimony is partisan, though I believe it will support sound generalizations.

The writer I want to single out from his fellows is an illusive creature, sometimes even to himself—self-knowledge being the treacherous knowledge it is. Besides which, our writer is not likely to practice his art from a position he has established firmly by dogma or ideology, though he may come to such a pass by the long labor of art. He is more likely intent upon looking at his immediate world with wonder and curiosity; he takes a delight in his immediate neighbor's multitudinous engagements of that world, both for his neighbor's and for his art's sake. He grows within that world, rather than choosing to stand outside it as separate from or superior to it. Certainly he does not suppose himself its creator when he is pleased by its reflection in the work he makes with words. One of his habits is that, though he may wander from his neighborhood, he is apt to return and settle down in it. That is, he does not long believe that in order to make artful use of his world he must live in New York City or on the continent. He does not feel driven, as James Joyce's young artist Stephen does, into "silence, exile, and cunning." Another sign of his peculiarity may be that he survives in his native, or even adopted, land in part through his sense of humor—without which he might well be left with only the resources of wit and irony to

9

reach an accommodation with the mystery of existence. For wit and irony, unmoderated by some humor, become modes of dissociation from existence. The point is difficult to refine briefly, but I'm attempting to define a humor in the writer himself that reflects his acceptance of the limits of his power to shape or create existence. This humor is necessary to the writer's acceptance of his own humanity, an act more difficult to the writer sometimes because he so easily confuses himself as maker of *a* world with God, the Maker of *the* world.

Compare the general attitude of two great writers, James Joyce and William Faulkner, toward the country and countrymen who fed their fiction. There are many likenesses between them, particularly the strong attraction they share to the immediate and local, to a history that is in their blood and memory, at every point adjacent to their senses in a most immediate way. Still, I at least sense in Joyce's fiction a feeling of discomfort with the ordinary Dubliner, almost at times an embarrassment in his presence, which seems to require the poet to distance himself through irony and wit, but not for his art's sake alone. Not just Stephen Dedalus but Joyce himself might fight against sounding like that agonizing Quinton Compson at Harvard who insists at the top of his voice that he DOESN'T hate the South. I'm suggesting that the distance between Faulkner and his Quinton is more marked than that between Joyce and his Stephen. In Faulkner one senses an amused acceptance of the ordinary Mississippian, an openness to the foibles of the simple, an attitude that sometimes rises to lyrical paeans or becomes entangled in a comedy of the ridiculous given an epic sweep, as in "Spotted Horses."

Incidentally, I am not suggesting that our Southern writer inevitably creates masterpieces—that such a fellow by his loving acceptance of limitations, the humility that evidences itself often as humor, is the superior of Joyce. In fact, irony and wit may be used to force a control of one's art as a means of self-protection, lest the writer's sentiment become sentimentality. The fear that sentiment may turn treacherous to art haunts Joyce, I think, but I think one must search hard to find instances of just plain bad writing in the body of his work; the task is easier in Faulkner's. Our Southern writer is not always the consummate craftsman, though he is often so. For craft has to do more immediately with the mystery of a writer's particular gifts and with his industry in the service of that limited gift. These more personal characteristics will always set him apart as discrete from any category like Southern or Irish or Russian.

We must not confuse our writer with the Southerner who may be said to write "about" the South, any more than we would confuse any writer using Irish matter with Joyce or Yeats. We certainly don't want to confuse him with those who intend to please a tourist curiosity—those who cater to an amorphous, deracinated audience whose number in this world is legion, whether they be titillated by "Too-alure-alure-a" or "Way Down upon the Sewanee River."

Frank Yerby or Margaret Mitchell may serve as example here of the writer who cultivates an audience's residual interest in the historical—our vague nostalgia for origins that so easily atrophies into an appetite for the fanciful and sentimental—the last sad state into which our ontological hunger may fall. Our writer to the contrary is intense in his concern for concrete reality as it may give body to his art, incorporate his word world. But that interest includes his concern for the hard complexities of history. He knows that our history, anchored in place, has both a threatening and a loving immediacy which our indulgent fancy violates at hazard to artist or audience. That is, he knows in words I borrow from T. S. Eliot that "A people without history / Is not redeemed from time, for history is a pattern / Of timeless moments" that bear inexorably upon this very moment, in this very place. Those moments may not be denied without fatal distortions of the present which, in a favorite Faulknerian word, "bequeath" deformations of reality to the future—a sort of congenital spiritual distortion of community, if I may be allowed a metaphysical trope.

Our writer, we are saying, has a strong sense of place and person in a relationship to each other, a nucleus to the growing body of a community in time; and such a community always bears deep down both the past and the future. He does not suppose that the particulars of either setting or character in his fiction are created ex nihilo by the artist, though he may and should enjoy those special freedoms Aristotle distinguishes in art as opposed to history, the freedoms of the *possible* or *probable*. He knows through his very breathing that, in the world he inhabits as man, the seasons of being are affected at a depth more profound than any empirical measure of time or place allows. Thus, although he is likely to focus upon a single house and family, a small town, a county, he does so not to lament social poverty or psychological isolation, as temporal uses of the world might be content to do, but to reveal a largeness hidden in the limited. Nor does he use the local—the "Southern"—to dramatize what turns out to be only a private, isolated version of the fabulous Self lost among the accidental stars. That sort of writer may write of any place or no place, since place is neither congenital to nor particularly relevant to his concern; he is a displaced person by preference. If he were to put the point, he might preach it as Haze Motes does in Flannery O'Connor's *Wise Blood*:

> I preach there are all kinds of truth, your truth and somebody else's, but behind all of them, there's only one truth and that is that there's no truth. . . . Where you come from is gone, where you thought you were going to never was there, and where you are is no good unless you can get away from it. Where is there a place for you to be? No place. Nothing outside you can give you any place.

The placeless writer may use the same material world as Flannery O'Connor, but it will not be used in the same way, for what Miss O'Connor sees and what our Motes-like writer sees are quite different, though they look at the same object.

Our Southern writer does not see himself as merely the creator of a textual world, a cage of words such as Haze's, which he builds to serve as an arena for the antics of that aberrant modern god, the Self. That Self has lost its belief in any reality separate from its own marooned awareness, and as Dante would find very appropriate, it is its own torment. And if our writer does not believe that his own consciousness occupies such a closed world, neither will he see art as so far divorced from his fellows that each lonely mind is forever trapped within its symbolic posturings—its symbols having no extrinsic referents and its order internally willed but irrelevant to any meaning, even to the trapped Self. That is the current fad in much of our criticism and philosophy and art, but our writer sees it as a fad, perhaps not unrelated to such mass isolationism as disco dancing.

Put in a positive, older, and intellectually more viable way: our Southern writer is mimetic. He believes that art, however else it may differ from the other modes of the mind's hymns to existence—the modes of science or philosophy or theology—also bears an appreciable relation to reality beyond itself. His position on art and its ends is a corollary to his belief that the individual Self has real and not illusional relations with other Selves in communities, wherever two or three are gathered together. That is, he believes we are bound in a mystery larger than his mastery of art, without which larger binding one's art or science or philosophy becomes only a form of magic. Such a binding is larger and more inclusive than any particular calling to us within the world—to be a doctor or lawyer or writer. And so our writer will very likely begin to suspect that we are bound not only in time but beyond time, in a calling that speaks to him through the one given, a calling which underlies all the structures of his awareness, all the symbols through which he may attempt to touch reality. That one given is *existence itself*.

That larger binding, he at least senses, is within an ordering of all being that should satisfy our desire for beginning and end; without the limits of beginning and end, particularity itself ceases to have any meaning. For there are deep hungers in us for a completeness of the Self, annulling worldly beginnings and endings, hungers buried essentially in the Soul. For *ontology* and *teleology* are not merely technical names of categories of thought created by the rational mind for its entertainment, though often so used. If the philosopher, scientist, and theologian wrestle in their several ways with these seemingly abstract terms, our writer attempts as poet to incarnate a reality that feeds the hunger, to give local habitation and a name to our desire—whether he presents his hero as struggling to return to some Ithaca, as a pilgrim with momentary vision of a multifoliate rose embraced by an inexpressible light beyond all our purgatorial struggles with dark and light, or as a possessed creature trying to subdue a hundred square miles of Mississippi wilderness to his own bent desire. The end we reach toward may be a false one; our struggles for origins within the middleness of reality may be quite misguided. But our beginnings within the complexity of reality stir a valid desire for large ends. Caught in the muddling middle, we begin where all drama of the spirit must begin, in that middle. As Flannery O'Connor says of us, recognizing our shared experience of this confusing *metaxy*, this "In-Between-ness" that threatens us: "There is something in us, as storytellers and as listeners to stories, that demands that what falls at least be offered the chance to be restored."

For our writer, man's being—man's Self—cannot be an absolute agent without an originating cause or a proper end, not an accident of accidents and thus always and only the meaningless victim of a meaningless middle. For he senses or believes or knows that even accidental existence must happen within some inclusive reference if the concept of the *accidental* is to have any meaning at all. And he cannot believe that his own mind is a sufficient inclusive reference. For him, the hunger for a "chance to be restored" will become foil, in his drama, to fallen man's several dreams of progress, spawned by gnostic presumptions against being that are as ancient as that first fall in the garden, the old presumptions of the Self as dominant power in this seemingly infinite, swampy middle. Thus pride or hubris—however low and common or high and royal his agents may be—becomes the high theme of his storytelling.

Now the modern reader hungers for the redemptive act, in spite of his being inhabitant of a world that tries to deny redemption except as it may be used metaphorically to describe some psychological or sociological recovery that implies man is either the ultimate god of the meaningless middle or a mechanical part of an unexplained mechanical world. And I contend that such a hunger is a sign of the possibility of his return to health. One hungers because there is such a creature as food, Saint Thomas says. One is ill because there is such a state as health. One founders or fails or falls only as measured against some high calling to a graceful dance. Such modern hunger speaks ancient origins. But, as Miss O'Connor adds in the passage just quoted, our writer's audience has largely forgotten the cost of restoration, for our "sense of evil is diluted or lacking altogether." From her own position, the cost of evil to the individual is an absolute beyond all worldly inflations, all relative scales. It is the absolute loss of the Self. Her Tarwater, in *The Violent Bear It Away*, discovers that the cost exceeds the Self's solvency. He is consumed almost to extinction, but also discovers some restoration through the terror of an absolute Mercy that beyond all reason buys him out of self-centered bankruptcy.

Our Southern writer may not, of course, be so resolutely convinced by faith and reason of a transcendent God. Flannery O'Connor is; William Faulkner is not. But it is in the light of such argument as she makes, I think, that one begins to recognize the considerable difference between the visions radiated by the God-haunted writer like Faulkner and those versions of existence made by Man-haunted writers like Flaubert, James, Hemingway, Fitzgerald. Or, nearer home, the difference becomes conspicuous between Flannery O'Connor, Andrew Lytle, Madison Jones as Southern writers and Carson McCullers, Shirley Ann Grau, Truman Capote as Southern writers.

To borrow from our writer's Eastern cousin, Nathaniel Hawthorne, we may say that he is reluctant to stray too far from the town pump or the well on the old family place precisely because, despite the reflections of the local in such waters, he knows they are deeper than time and more healing than any words the Self may speak of and to itself alone. Still, this inclination to the local is easily misunderstood by those who would believe the homeplace-well polluted by provincialism. As I have already hinted, there is misunderstanding not only by the postmodernist anarchist mind that would drink of any muddy puddle and smack in delight to outrage the supposedly innocent among us, denying the existence of thirst even as he does so. I say supposedly innocent, remembering the Bible salesman in "Good Country People," who shatters Hulga, the existentialist with a Ph.D.: "you ain't so smart. I been believing in nothing ever since I was born."

In another direction, our Southern writer is misunderstood by that postnaturalist mind which is so heavily at home in the academy, particularly by those who see literature as a sector of our intellectual estate to be seized by the pseudosciences of sociology and psychology and turned to social and political ends. The anarchist of whom we spoke first sees mimesis as an illusion. For him, in Gerald Graff's words in *Literature against Itself* (1979), there is "no such thing as a real object outside language, no 'nature' or 'real life' outside the literary text, no real text beyond the critical interpretation, and no real persons or institutions behind the multiplicity of messages human beings produce. Everything is swallowed up in an infinite regress of textuality." Such anarchy, while destructive of the fabric of society, is not so conspicuously destructive as the alliance of sociology and psychology when turned upon the social fabric. One is tempted to remark on these pseudosciences with the irony Chaucer uses about his Physician and apothecaries: "ech of hem made other for to winne." The socio-psychologist or psycho-sociologist takes our writer's work as a local naturalism which may be made to yield evidence suited to his own gnostic ideology.

Yet his denial of nature or life is only partial in contrast to the anarchistic structuralist's. The pseudoscientist must admit the existence of some reality—the social world for the sociologist, the psychic world for the psychologist. Still, he sees it existing for the sake of being shaped, of being restructured to suit some primarily human dream. It is no accident that sociology and psychology have become dominant forces in the civil state since World War II, subordinating even Harvard economics to janitorial status in the halls of Congress and in the White House. For since the days of Auguste Comte the State has been gradually transformed into the gnostic Son of the world, the substitute Emmanuel, and the Holy Spirit of social humanity has been increasingly called into a presence as lord and giver of life to individual man, filling the embarrassing gap between human knowledge and human power in the ideological struggles to subjugate existence to human will. A humanistic priesthood has emerged, through which one is required to worship an abstraction—Humanity—as the official state religion under the threat of exile for both heresy and treason. Its principal established college of priests is called HEW, pronounced *hew*, as you know, and its energy and our substance are spent largely in hewing individual persons to fit its vague dream of an ideal citizen.

ii

We must observe carefully, then, how our Southern writer differs in his address to reality, not only from the anarchist mind, but from the gnostic directors of social and psychic being also. No matter how particular or how local his material, however deeply colored by literal social and psychological aspects of man's being, he is not so much reporter or statistician of particularity as he is witness to depths in reality beyond all facts or photographs. For he knows, again to summon Flannery O'Connor, that a "view taken in the light of the absolute will include a good deal more than one taken merely in the light provided by a house-to-house survey." One is not likely at this late date, despite those large forces that distort reality, to miss this point in Faulkner's postage-stamp county, unless one's intellect and sensibilities have been fatally atrophied. To cite once more that very articulate spokesman for our Southern writer, Flannery O'Connor, "the longer you look at one object, the more of the world you see in it; and it's well to remember that the serious fiction writer always writes about the whole world, no matter how limited his particular scene." That is why the dedicated, unblinking naturalist will always write more largely than the academic definition of *naturalism*—assuming in him a talent and industry in support of his courage in the presence of creation.

To misunderstand this point, as many critics have done in attempting to come to terms with the complexity of the Southern Renaissance, is to see this

Southern phenomenon only at its social and psychological level, the point at which our Southern writer himself begins. That is why I keep underlining my theme: for our writer, the slant of the sun upon a particular person in a particular place is more deeply significant of the large mystery of creation than is any conception of existence as a continuous accident or dead mechanism with which man is forced to struggle for an order of his own devising. He sees both the postmodernist anarchist and the gnostic disciple of old Enlightenment thought attempting to reorder creation under their Banner of Progress, when he is seeking the dance. We turn toward an immanence that denies transcendence with the coming of nominalism, of Machiavelli, the Philosophes, and their disciples. It is a turning Chesterton capsules in remarking the difference between Chaucer's world and ours: up to a certain point in the West, life is understood as a dance, after which we decide it is a race.

The Southerner of whom we are speaking is going to be suspicious of any appeal to Progress as substitute for a profound teleological object. He remembers something of the grace of the dance. He will know, in his heart if not his head—by *intellectus* if not by *ratio* as the medieval man of letters might put it—that the anarchist or the Sons of the Enlightenment dedicated to power operate out of the same false ground. For both of them the In-Between they wish to manage is an accident that has inexplicably thrown them up on the shores of a dead world. Our writer, to the contrary, sees both being itself and the conditions of man's particular being as givens. And the given implies a Giver, however confounding the approach to the Giver through the agency of those gifts. Therefore, our writer by his art opposes those violations of the world that proceed from any premise of existence as either random chaos or the order of a spiritless mechanism.

A reading of his work at what criticism has called the naturalistic level, as a ground for exercising social or psychic manipulations of complex existence, will overlook the spiritual dimension of that work, particularly its reverence of person and place and thing. For our writer, whether the version of community he presents us is on a scale so small as one of Miss O'Connor's decimated families or so large as Faulkner's rich Yoknapatawpha County, reflects the community as a spiritual organism, though fallen from fullness. Nor need one be the Thomist Miss O'Connor is to realize that in man's limited estate he necessarily approaches the spiritual in the concrete, created world that is always just at hand. To touch that world is already to reach toward its Cause, even if one realizes only feebly that his reaching is a spiritual one or is completely oblivious of the deeper hidden end that is the Cause of his reaching. The gnostic manipulator is himself subject to such a shock of recognition, as occasional conversions suggest. Man has believed for a very long time that the first intellectual step along the spiritual road is made within the country of naturalism, through one's body; it is a step made within a context of our sensual response to some reality separate from the self. The belief is in Homer and Aristotle, in Dante and Saint Thomas.

So the Southern writer we speak of observes that the increasing power claimed by a denatured naturalism these past hundred years or more—*denatured*, since nature divorced from its cause by gnostic will can be seen only as unnatural—has strangled the spiritual dimension of creation itself. Or rather, it has estranged us from that spiritual dimension, for such gnostic reconstructions of reality are fundamentally illusions and do not affect reality essentially. Our writer understands such a power to be a retrogression into a provincialism, into a primitivism, more limited than that we encounter in Homer or find revealed by the highly sophisticated explorations of scholars like Mircea Eliade. It is a provincialism exposed to us by Richard Weaver, Gerhart Niemeyer, Eric Voegelin—such scholars whom our writer may or may not have read. Our writer sees the distortions of reality, but he knows also that it is still at the level of nature that he must work. That is where the artist begins, and particularly at the level of human nature with its spectacles of the psychological and sociological and historical upon which he depends heavily for his incarnational act as artist. Each person, he says along with John Donne, is a little world made cunningly of elements and an angelic sprite. And through representations of that little world—which he places in the larger context of family and community in nature—a much larger world is revealed by his practice of similitude and dissimilitude. The more fully he reveals that little world, the more largely he speaks outward to a world beyond the boundaries of any literal time or place.

He recognizes, in words I adapt from Stark Young's contribution to *I'll Take My Stand*, that he is called to witness certain principles intrinsic to creation, not because those principles belong to him, but because he belongs to those principles. To put the point as Allen Tate might do, he is a spiritual regionalist, not an intellectual provincial, that secular gnostic of whom Eric Voegelin has written so revealingly. In Voegelin's sense of the term, which we have used more than once here, our writer finds himself deeply engaged by the "In-Between," the only immediate source for the material of his made world.[1] But he does so

1. "Existence has the structure of the In-Between, of the Platonic metaxy, and if anything is constant in the history of mankind it is the language of tension between life and death, immortality and mortality, perfection and imperfection, time and timelessness, between order and disorder, truth and untruth, sense and senselessness of existence; between *amor Dei* and *amor sui*, *l'âme ouverte* and *l'âme close*; between the virtues of openness toward the ground of being such as faith, hope and love and the vices of infolding closure such as hybris and revolt; between the moods of joy and despair; and between alienation in its double meaning of alienation from the world and alienation from God." From "Equivalences of Experience and Symbolization in History," an unpublished manuscript quoted by John H. Hallowell in his "Editor's Preface" to Eric

with an openness of mind and spirit toward the complication of existence, in consequence of which he finds himself inevitably anti-gnostic. Thus he celebrates the rich complexity of existence, although to celebrate that complexity does not mean to present it with an artificial sweetness and light. We may see this point everywhere in William Faulkner's work. In *Absalom, Absalom!* Thomas Sutpen attempts to limit existence to an arena of a hundred square miles by sheer dominance over the land and the creatures bounded by that artificial measure of nature; his attempt to manipulate man and nature is tragically shadowed. And in *Go Down, Moses*, Ike McCaslin attempts to reject any binding by place or history, abandoning his inherited land and sacrificing persons dear to him beyond his romantic imaginings, as he comes at last to realize. For Faulkner distinguishes between the responsibility of a man's stewardship within the grounds of being and man's old temptation to control being itself, the gnostic principle that Christian orthodoxy sees in our first parents' violation of creation in the Garden. There is a very complex dramatization of this distinction in *Go Down, Moses*, which I may only touch upon here to make my point a little clearer, though the rich texture of Ike's place in nature and history warrants a longer devotion.

In those stories we witness two gnostic forces in conflict. There is the obvious active destruction by the invading timber companies that ravage the Big Woods, but it is an encroachment upon a world Ike McCaslin has already abandoned through the illusion of his sacrificial act. Ike McCaslin may be described as a passive gnostic; in an ultimately destructive way he abandons his responsibility as steward of place in time. Caught between these two forces, trying to rediscover and redefine man's ordinate responsibility in nature, is McCaslin Edmonds, who must bear Ike's name even more heavily in consequence of Ike's refusal of responsibility. For he is an Edmonds and not so directly descended as Ike. Ike supposes that by relinquishing his title to Old Corothers McCaslin's land, he may separate himself from tainted history by repudiating it and in some degree "anneal" the wrongs of his forefathers. He intends a sacrificial act, but he presumes to rescue the world he inherits, to redeem time as it were, as if he could command grace. As he comes to realize at last in the story "Delta Autumn," man may be a waster of the world through the ravenous appetites so general in community, but man may also mistake himself as sufficient agent of grace, whether grace will or no. That is, Ike presumes a role that orthodox tradition allows only to Christ.

If we call this kind of Southern writing mimetic, we acknowledge that its

---

Voegelin's *From Enlightenment to Revolution* (Durham: Duke University Press, 1975). See also Voegelin's extended exploration of the idea in "Experience and History," part 2 of *Anamnesis*, translated and edited by Gerhart Niemeyer (Notre Dame: University of Notre Dame Press, 1978).

limits are determined by the order of creation. Its limits must also be distinguished from those of science or philosophy or theology. The possible or probable are displayed as dramatic speculation upon the complexity of existence in a way quite separate from those explorations made by biochemist or historian or metaphysician, as the artist slowly learns, sometimes with great difficulty. He may nevertheless present our nature in such a way that it becomes increasingly difficult for the sensitive mind to deny a spiritual dimension to reality, most particularly that spiritual dimension in man that is man's by virtue of the elemental gift of his existence. For it is out of this gift that scientist or philosopher or historian or poet fashions his responses to creation. Whether one clear and plant a few acres or exercise civil authority in Washington, D.C., the gesture toward order and growth is inevitably a gesture beyond the Self and toward the Cause of order, however willful or blind one is to the root cause of his gesture. It is the gift of being that makes gesture possible, and within this gift we are inexorably bound one to another.

For this reason we must not overlook, in our brief sketch of the Southern writer, his appearance in places other than the American South, as if we supposed him to be found only south of the Potomac River and east of the Mississippi. Thus, one may well put "Southern" in quotation marks. I have, for instance, called attention to a close kinship between those Soviet dissidents who published a collection of essays titled *From under the Rubble* in 1974 and those Southerners who published *I'll Take My Stand* in 1930. Allen Tate's late essay called "The New Provincialism" has passages strikingly interchangeable with Solzhenitsyn's much later essay "The Smatterers," particularly as they each express a mutual reverence for place and a concern for man's stewardship in place as that commitment to the created world relates to man's spiritual nature. Solzhenitsyn, like our Southern writer, recognizes in the aberrant refusal to serve, or in the rapacious pursuit of self-service, the shadow of an evil inclination in man's will that neither anarchy nor gnostic reconstructions of reality have succeeded in explaining away.

It is to this problem of evil in man that we might turn in detail, given world enough and time, to suggest why the Southern writer's very conspicuous concern for willful violence reflects a failure in man not peculiar to the South nor to recent history, though modern responses to violence are so confused as to make it appear that we here encounter a new problem. It is a sign of hope in a dark time that this literature speaks resonantly to the world in general. It is a prophetic literature, prophetic in the sense that it recalls us to the once known but now largely forgotten gifts of being. And it is this aspect of our writer's work, as well as his superb craftsmanship, that attracts attention outside the South. Man's deliberate and random evil, in the face of his obligation to pursue the good, speaks to the large confusions all about us—wherever man touches the created world. But wherever man touches the world, somewhere among his number will be found this creature we have been pursuing, the so-called Southern writer. He does not turn away from the problem of evil, or attempt to explain evil away in such a manner that we may be left comfortably irresponsible, the self-made victims of appetites we tend to elevate to the role of spiritual callings of the Self to the pathetic Self.

iii

I begin with a quotation from Richard Weaver's *Ideas Have Consequences*, that very large little book which traces the intellectual decline of the West back to William of Occam. But let us recall here that Weaver's small book was written after his intense study under Cleanth Brooks and Robert Penn Warren, published posthumously as *The Southern Tradition at Bay*. The intrusion of Occam's nominalism into that larger realism which held creation in relation to its transcendent Cause, Weaver argues, is an intrusion whose consequences divided man against himself. Early on in *Ideas Have Consequences*, Weaver says that we moderns find ourselves trapped between sentimentality and brutality: "sentimentality, with its emotion lavished upon the trivial and the absurd; . . . brutality, which can make no distinctions in the application of violence. Those who [base] their lives on the unintelligence of sentimentality fight to save themselves with the unintelligence of brutality." Thus our senseless affections and hatreds, rising out of the "unintelligence of sentimentality," lead to the large destructions of recent history with which we are so familiar, effects out of our struggle for self-justification. In our time—that is, from the time of Adolf Eichmann and Auschwitz down to the Reverend Jim Jones of Jonestown, Guyana—the gnostic's detachment from being seems increasingly to assault our residual sensibilities in terrible tableaux. It disturbs us particularly when the effects reach a level of sensational action whose spectacle no longer allows our inattention. The horror at Auschwitz or Jonestown seems a personal assault because we have forgotten the evil that is potential in each man's power over nature but are reminded by events beyond our understanding that we are nevertheless members one of another, even in such dark displays of community as mass murder. The gnostic manipulators of being, Voegelin's "directors" of the reconstructions of reality to fit millennial dreams of an infinite variety, find it expedient to obscure that potential evil common to all men, for in order to distill power from the ferment of the "popular spirit of the age" it is important that they not disturb that volatile source. Otherwise their reductions of being in *why is it important to supress the evil in man for marxist, knogstics?*

the name of Humanity make the power highly unstable. Not only must the dreamed end be persuasively presented as a common good, but the source of that power to be directed to the good end must be assumed uncontaminated, lest the hint of spiritual pollution at the source of power affect the consent of our will that the power be used to construct the dream. Little wonder then that "original sin" in that source—individual man—as either metaphorical or literal must be removed from our reflection. It can be admitted only as a lingering species of Neanderthal theology. But when an Eichmann or a Jones at last stands before us as agent of murder on a statistically grand scale, we are astounded by the seeming disparity between the destruction and the insignificant, obscure agent. Our easy dreams become disturbed. And the popular spirit stirs in a threatening way. The death penalty might even be reinstated.

We are shocked, I suggest, because we have been willingly led to forget the complexity of human nature spoken to by the concept of Original Sin, a doctrine many Southern writers are loath to abandon. For if the hero need not be an Oedipus or a Count Roland or a King Richard I, neither must the villain be so conspicuous a figure on the stage of our awareness as Iago or Count Ganelon, a point Faulkner makes with disturbing effect through his unfolding of Flem Snopes and Popeye. We tend to come to terms with a Sutpen, or with a Stalin or Hitler, our anger and bafflement assuaged as our understanding is flattered by submerged Hegelian thought. These agents are instances of a coincidence of power in dynamic if terrifying figures, when seen in that reduction of reality into the myth of our age, historicism. Through such figures move the great contending forces of an age. They become "archetypal," like Attila or Robespierre or Napoleon. Their great acts of destruction underline climaxes in the flux of history, seeming to give history a godlike direction in the flow of time when measured by our post-Hegelian mind. But then comes such a functionary as Eichmann, a high-school dropout, the failed son of a tram company accountant, who becomes an efficiency expert in transporting millions beyond time in a "final solution." He becomes an absolutist of ordered fact beyond his father's fondest dreams. And what of such a peripheral figure as the Reverend Jim Jones, who scatters the random lees of our progressivist social world on a jungle floor to be displayed in unliving color on the cover of *Time*? What of such an inconspicuous West Virginia child as that small boy buying candy at the corner store in West Virginia who suddenly blooms darkly in our evening papers out of California under the name of Charles Manson?

Anonymous, hidden evil breaks out, rises to the level of a name no longer inconspicuous, for the name itself gains a magnitude by the enormity of effect wrought by the obscure agent of history bearing that name. *Adolf Eichmann* is to be forever a substitute for the millions of nameless common and uncommon people he helped destroy in the name of an apocalyptic "final solution." Han-

see argument above

nah Arendt, having attended the Eichmann trial in Jerusalem, is arrested by a new idea, "the banality of evil." The apparent contradiction between her new concept of evil and what she calls "our tradition of thought" which sees evil as "something demonic" led her to a two-volume reconsideration of the problem, *The Life of the Mind*, in which she examines the nature of thinking, willing, judging. Whether she would have held to her new concept is problematic, since she did not live to complete the section of the work on judging. But in setting out she says of Eichmann: "I was struck by a manifest shallowness in the doer that made it impossible to trace the uncontestable evil of his deeds to any deeper level of roots or motives. The deed was monstrous, but the doer . . . was quite ordinary, commonplace, and neither demonic nor monstrous." The "only notable characteristic one could detect in his past behavior as well as in his behavior during the trial . . . was something entirely negative: it was not stupidity but *thoughtlessness*." And reflecting on the "macabre comedy" resulting from Eichmann's helplessness, caught as he is in his "cliché-ridden language," she adds: "Clichés, stock phrases, adherence to conventional, standardized codes of expression and conduct have the socially recognized function of protecting us against reality," lest we exhaust ourselves by the necessity of a constant intellectual engagement of the events and facts always pressing upon us. The consequence of such a withdrawal from reality is the disjunction of thought and action, leading to such macabre comedy as that of Eichmann standing before the Israeli court.

That staged spectacle leads Miss Arendt to the questions she pursues in her two volumes:

> Is evil-doing (the sins of omission, as well as the sins of commission) possible in default of not just "base motives" (as the law calls them) but in any motives whatever, of any particular prompting of interest or volition? Is wickedness, however we may define it, this being "determined to prove a villain," *not* a necessary condition for evil-doing? Might the problem of good and evil, our faculty for telling right from wrong, be connected with our faculty of thought?

If the answer to these questions is *yes*, as Miss Arendt implies, then we are left with an enormous problem in attempting to deal with an Eichmann. For we must conclude in this line of thought that he is innocent of wickedness, that his participation in the slaughter of other innocents is an accident of forces loosed by history but not yet subjected to the control of gnosis. Even the ground of our outrage at brutalities is eroded, since outrage is itself presumably susceptible to the control of knowledge.

Now the supposition that wickedness is not necessarily a condition for evil-doing is scarcely new; it is a doctrine progressively advanced these past two hundred years till it has in fact become the new orthodoxy. But tolerance of evil as a social principle growing out of philosophical determinism has had little support in the American South, at least up to the present. Indeed, the fierceness with which the South has resisted such a principle has intensified some judgments of the South as evilly and sinfully inclined, in a blatant violation of the principle of tolerance on the part of the principle's most rabid partisans. The murderer, an old argument said, is no more guilty of his so-called crime than is his knife, an argument still generally rejected as nonsense by most Southerners. What some Southerners observe, with irony, is that the principle is most selective when used by some of its advocates. That is, some of those who exonerate the criminal because he is a victim of generic or social determinisms seem to have little difficulty concluding to the contrary that the South is quite actively evil in its traditional understanding of evil as an effect of aberrant will.

What brings Miss Arendt's question into arresting focus is not that it is a new doctrine, but the enormity of its effects upon our world in recent history. And what is called into question most particularly is our growing tolerance toward evil, a tolerance established as one of the conditions of millennial progress from the days of Machiavelli into our own recent machinations of human rights as a political instrument in foreign policy. It is one of history's little ironies that we recently witnessed a president from the South operating within this new tradition, though professing its opposite.

When the Machiavellian figure is discovered operating in the large movements of history, our judgment is tempered by questions of net gain. Evil effects, in pursuit of progress, are a consequence of high motives. But when a figure who in his effects looms large and Machiavellian is discovered among the ordinary everyday members of humanity, rather than in the pantheon of the gods of progress, we are likely to reexamine our intellectual tolerance of evil. An Eichmann, a Jones, a Manson may be sleeping in the room upstairs or sitting down with us at our last supper. We might even encounter him on a deserted dirt road in Georgia, as Flannery O'Connor's grandmother does in "A Good Man Is Hard to Find."

The argument that wickedness is not the necessary ground in the individual out of which evil deeds grow is the line of thought that has, of course, been overwhelmingly advanced by those new sciences, sociology and its handmaid psychology; the arguments of those disciplines have generally narrowed the possibilities of individual freedom and responsibility until, in the clichéd language of Miss O'Connor's Rayber Tarwater in her novel *The Violent Bear It Away*, such a creature as Eichmann must be logically excused on the ground that he is somehow "an accident of nature" no less than Rayber's own idiot child-ward, Bishop. If action is forced upon society by the enormity of an evil deed, that action is considered a corrective of nature, execution or incarceration thus being severed from any relation to retribution. For neither anger nor love finds any rational role in such actions. Rayber Tarwater in spite of himself is so moved by love for his idiot son that he cannot kill the child, but he can understand his love only as an aberration, an encroaching insanity.

There is a growing body of revealing literature, some of the most cogent of it from within the preserves of sociology and psychology, on the theme of these new sciences' obfuscations of the mystery of evil, the distortions that remove evil from individual responsibility into the abstract country of personal and social adjustment. For instance, Professor Donald Campbell, a recent president of the American Psychological Association, shocked many of his colleagues when he said in his presidential address:

> There is in psychology today a general background assumption that the human impulses provided by biological evolution are right and optimal, both individually and socially, and that repressive or inhibitory moral traditions are wrong. This assumption may now be regarded as scientifically wrong. Psychology, in propagating this background perspective in its teaching of perhaps 80 or 90 percent of college undergraduates, and increasing proportions of high school pupils, helps to undermine the retention of what may be extremely valuable social-evolutionary inhibitory systems which we do not yet fully understand.

If this late admission from an authority in the field leaves the person still entangled in "social-evolutionary systems" and the question of evil still rooted in "biological evolution," Professor Campbell does at least admit "social functionality and psychological validity to the concepts of sin and temptation and of Original Sin due to human carnal, animal nature." To remember sin and temptation in such terms is but small advance toward the spirit's territory, but it is a beginning.[2]

Walter Berns, in the April 1979 issue of *Harper's*, has urged us to consider that anger directed against those who commit evil deeds at least "acknowledges the humanity of its objects: it holds them accountable for what they do. And in holding particular men responsible, it pays them the respect that is due them as men." The failure of his fellows to hold that degree of respect for him, their choice rather to explain him away as a mechanistic creature of nature, is the

2. For a searching critique of psychology's deconstructions of reality that call forth Campbell's carefully hedged warnings, see Paul C. Vitz's *Psychology as Religion: The Cult of Self-Worship* (Grand Rapids: Eerdmans, 1977), or the redactions he made of his book in "Psychology: Advocate of the New Narcissism" and "Psychology: Enemy of the Family" in *The New Oxford Review*, April 1979 and May 1979.

maddening pain in Miss O'Connor's Misfit. Good having been explained away, he has only his evil to give him any sense of being. Ironically, he's a better "Christian" than many who profess the faith, since his sense of loss is a sense of having lost the *good*. It would not be difficult to persuade the Misfit of the reality of original sin, as the grandmother discovers with shocking finality. Berns puts the conclusion to be drawn from our absence of anger: "If, then, men are not angry when someone else is robbed, raped, or murdered, the implication is that no moral community exists, because those men do not care for anyone other than themselves." It is a conclusion that the Misfit feels forced to: "it's nothing for you to do but enjoy the few minutes you got left the best way you can—by killing somebody or burning down his house or doing some other meanness to him." Even then, "It's [there's] no real pleasure in life."

One is struck on reading Miss Arendt's characterization of Eichmann by its aptness to Miss O'Connor's Misfit. "A Good Man Is Hard to Find" is, from its title to its concluding words, a story whose texture of clichés develops a macabre comedy; but that story suggests that clichés are something quite other than a means of protecting one "against reality," in their origins at least, though her characters pay a terrible price again and again for using them as a shield against reality. The relation of manners to mystery is a constant one in Southern literature as it attempts to rescue cliché in its origins. The sense of community as a body in time and place—of members dead and dying and to be born—focused upon a geographical point, is strong in that literature's anti-gnostic stance. For what is implicit and often overt is the attempt to reaffirm the order of creation as transcendent in origins.

What we wish to remark here is that the language which entraps an Eichmann is one which Eric Voegelin would describe as residual symbols that have become opaque; it is this aspect of cliché that effects one's removal from reality. A recovery of translucence in those symbols would lead us back to reality, a point Miss O'Connor repeatedly dramatizes. But most important to our concern, we must remember that the individual, in the very act of using such language, participates in evil—bears false witness—and the incommensurate distance between the doer and the deed that is revealed in startling events awakens in us the realization that there is a mystery in evil itself, toward which we are often willingly drawn, since we do not will otherwise. The neutrality of the will is, alas, one of those comfortable illusions we cling to so that the tensions within the world will seem relaxed. We wish, in the words of a popular song to this effect, to go "rolling with the flow."

The mysterious attraction of evil is a principle in human nature that our Southern writer has rather constantly addressed himself to as he bears witness to the reality of man in the world, for he sees in each of us some degree of participation that makes each in some degree a Misfit. I have suggested that there is a celebration of good in the drama of our desperate fight to establish at least some claim to evil against social and psychological and philosophical attempts to deprive us of that birthright. It is only through a blinding pride, which may exhibit itself as a banal disjunction through cliché from the reality of the evil in our deeds—as with an Eichmann or a Jones or a Manson—that we are able to deny our kinship to such arresting figurings of man as Miss O'Connor's Misfit. In the Southern literature we have been talking about, we find ourselves already revealed in grotesque distortions that elicit both terror and laughter.

Our writer, then, is the prophetic poet, about whom I have had much to say on other occasions. I repeat in closing that he bears witness beyond the limits of art's projections of man's struggle within the *metaxy*, the "In-Between." He knows this in his blood if not in his head, even as Haze Motes knows it in resisting his own calling to prophecy; even as so sophisticated a poet as T. S. Eliot comes to know it in his heart when he is at last able to make that gesture celebrated at the close of *The Waste Land*, that "awful daring of a moment's surrender / Which an age of prudence can never retract." I emphasize that distinction, the old difference made between the *reason* and the *understanding*. One is required to bring those complementary faculties of the soul into an ordinate support, each of the other, for the good health of the soul. The failure to do so leads us to a dissociation of sensibilities at a greater depth of the soul than those spectacles of the soul—our symbolic orderings in art or government. *Ratio ET intellectus*, says the old scholastic formulation, grown out of Heraclitus through our principal thinkers into its scholastic formulation in Saint Thomas. The loss of that relationship may set any man at any moment on the road away from reality. But when a whole civilization loses it, that civilization has secularized the spiritual faculty of the reason or of the understanding and becomes secular gnostic, whether it be categorized as Rationalist or Romantic. There follows an inevitable abandonment of the dance in favor of the race toward apocalypse, spectacles of which are everywhere about us, as in that encounter in Tennessee recently between the would-be saviors of the snail darter and the champions of a water power such as Hawthorne would not understand. We have moved rapidly in this race of Progress, from Monkey Trial to Minnow Trial, in confusions beyond the art of satire.

If we learn this basic truth about Western man from our Southern literature as we enjoy its various gifts, we will have begun to move toward a participation in community, the living body of humanity. As misfits all, we may encounter with the shock of joy a recognition of "a good under construction" in us, to use Miss O'Connor's phrase. Her Hulga, we remember, was christened Joy by a mother given to cliché, and so changes her own name to the ugliest she can think of, as if that might change her nature. The story "Good Country People" leaves Hulga thunderstruck by the Bible salesman. That tempter, walking up and down in the earth, is right about Hulga's futile attempt to raise nothingness to an absolute by reason. His prophecy fits us all in a special way; we're all born believing in nothing, a condition of the fortunate fall. The question is whether we have believed in nothingness "ever since." At that level, of course, there is no such thing as "Southern" literature.

II. Flannery O'Connor's Sacramental Vision

If a writer is any good, what he makes will have its source in a realm much larger than that which his conscious mind can encompass and will always be a greater surprise to him than it can ever be to his reader.

—Flannery O'Connor

It has been one of the most popular critical assumptions in our century that the realist's art is incompatible with a spiritual vision, an assumption endemic at the level of the academic intellectual. Especially, the assumption holds, an artist professing an orthodox Christian vision cannot adequately deal with the "real world." Just why our unreal modernist world should inherit and treasure this disease of the intellect has a long and intricate history in the Western mind, one that we must touch upon in considering why that poet of a Catholic vision, Flannery O'Connor, calls herself a "realist of distances." (I have explored the infection in its historical background in three long volumes, called collectively "The Prophetic Poet and the Popular Spirit.") We may note that Miss O'Connor is herself acutely aware of the disease. She attempts to remedy it, as prophetic artist, by recalling us to known but forgotten truths about our existence in the world. And the concern is a constant theme in her *Mystery and Manners*, as in the letters she so generously wrote to a spectrum of the popular mind, collected by Sally Fitzgerald in *The Habit of Being*. Flannery O'Connor is concerned with our world's deliberate exorcism of the spiritual from creation, a deconstruction of reality which she speaks of as modern Manichaeanism.

The modernist version of that ancient heresy denies the spiritual dimension of creation in the interest of conquests of nature to please appetites, those appetites as various as the inordinate hunger for things and the more diabolical hunger for power over things. (*Things* here includes persons reduced from any spiritual dimension.) The ancient Manichaean tended to a gnostic rejection of material being. Miss O'Connor finds evidence of a similar reduction of reality in our separating *reason* from *imagination*, *judgment* from *vision*, and (particularly important to the sacramental question at hand) *nature* from *grace*. She affirms a complementary necessity in these pairs, urging our return to a larger reality through them; that is, she argues for a reassociation of sensibilities that

28

goes much deeper than literary categories. To read her well, then, requires that we understand carefully what she sees as a larger-than-literary dimension to such literary shibboleths as image or metaphor or allegory.

At the same time she insists that the artist's primary responsibility is to the thing he makes. This is to say that her understanding of the artist's role is delicately refined, most carefully precise. She is uncompromisingly committed to a vision; she would reflect that vision by her art, but only within the limits set by the nature of art itself. For her, reason and imagination are complementary aspects of a fundamental gift—namely, *being*, *existence* itself. They are not to be separated by the rational intellect as they generally are in our world, either in the interest of power (when reason becomes independent of and elevated over the imagination) or in the interest of feeling (when the imagination unbridled by reason becomes capable only of some form of sentimentality—pornography being the dominant mode of sentimentality at this juncture).

She is, preeminently among modern writers, a realist. In her own phrase, she is a realist of distances, though as one knows from having read her stories her sense perceptions of the immediate world are striking in themselves. The epithet *realist of distances* is one she embraces directly out of her fundamental Thomism, about which a brief but necessary word.

First off, as we have said, Flannery O'Connor understands the artist's overriding responsibility to be to his art, since his is an exercise of a peculiar gift, though one for which he may take no primary credit. (The artist is, of course, responsible for perfecting his gift.) She sets aside art defined as an imitation of nature, art as a mirror or as history. In its true definition, art is rather an imitation of the *creative activity* of nature. This is a crucial distinction which she finds explicated by Jacques Maritain in his *Art and Scholasticism*, the primary source this side of Saint Thomas's own work for anyone exploring Miss O'Connor's aesthetic vision. As an artist imitating the creative activity of nature, she (like Maritain, and like Saint Thomas before him) focuses upon reason's relation to imaginative vision. The consequence of these complementary faculties of the intellect in the artist is the made thing—the poem or story. The artist's necessary devotion is to the action of making, but always in the interest of the good of the thing made. The mutual accommodation of reason and imagination, then, is what she is talking about when she says—again and again—that "art is reason in making."

The responsible artist, in her view of the matter, is obligated to what we in the academy recognize as fundamental Aristotelian aspects of artisanship. If we read *Mystery and Manners* carefully, we hear her deliberately echoing the *Poetics*. She is concerned with order, unity, clarity, proportion, as those concerns apply to her fiction; she is particularly concerned with questions of the *possible* or *probable*. In short, she is aware of those abiding aesthetic categories that attach to questions of *craftsmanship*. But she is concerned at the most homely level of craftsmanship with more than theory's more intoxicating reaches; for those higher reaches of theory will take care of themselves if the artisan takes care of his peculiar homework. She speaks of the labor of finding the next word, remarking that "The Theories are worse than the Furies." Her reason pursues form at the level of *syntax* and *diction* and *image*, tuned to the immediate world, working from that level toward the complexities of metaphor. On occasion she will speak beyond this level—at a metaphysical level of metaphor. She will speak of a good metaphor's resonances at that highest allegorical level, the *anagogical*, a word one encounters rather often in her essays and talks and letters. That word reminds us of the parallels she sees between her own concerns and Dante's. To a beleaguered graduate student, working on a thesis on Miss O'Connor's work under a director who allows no theological terms in relation to that fiction, she says,

> The writer whose point of view is Catholic in the widest sense of the term reads nature in the same way the medieval commentators read Scripture. They found three levels of meaning in the literal level of the sacred text—the allegorical, in which one thing stands for another; the moral, which has to do with what should be done; and the anagogical, which has to do with the Divine life and our participation in it, the level of grace. Now if you use the word anagogical long enough, the idea of grace will become sufficiently disinfected for [those who reject the mystery of grace] to be able to take it.

Put another way, because Dante has been thoroughly academized, his terms can be taken as part of a critical system by those for whom (as she says in another context) "Every story is a frog in a bottle." One recognizes in her fiction itself, then, that she eschews the moral and allegorical levels as here presented, but the anagogical, the level of grace in relation to nature, is the very center of her dramatic concern. Nevertheless, she always turns such discussions back to the homely level of the artist's labor. Before a wooden crutch may be a symbol, she says, it must first be a wooden crutch. "Fiction," she says in *Mystery and Manners*, "is an art that calls for the strictest attention to the real." To the neophyte she advises, "Don't be subtle till the third page." Given the writer's attention at this level, the resonances of the anagogical will be available to the good reader, not because the writer has built the anagogical into his story, but because he has been true to the reality of existence immediately at hand. She reports with approval the response of a country neighbor who read her stories: "She said, 'Well, them stories just gone and shown you how some folks *would* do.'" Aristotle said it only a little better than this Georgia country woman when he speaks of the possible or probable.

If we recognize Aristotelian dimensions to her concerns, it is necessary to remind ourselves that hers is an Aristotle baptized by Saint Thomas. When she speaks of the *possible* or *probable*, she is aware of the artist's temptation to assume a false prophetic power in moving from the possible to the probable, from what some folks *might* do to what they *will* do. It is a temptation that in itself may lead the artist to assume that his responsibility to the world requires him to be Moses, leading lost children out of whatever desert. We may recognize Milton's struggle with this temptation, I believe, in that most personal of his poems, *Lycidas*. Recognizing the danger, Miss O'Connor insists: "The lord doesn't speak to the novelist as he did to his servant Moses, mouth to mouth. He speaks to him as he did to those two complainers, Aaron and Aaron's sister, Mary [*sic*]: through dreams and visions, in fits and starts, and by all the lesser and limited ways of the imagination." This being so, it is reason that one must depend upon to clarify whatever fitful vision comes to the artist through the lesser and limited ways of the imagination. The artist has more than he can perfectly concern himself with in paying attention to the meticulous exercise of his gift, and he should leave Moses' labor to Moses, Cromwell's to Cromwell.

In speaking explicitly of the Catholic writer's responsibility, Miss O'Connor cites the angelic doctor: "St. Thomas says that art does not require rectitude of the appetite, that it is wholly concerned with the good of that which is made." She knows all too well those artists who are dominated by a concern for "the rectitude of appetite," for articulating a moral message. They range from Marxist ideologues, whose materialist god inflames appetite, to Sunday-school tractarians, many of whom would not simply rectify appetite but abolish it altogether. Those artists advance programs disguised as fiction on occasion, practicing a species of sacrilege against art and nature, and inevitably thereby distorting reality. She complains, in one of her reviews in her diocesan paper, of a novel that is evidence of "a depressing new category: light Catholic summer reading." And she advises that one might indeed buy a copy of Cardinal Spellman's novel *The Foundling*, since the proceeds go to charity, so long as one has the good sense to use it as a doorstop and not value it as a novel.

There is for her a piety proper to her calling as artist, but it cannot be discovered through tracts of whatever sort disguised as art. Nevertheless, she believes that what is good in itself glorifies God, whether that good thing be a person *becoming* or a poem or table or garden *made*. Man, because created in the image of God, is therefore inescapably a maker, and each of us is a maker according to our peculiar gifts. That principle, deduced by reason out of faith, returns us to our earlier definition of art. For in the action of imitating nature in its creative activity, rather than attempting merely to mirror nature on the one hand or distort nature on the other through an art turned to some gnostic program for restructuring the world, the creative action realizes a potential within the thing—poem or story—even as that same action becomes a realization of the maker's own potential being.

When she speaks then of good as something under construction, she understands her point to apply whether one is speaking about a person or about the peculiar work that such a person does. The poem or story is an artifact projected by the imagination and brought through reason's labor into an existence of its own, more or less good. In either aspect of action's effect (and the effects are inextricable)—whether of a person's struggle to become or his struggle to make a thing beyond himself—a *given* is presupposed. It is first of all the gift of being itself that underlies all creation and binds all creation together. Existence is the common ground in creation. But all creation necessarily includes the person, the artist and gardener no less than poems or trees and shrubs and earth and stones. This aspect of the given is formally spoken of as *esse*. There is an additional gift beyond being, beyond *esse*, whereby a thing (*res*) exists and is the very thing it is. That additional given is particularity, which in individual men includes the special calling to act within the limiting gift of one's particularity. The point is summarized by Etienne Gilson in *The Spirit of Thomism*: "Actual existence, which [Thomas] calls *esse*, is that by virtue of which a thing, which he calls *res*, is a being, an *ens*."

The point is not so esoteric as it may sound in our taking recourse to Saint Thomas through Gilson. And it is a point absolutely central to Flannery O'Connor's understanding of her own calling to be a realist of distances, as it is to our concern to understand her sacramental vision. What the scholastic point means by extension to the artist and his art is that man, in every instance of his action, is operating as a creative agent participating in his own existence, but at a secondary level. It is the refusal to accept our participation in our own being at a secondary level that is the wellspring of Sartrean existentialism, a philosophy as old as the fall from grace in the garden. Though man be given a freedom through which he may easily suppose himself the first, the sole or primary cause of his free actions of creation, reason will tell him at last that he is *himself* a given and that even his freedom is a given. In this view there can be no such thing as the self-made man, only the self-unmade man. For whatever the nature of his action as maker, man is always operating *upon* givens *with* givens *from* his own givenness.

Because Flannery O'Connor understands her own talents to be a gift, she is freer than most of us. She feels a joyful obligation to actions out of that gift, even as she supposes the same required of us all. She says in a letter, "You do not write the best you can for the sake of art but for the sake of returning your talent increased to the invisible God to use or not use as he sees fit." That is—as the Apostle Paul reminds us—we are called to imitate into being our own given natures, each according to his gifts. Thereby we discover ourselves members, one of another. Thus it is that we become a body, the Church, whose head is Christ. This is the vision of community Miss O'Connor never wavers from. And it is in the light of this vision that one sees her answering the endless seminar question, spawned by psychology—why do you write? Because I'm good at it, she says. And does the burden of the disease she suffers (disseminated lupus, which increasingly made her invalid) affect her calling? Not particularly, she says, since she writes with her head and not with her feet. Her gift was not that of the bicycle rider.

If one understands the artist's gifts and powers as Flannery O'Connor does, he approaches the question of reality with a piety toward creation that will be reflected in his actions as artist. His address to existence does not presume the existential world, in which he is caught up, to be merely a reservoir of prime matter out of which to make whatever worlds he fancies. That world is a creation at a primary level. In this view, all creation must be seen as *creaturely*, depending in its being from the Prime Creator. Whatever *man* as *maker* manipulates requires of *man, the made*, a reverence for its being. From this creature— the created world—the artist borrows to build what J. R. R. Tolkien calls Secondary Creations, the poem or story. In doing so, the artist discovers a responsibility for a careful attention to the created world. And the degree to which he exercises this responsibility makes all the difference to that fullness, to the resonance, of any Secondary Creation he attaches his name to.

It is inevitable, Miss O'Connor believes, that even if the artist does not recognize and venerate the Cause of Primary Creation, his Secondary Creations will nevertheless carry larger resonances that he may suppose or intend. They will necessarily do so insofar as he makes his poem or story with a close eye upon the immediate world and with a careful respect for craftsmanship. As she puts the point in one of her essays:

> If [the novelist] believes that actions are predetermined by psychic makeup or the economic situation or some other determinable factor, then he will be concerned above all with an accurate reproduction of the things that most immediately concern man, with the natural forces that he feels control his destiny. Such a writer may produce a great tragic naturalism, for by his responsibility to the things he sees, he may transcend the limitations of his narrow vision.

By his responsibility to the things he sees. That is the necessity she keeps insistently before her, and it accounts for her realistic dimension. For as we have said, the artist has precisely this limit upon his power to create: his Secondary Creation is unavoidably dependent upon Primary Creation. Therefore, if he is attentive, what he makes must in some wise echo the Cause of Primary Creation. (Ironically, science fiction usually struggles to sever those bonds through imaginative extremes; the result is nevertheless a grotesque imaging of reality, any grotesque always reminding us of reality itself.) Insofar as the artist is true to the Primary level of existence, including his own fallen nature and its particular gifts of becoming through making, his art will echo with anagogical resonances. The theologian or philosopher must concern himself with questions searching into the causes and ends of things; the artist need not worry about proving anything by his art. He must, however, be responsible to the thing he would give its certain existence—the made thing.

With eyes open, with the confidence of her faith that existence has meaning, however deep the mysteries of existence, Miss O'Connor responds to the various world in imitation of its creative activity, under the guidance of reason.

> I try to satisfy [she says] those necessities that make themselves felt in the work itself. When I write, I am a maker. I think about what I am making. St. Thomas called art reason in making. When I write I feel I am engaged in the reasonable use of the unreasonable. In art reason goes wherever the imagination goes. We have reduced the uses of reason terribly. You say a thing is reasonable and people think you mean it is safe. What's reasonable is seldom safe and always exciting.

Reason reveals to her that, in engaging the particular, she is committed beyond the imagistic level, and in this respect her vision coincides with Gerard Manley Hopkins's. Again, she says, "The longer you look at one object, the more of the world you see in it; and it's well to remember that the serious fiction writer always writes about the whole world, no matter how limited his particular scene." The Cause of creation must inevitably (for her) be reflected in art's inscape, insofar as the artist's eye is steady and his craft sure. The *instress* of Primary Creation will be caught by the *inscape* of the particular Secondary Creation, the poem or story, an additional effect of which is the deepening of the artist's *instress*, the realization of his own particular potential being. Catholic critics, she wrote to Sister Mariella Gable, should look in a work "for its sort of 'inscape' as Hopkins would have it. Instead they look for some ideal intention and criticize you for not having it."

An artist who is troubled about the large questions—about whether the universe is random accident or a self-determined closed order or a caused creature—may well find himself engaging art as if it were an instrument of empirical value, directing him to conclusions beyond the reach of the philosopher or theologian. It is a conspicuous inclination in the poet to assume the role of philosopher or theologian or scientist, usually with bad effect upon his art. Indeed, such an untroubled writer as Miss O'Connor is a rarity, at least since the Renaissance (that childhood of our art during which there could be such free playfulness); she has an adolescent exuberance with metaphor, for instance, such as we see in Donne's love poetry. I sometimes suspect that in Donne's love poetry we see a desperate last fling of high fancy before metaphor is to be denied its joyfulness, before poetry turns serious and solemn in Milton's great poems—after which point the poet is never again quite so free, never again quite so trusting of language itself. (The audacity of language in such extremes as Surrealism is as much an action *against* as *with* language.)

Because she understands the nature of and the limits of her gift, Miss O'Connor can make such responses with humor and wit, but without arrogance. She never confuses herself as the first cause of the thing she makes; she is mediate cause. That is the point that concerns her when she says in a letter, "The hardest thing for the writer to indicate is the presence of the anagogical which to my mind is the only thing that causes the personality to change." She adds, "We are not our own light." Nevertheless, the artist has tended, in an accelerated way at least since Shakespeare, to see himself as absolute cause of his art—to see himself as his own light. It is no accident that Milton's Lucifer has become the patron saint of the artist in the nineteenth and twentieth centuries, a role Joyce's Stephen Dedalus celebrates when he becomes strong enough in his willfulness to declare, "I will not serve." One may see the temptation easily enough: in imitating the action of nature through art, the maker may mistake himself as the artifact's prime cause; forgetting his own nature, he mistakes himself for God. It is, of course, a temptation to which all are susceptible, but in our limited concern with the writer as maker consider that the sharp revolt against reason— as reason came to be abused in the seventeenth and eighteenth centuries—has led many poets these past two hundred years to a denial of reason's central service to art, even as they have insisted upon their own rebel status in nature and society. Among the excessive growths of romanticism in revolt, we recognize Surrealism and Dadaism as symptoms of the distortions whereby grace is separated from nature and the subjective becomes the only valid response.

So long as the artist's divine madness has some sense of limit implied, as when he serves under the authority of Apollo and his especial muse, he may retain some sense of his powers as limited. But rebel powers have overthrown even Apollo, while Dionysus is allowed at best a proconsul role. (Perhaps the muses have been smuggled back into the country of art, under the auspices of the subconscious.) Now when the faculty of reason itself is sent in exile from the artist's province, the artist may forget that he does not create ex nihilo. Of course, since he is not his own cause, he cannot do so. And since he is not the cause of the larger created world, from which both he and his made thing depend in very literal ways, he is thus demonstrably limited by creation itself— however much he may insist that his powers are godlike.

When Dr. Johnson regrets the "improper and vicious" in Cowley, and by extension in the other metaphysicals, as produced "by voluntary deviation from nature in pursuit of something new and strange," he is not being simply prudish; he is rather recognizing an incipient romanticism in art which, as it loses its firmer anchor in reason, will drift loose to fancy's extremes—to Dada for instance, that spectacular recent spiritual rash on the body of art. That rash is a symptom of a spiritual disorder in man when he has turned the world upside down, when Sartre and others succeed in turning Saint Thomas on his head. (Sartre is a presence Miss O'Connor contends with in her fiction, as we recognize in "Good Country People.") I think Dr. Johnson recognizes in the extremes of metaphysical poetry a growing effect upon art consequent upon the shifting of reason to the especial province of an emerging empirical science. He sees an audacity on the part of the poet as the poet responds to science's encroachment. (I've mentioned science fiction earlier, and one might consider whether it as a genre doesn't represent the metaphysical poetry of science.) One might note in contrast to Donne's metaphorical audacities in his love poetry a sense of the joys and terrors of the beleaguered spirit in his meditations and sermons, as if he is becoming consumed with spiritual responsibilities to himself and to the world.

There is deep in Donne's poetry an instinctive, if not conscious, sense of a world threatened, a refuge from which comes refined wit, a most effective defensive weapon. Dr. Johnson charges that the metaphysicals reveal through their audacity in yoking "the most heterogeneous ideas . . . by violence together" a certain poverty of spirit. He concludes, "Their courtship was void of fondness and their lamentation of sorrow." Whether one agree with Dr. Johnson's judgment without some modification of it, I think it safe to observe that wit becomes the rescue of the poet whose world seems to be dissolving—the world of nature after Descartes; the world of spirit in nature after Bacon. The new world in the making—or rather the new worlds—are ones in which the old confidence in image and metaphor rapidly disappears. Little wonder that the wilder extremes of wit developing between Ben Jonson and Samuel Johnson would appear to the good Doctor as something of a betrayal of old valid causes once presumed in the keep of language itself, betrayals increasingly in need of reason's stay.

In the Elizabethans' free and open participation in creation in the childhood of our poetry, there had been a humor out of which wit became distilled as antidote to gnostic advances of mind upon nature. (Lest it be supposed I'm deprecating our Elizabethan childhood, let us remember Mrs. Lucynell Crater in the "Life You Save May Be Your Own," who speaks for that progressive gnostic mind: the monks of old [she says] "wasn't as advanced as we are." And remember as well the visionary powers of Miss O'Connor's children.) But that Elizabethan humor rapidly disappears, while wit turns increasingly toward sardonic irony, a clear symptom of the satirist's isolation from the world. Thus in Swift, wit becomes a weapon of fury—a deadly rapier replacing the more generous if more barbaric Elizabethan broadsword. My metaphor here is quite deliberate, to suggest those precisions of mind that turn to serious contention with those other minds for whom theology and philosophy and art are increasingly subordinate concerns, if concerns at all.

Wit, let me suggest, does not necessarily include the fullness of reason, in that it may come to rely too heavily upon strict logic or, in its more desperate manifestations, upon verbal acrobatics. And do we not notice a shifting of the poet's confidence in the faculties of mind itself, a shifting reflected in the range of poetic effects attempted between the time of Donne and that of Wordsworth? Included in that shifting are changes in prosody toward the mechanical and an increasing dominance of poetry by rhetoric. (Both Swift and Pope offer evidence of what I mean.) One is tempted to say that the shift in poetic mode is art's imitation of the emerging science. But in the end the poet finds himself more and more an exile. By the nineteenth century, he feels compelled to resort to radical changes in prosody, abandoning rhetoric's formalities because rhetoric seems an instrument of suppressive reason, as meter once seemed evidence of a possessive muse.

It is in the admittedly partial light of my oversimplified account of the poet's progress from Shakespeare to O'Connor that we turn back toward Miss O'Connor and her art. And we shift one term of our metaphor for wit in doing so (why should the metaphysical poet have all the fun?). Let us say that from Swift to Joyce runs a thread holding the artist more or less tenuously to creation. Finely, intricately spun and woven, this thread of wit may allow the poet to make a magic carpet on which increasingly he has attempted to sail free of creation. In such detachment, maintained through several species of wit's irony, the poet more and more severely judges God, nature, and man. And he is increasingly tempted to reject all three, if he is Joyce, for instance. If he is the young Eliot, he finds himself isolated beyond any comfort of wit, as in that pathetic intellectual J. Alfred Prufrock.

What I see in Flannery O'Connor is a rescue of the artist back to the fullness of reality. She appropriates metaphysical wit and some of its subsequent refinements, such as a Swiftian incisiveness, though she excludes the sardonic that so often threatens Swift. Because she accepts man for what he is, a creature fallen in his nature, within the mystery of pitiable, irritating man as he exists under the generous auspices of grace, she is able to complement wit with humor. She is very Chaucerian in this respect, it seems to me. Consequently, one may discover that her use of cliché, which is like Swift's and Joyce's in precision and incisiveness, is accompanied nevertheless by a tolerance of man's willful stupidities of mind and spirit. Hers is not a responsibility for the rectitude of appetites. Her tolerance is judgmental, for she says what she sees. But there is none of the scorching acid of Swift nor the divine aloofness of Joyce. This difference in the effect of her wit as we encounter it in her art lies in her not having succumbed to the temptation to separate judgment from vision. She does not, since she sees that man's fallen nature is not to be separated from the possibility of a rescuing grace. (Not *probability*, but *possibility*.) Firm of intellect, cautious of presumptuousness, she judges, but not without her own mercy toward that pitiable, even disgusting figure, man. The exercise of that mercy we discover in her stories and call it humor. The meanest of her characters is not, in her view, beyond rescue, and indeed she delights in protagonists who seem most nearly beyond the reaches of grace to the secular human eye, as she delights in the most ordinary mediums of grace to those agents of her fiction—a modern, clean pig parlor; a water stain on a bedroom ceiling. She is equally cautious, of course, about affirming that such characters are rescued. The Misfit, even Rayber, may or may not be damned. As artist, then, she does not feel called upon either to force the rescue of foolish or willful man or to deliver him over to an annihilation. The novelist or poet, she says, "feels no need to apologize for the ways of God to man or to avoid looking at the ways of man to God."

She looks very closely at the ways of man to God, and comedy both in Dante's high sense of the term and in its more popular meaning is her inevitable mode of presenting the tragic dimension of man's struggle with grace. Having demurred from Milton's theme, she goes on with her point: "For [the artist] to 'tidy up reality' is certainly to succumb to the sin of pride. Open and free observation is founded on our ultimate faith that the universe is meaningful, as the Church teaches." What she urges as the necessary responsibility of the artist may be summed up as follows: believe, and look where you will—so long as the actions of nature are not violated by the actions of art; so long as one sees clearly; so long as one does not distort his seeing by the arrogation of final judgment or by the presumption of rejecting the complexity of existence in which the mysteries of good and evil are in contention.

These, then, are the reasons—put in very abbreviated form—that Flannery O'Connor says with such confidence, "If a writer is any good, what he makes will have its source in a realm much larger than that which his conscious mind can encompass." That larger world she accepts sacramentally, a gift of being, as she accepts her calling to be a writer with the old depths of the religious vow.

III.   Cleanth Brooks
and the Life in Art

. . . the community is still in being.

—Cleanth Brooks

At some point in one's encounter with the imposing work of William Faulkner one will come to the advantage of reading Cleanth Brooks's large studies, *The Yoknapatawpha Country* and *Toward Yoknapatawpha and Beyond*. But it is a later and smaller book, growing out of these studies, that might prove more helpful in the attempt to recover literature as a civilized pleasure rather than a professional speciality. I mean his *William Faulkner: First Encounters* (1983). Its special value is Mr. Brooks's gift in sharing such pleasure. We may learn from him that literature is not a deadly necessity to our programmed learning, as our attenuated academic disciplines have inclined to make it in the feeding of what C. S. Lewis in his "Interim Report" called "the incubus of Research, . . . devised . . . to emulate the scientists." As Brooks has known and said to us for a long time now, literature is important to our well-being as persons. In the academy since World War II, as both he and Lewis know, there has tended to be a crippling separation of literature from life. Our curricula reflect, for instance, a chasm between graduate and undergraduate teaching, and if one should as academic find oneself most rewarded and celebrated on the more specialized side, he is likely—except for an occasional missionary gesture—to remain on that plateau, raised above the undergraduate level. Even the faculties are separated, those heavily involved with undergraduates far less willing to be called to (or to have time for) the feeding of that sphinx or incubus or whatever epithet best fits it, Research.

I know from long experience that some faculty consider the task of teaching undergraduates an onerous one, though it is the price one sometimes must pay for an occasional opportunity to teach literature at the level of real importance, to intending specialists like oneself. The high dream is of a "chair," which allows an escape from the great unwashed undergraduate hoard that now swamps the academy. The occasion of a graduate course, and even perhaps of a seminar, allows a sharpening of the project underway, toward whatever article or book might satisfy the ravenous incubus for a very brief moment. One need not deny some validity to these concerns for research, given the intellectual chaos we call the academy. A university has many ends and none in our day, and the political and economic civil wars within it make refuge in a seminar welcomed, perhaps even calming of spirit on occasion. It is only that, when the concern for happy residence on the plateau of graduate education becomes itself the primary goal, a concern for education in relation to the social body degenerates to clichés not believed. The full exercise of intellect, required if we are not to be victim of society as a machine whose parts are specialists of one sort or another, is sacrificed to private expediency. If we are speaking of the specialist in literature, his teaching of undergraduates may incline him to a reduced measure of his specialized concern, such as may be palatable to the uninitiated, applied to Homer or Shakespeare or Dante. Or he may by rote and routine present such texts in a deadly literal way and so arrest any potential interest in the sleeping undergraduate minds before him.

I do not discount another aspect of our exhausted system that might well make one long for the academic plum, the graduate course, or that plum of plums, the seminar. I mean the greater likelihood that at the graduate level there will be students who are arrived at at least a college level. In a graduate course in Faulkner, one is likely to have students who have read some Faulkner. But except at a few exceptional places, and sometimes by rare accident at many places, the chances of teaching undergraduates minimally prepared for some delight in literature, seriously taken, are rare. It is a larger question, which we won't go into here, as to whether this parlous state of student mind in the academy is an effect of the specialization in academic disciplines such as literature and history and philosophy in imitation of science, or whether the specialization is a late refuge for professors fleeing the intellectual incapacity of students. My own position on the question would indict specialization as culprit.

Which brings me to Mr. Brooks and his little book on Faulkner's fiction, a book which should be a delight to any professor or graduate or undergraduate suited to the academy in the first place—for reasons I want to explore briefly. *First Encounters* is a prologue to Faulkner's work, written after Mr. Brooks has made a long journey and returned to share it. He shares generously, as one bearing a valuable gift, and considerately, as one knowing the realities of the modern academy in which he would share that gift. One may start here not simply to learn how to read Faulkner's great work and see its greatness. The deeper lesson is how to move beyond Yoknapatawpha, to understand an ancient relation between life and art. Mr. Brooks, who has been called "the best critic of our best novelist," knows that literature provides a resonant ground in which may flourish serious social pleasures. Through such growth of mind and spirit in ourselves, we pay homage to the community of man—to our strengths and weaknesses individually and in concert at this moment and throughout history. The end of such social encounters through our person is not simply knowledge, but understanding. Now reading this "little book" (as Mr. Brooks calls it) is like listening to good conversation about life itself truly seen, a conversation between a great artist and his best reader. It is to learn what it means to be civilized. And one learns as well what it means to be well-mannered in good company, for Mr. Brooks includes us in the colloquy as both equal to and hungry for the serious pleasures at issue.

There is a much more important point at stake, then, than that Mr. Brooks is a native Southerner speaking of Southern things. In commending good manners as governing good conversation about good literature, I am not describing him as a civilized "good old boy"—though none of these adjectives is necessarily inappropriate. There has been a growing tendency among students of American criticism to misunderstand this gentleman as a "New Critic," by that very title removed from the virtues just ascribed to him. A reductionism of what he is about, and has been about for a long time in his interest in literature, is consequent upon those very specializations of literature in the academy that we spoke of, and he has not himself escaped such a characterization. So a clarification of Mr. Brooks's "Southernness" in relation to him as "New Critic" is in order. His "Southernness" is of more ancient lineage than any superficial anchor in geography, politics, or history, though he is very firmly anchored in the historical South— intellectually, socially, and in any department of his existence as a person. But as critic, his work is rich far beyond the accidents of the local. Now he is so precisely because he is anchored in the local at levels his biography would not seem to suggest as likely, if we should misunderstand such accidents of the local in his biography as his long sojourn at Yale. Good art, he knows, is anchored in the local, whether one is reading Milton's *Lycidas* or Donne's "Canonization" or Faulkner's *As I Lay Dying*. That realization has meant for him an immediacy of the text to the art of his criticism, but it is also a first principle that has resulted in misunderstandings of him as critic, by other critics, as we shall presently see.

That is why his *First Encounters* proves valuable to us. One knows that his conversation about Faulkner's text has an added dimension as it touches upon Faulkner's own Southernness, out of the circumstances of their both having been born and formatively reared in the South. In the *Summa theologiae*, Saint Thomas remarks those circumstances as "accidents," as particularities pointing to the essential, but not themselves the essential: the "particular conditions of any singular thing." It is a point Mr. Brooks understands about himself in relation to literature, I would say, though he needs no recourse to Saint Thomas. As wise elder reader speaking to us about the nature of the community of man, he reveals that we must make discoveries about a larger "Southernness" than simply the American South. But he does so without abandoning the necessity of particularities (the local) in that discovery. It is in respect to this witness he bears as critic that we listen to him talking about theme, character, plot in selected stories and novels of a great novelist. The community of man, as situated by Saint Thomas's accidents of the local, we discover to be universal to man. For being comfortable with the local makes it possible to move toward that universality, which is never itself abstract, properly speaking.

And that brings us to mention in connection with *First Encounters* a significant companion, a "New Critic" text that revolutionized the teaching of literature in the academy at the close of the 1930s, the famous or (in some quarters) notorious Brooks-and-Warren book, *Understanding Poetry* (1938). It is easy for us to miss an important point about that revolutionary text now, given recent developments in criticism: what was underway in it was a recovery of literature to the immediacy of life, a concern with the text now generally denied. It was a recovery Yeats called for as poet, against those who, as

> Old, learned, respectable bald heads
> Edit and annotate the lines
> That young men, tossing on their beds,
> Rhymed out in love's despair.

If literature as a livelihood, that is, as a "profession" practiced in the academy under the sudden pressures of the exploding university after World War II, took criticism away from the immediacy of life by appropriations of and then manipulations of such approaches as Brooks and Warren make in their text, we must be careful not to pillory them. That would be as wrong as to charge Milton with corrupting subsequent poets, as Eliot did and then regretted doing. If that "revolution" of New Criticism signaled in *Understanding Poetry* has fallen on evil days, we may not blame Mr. Brooks certainly.

How considerate he is of his reader, inviting him to a first encounter with Faulkner's work, even as with the poems of the textbook. He encourages one to rely first on one's own latent sensibilities, rather than on the considerable body of Faulkner criticism, much of which he nevertheless praises by the way. (And some of that work is, alas, by some who "cough in ink," as Yeats or Faulkner might complain.) Mr. Brooks assumes that his reader, sensibilities stirred, will come to distinguish in these matters. As for himself, assuming that the reader has first read the story or novel, he suggests just enough about it, quotes just enough of the work itself, to turn the reader back on his own memory and to fresh discovery in the work itself. It is that balance which gives the impression of colloquy among Faulkner, Mr. Brooks, and the welcomed reader. And so one recognizes Faulkner to be a great artist, whose work has an immediacy beyond the surface complexities of style and technique over which so much ink has been spent.

One discovers those complexities in a great writer to be organic and not surface. They are of the work's body and not a clothing provided to display the artist as haberdasher, as so many of our undergraduates seem to conclude when their teachers present form as *form*, rather than arriving at the more complex discovery of *substantial* form. One learns, for instance, to consent to Benjy's monologue in *The Sound and the Fury*, rather than seek refuge from its strangeness as discourse through exhaustive exegetical criticism that ends up emphasizing the debt Faulkner owes Joyce. Without an informed consent to that literature of genius on the part of the reader, as Mr. Brooks knows, one may lose the resonance of life itself that Faulkner turns us to through art. Thus, with Mr. Brooks's leisurely patience, which speaks his confidence in the intelligence of the young and uninitiated (as the good teacher or father must), the growing reader discovers the Benjy monologue to be much more than a tour de force by a gifted writer. He discovers the possibility, even probability, of a sensitive nature in such a seeming aberration of nature as Benjy. It is the sort of discovery that enlarges a reader's own sensibilities. Such enlargements upon the prospect of life itself by literature will find their complement more widely than in literature compartmentalized through specialization. One will be the better prepared, for instance, to respond to such sensitive work as that of Oliver Sacks, the clinical neurologist whose *The Man Who Mistook His Wife for a Hat* speaks to the mystery of mind beyond neurological science's capacity as science. One begins, that is, to discover oneself member of a community larger than his restrictive "major" in this or that "literature."

It is of course our good fortune (and Faulkner's) that Mr. Brooks shares with his author the accidents of being Southern. This allows him to take advantage of those accidents of his being as is proper to intellect. He knows firsthand the language and customs that Faulkner draws upon in presenting us a man like Sutpen, who mistook his Hundred for himself. Faulkner, as the good artist is like to do, assumes a ground supposed common to his reader, and that means necessarily a local ground, not that the reader is required to share those accidents of the local common to Mr. Brooks and Faulkner. It is rather that Faulkner, by being true to that local, makes it possible for any reader to judge the vision of the art as anchored in existential reality. As reader, one may come very close to that local reality himself—if not actually, then by its analogy to his own accidental circumstances of the local. For *being* is a common ground within any accidents of the local. This discovery is one Mr. Brooks is helpful to our making, and he does so through his recognitions of the actual, in which Faulkner anchors his vision. For instance, given the inevitable lapse from old ways and words, Mr. Brooks can provide a continuity that helps us avoid misunderstanding, whether or not we are fortunate or unfortunate in sharing Southern accidents of being with either author or critic. Thus one needs to know that the journey undertaken by the Bundren clan to bury Addie (in *As I Lay Dying*) is not a "custom of the country." Otherwise one might take as merely comic the community reaction to this strange caravan in a Mississippi countryside. And Mr. Brooks teaches a little history also, reminding us of forgotten circumstances important to Faulkner lest we overlook the ironies of history implicit in Faulkner's drama: "After all, General Lee owned no slaves, having freed those that he had inherited, whereas the great commander on the other side, General Ulysses S. Grant, did own slaves, slaves that had come to him through his marriage."

And how refreshing is our critic's delight in *The Hamlet*, how eager to share its rich fullness while remaining considerate of the reader's rights of discovery, the balance of which is the healthy enthusiasm of the generous patron. It is as if Mr. Brooks has practiced his art for a long time to be prepared to render homage, not only to a great artist, but to us as humane creatures in a shared life. That ordinate homage is a gift to us. But alas, this book is of a kind made almost impossible by modern academic concerns for civilization, which dictate to the academic mind the habit of a detachment from existence, a detachment which is called "objectivity" but which most often proves only a sterile abstraction of the mind from both art and life. It is an atrophy highly suited to the mechanics of publication, to be practiced lest the scholar perish in the academic marketplace. Such has become the curse of specialization, in our lives generally. If we were wise in our concern for civilization, we might even prohibit or at least discourage young scholars from publishing books. To publish out of one's gifts rather than as a necessity dictated by the Job Description might produce many more such wise works as this, books in which one might meet a civilized host serving our mutual humanity to its good health.

We said earlier that Mr. Brooks as "New Critic"—and indeed that whole amorphous movement—appears increasingly misunderstood. At the moment, the movement is being blamed for a range of literary ills, from the blight on language and life called "deconstruction" (a fad now fading) to the death of poets like John Berryman and Robert Lowell. New Critic porridge can be deadly, of course, depending upon the digestive systems of the partakers. But the "Southern" members of that movement are increasingly misrepresented by some, even though in doing so they may properly lament literature's turning against itself into such wayward intellectual culs-de-sac as deconstructionism or bewail the suicides of gifted poets. I think we may the better explore this point by introducing here a second author and her own "little book," an author who partook of the waters of the New Criticism. Flannery O'Connor's *The Presence of Grace* is a posthumous collection of brief reviews she contributed to her local diocesan paper, the *Georgia Bulletin*. In these she is speaking to a more local, but more varied, audience than does Mr. Brooks, since she is speaking to minds not necessarily interested in literature or philosophy at all. Her audience is that body of diverse members in a community of life sometimes touched by the academy but not directly related to it. But her address to that audience is rather closely related to that of Mr. Brooks to the readers of Faulkner.

Miss O'Connor's reasons for writing these reviews are interestingly complex. She is a fiction writer, not a critic such as Mr. Brooks by calling is. And as the good artist must be, she is primarily concerned with the good of the art she fashions, not with an audience for it. Nevertheless, she is concerned with "the generally low level of Catholic taste"—in art, history, theology. She refers to these brief reviews with sardonic humor as acts of penance, but there is the cutting edge of a serious concern for the other members in that body of which she is a part, the Church in its local manifestation. In the interest of its good health, she knows that one must engage that body at the most local of levels, intellectually as well as geographically. Hence her reviews. Even so, she is aware of how ineffective those reviews are likely to be. (I dare say Mr. Brooks does not expect his own book to recover academic criticism to good health.) But her reviews at least allow her a self-disciplined concern for that body, a concern thus made ordinate to her own practice as artist. She pursues her interest in Old Testament studies as a dimension of her fictional concern for present prophecy. And who knows, these brief notes may even strike some spark in the varied readership of the *Georgia Bulletin* (as indeed they did). In disciplined, but not esoteric, descriptions of work by Maritain and Gilson and Voegelin and others, she confirms her understanding of art and history as healthful to that body of which she is member. For those who savor the compact incisiveness she everywhere presents in her writings, even if not themselves professed members of her elected audience, this collection is a delight. In it one finds her genuine concern for the common good, under the firm control and pressure of her own remarkable intellect.

There are the delights of humor and wit characteristic of her person. She castigates a new novel as "fictionalized apologetics." She observes in another book "the clerical gift for bringing forth the sonorous familiar phrase of slowly deadening effect." Zen, she observes, is "non-conceptual, non-purposive, and non-historical" and therefore "admirably suited to be exploited by the non-thinker and pseudo-artist." She advises her local audience that Caroline Gordon's *How to Read a Novel* "along with Maritain's *Art and Scholasticism* should be studied by any Catholic group making public pronouncements about literature." In reviewing a novel by Julian Green, she laments, "Spokesmen for the deliver-us-from-gloom school of Catholic criticism have found that this novel commits the unpardonable sin: it is depressing." She to the contrary declares it written "with great deftness and delicacy and with a moral awareness that comes only with long contemplation on the nature of charity. . . . it offers no solutions by the author in the name of God," being "completely lacking in false piety." Above all, she warns her Southern Catholic audience to protect itself against the "assumption that there is a brand of criticism special to Catholics rather than that any good criticism will reflect a Catholic view of reality."

The collection, being the work of a gifted and devoted observer of humanity, is a delight in itself. It is also a rich mine for those students burdened by term papers and theses, though she would most likely regret such uses. Her interest in Hazel Motes of *Wise Blood* or young Tarwater in *The Violent Bear It Away* is reflected in her remarks on grace, especially in her concern for distinctions between Catholic and Protestant understandings of grace. But our principal interest in introducing Miss O'Connor and her own "little book" is its evidence of an indebtedness to the New Criticism as practiced by Mr. Brooks. Her uses make interesting contrast when juxtaposed to those of her contemporaries like Berryman and Lowell. To do so, I shall introduce here a critic not of the "new" school. Concerning these poets, whom Berryman's widow gives us some history of in her memoir, *Poets in Their Youth*, there is a generally perceptive critical essay in the May/June 1983 issue of *American Poetry Review*. But the essay makes such simplifications of the role of the New Criticism as contributing to their youthful misery that we must remark them.

First let us observe that this essay illustrates a current critical position on the New Criticism that has been distilled from forty years of academic study and counterstudy of that movement. So vast has been this criticism of criticism, by an exponentially growing body of the critically concerned in the academy, that one begins to suspect the current understanding a received opinion now, removed by two generations of scholars from what was in the beginning a very pluralistic movement that John Crowe Ransom dubbed "the new criticism." As our essay at issue suggests, the received opinion is now removed into the popular mind beyond the academy, for the *American Poetry Review* has been quite deliberate in removing itself from "academic" concern. It has tended instead to consider the artist who happens to be in the academy as occupying an outpost which, if not in a no-man's-land between society and the academy, at best occupies a beachhead in enemy territory. Such generally, one dares suggest, is the attitude toward the academy that one finds in "creative writing" departments or lesser enclaves of "life" in the academy.

But to our essay: Marjorie Perloff examines those young lost poets like Lowell and Berryman as "*Poètes Maudits* of the Genteel Tradition" and finds them poisoned by the "brooksandwarren" (Lowell's own biting word) approach to poetry. She finds the young poets themselves (more accurately middle-aged waifs) inheriting a principle "codified by the New Criticism, . . . the rigid separation of *art* from *life*." She says, "If Lowell hadn't existed, surely the New Criticism would have had to invent him." She mimics Lowell's self-justification:

"For wasn't poetry, as Ransom and Tate had taught him, wholly unrelated to life?" Well, no. And Lowell's position as here reflected, we must remember, is that of a poetry with no regard for the violation of persons, including himself— a lesson never learned from Ransom or Tate.

Lowell's considerable gift as poet has established what seems now a mythical figure of the poet—the American *poète maudit*—as a very present ghost haunting our post–World War II poetry. It is probable that his own position as poet in our pantheon will increasingly require rearrangement, precisely because he could not at last come to terms with the relation of poetry to life. But his failure, I contend, is in not having learned of his teachers, "old and contrary" as they might have been. His inability to do so is not so easily laid at the feet of those mentors he himself chose, as our essayist and Lowell himself might wish to do. At the level of his personal struggle as poet (revealed in the private, intimate, discrete events in his life now rather fully reported to us), he could not reconcile the virtues of art and the virtues of prudence in his *person*, a consequential dilemma not only to his poetry but also to his person. Now Flannery O'Connor was, through the Robert Fitzgeralds, "Cal's" close friend. She was troubled by his growing troubles, reported to her by mutual friends. The root of Lowell's difficulties may very well have been his inability to reconcile a certain "Protestant" heritage in respect to his person's relation to grace and a "Catholic" inclination in him to that relation, to speak here in part metaphorically, but in terms familiar to his friend Flannery. On the point, see O'Connor's remarks on Lowell in her collected letters, *The Habit of Being*, considering them in the light of this apt title chosen from a letter for the posthumous publication. Lowell could not come to terms with his calling as poet, as he might have through that work Flannery O'Connor herself found crucial in clarifying her own thoughts on the relation of prudence to art, Maritain's *Art and Scholasticism*.

We are talking about Lowell and Berryman and Blackmur and Jarrell and Schwartz and Roethke and others as a second "Lost Generation." They were very much expatriates, though they seldom left the North American continent. They did travel widely in it, as if seeking a place, but always drawn back to the Northeast (except for Roethke perhaps) again and again. They took up a variety of causes, including active participation against the Vietnam War. It is in the climate of this late activism that Lowell turned to his *Notebooks*. He was struggling to reject, it seems, his earlier inclinations rooted in a Western intellectual history larger than his immediate New England origins. Eliot had been there before him and had recovered (for himself at least) that larger tradition. But Lowell attempted, with a violence to his poetic gifts, to reject Eliot and Tate and their commitment to an older tradition of which Lowell's Boston Brahminism was an aberration. He embraced Allen Ginsberg and Whitman. It was as if he had concluded that Eliot (the poet of "Ash-Wednesday" and the *Four Quartets*) and Tate were captives of an intellectual heritage that, differing as it did from his own immediate history out of Henry Adams, was equally as untenable as his own immediate intellectual origins.

Lowell and his fellows, and particularly Blackmur, were burdened by discovering themselves most immediately heirs of Henry Adams. Lowell's attraction to Ransom and Tate and "brooksandwarren" had been a part of his earlier attempt to come to terms with that legacy from Adams. One finds the same struggle in Adams, of course, a struggle to reconcile the dynamo and the Virgin, a struggle to resolve the conflict of traditions he finds represented in contests of architecture, as between Mont-Saint-Michel and Chartres. Adams's late Stoicism as a response to his family and cultural heritage in the Boston world proved an insufficient rescue for him, a considerable pathos of spirit permeating his life in consequence, a pathos Eliot would come to recognize in himself through Baudelaire's ennui. It is this spirit unreconciled to the world that Eliot had also discovered in Adams, as well as in himself. Henry Adams's mind is very much present in the intellectual community at Harvard, including that bold attempt at its rescue through a New Humanism by Babbitt and more especially by Santayana. Puritanism reduced to Stoicism resulted in spiritual defeat for Adams, in contrast to a more viable Western tradition which Eliot slowly came to accept, that of orthodox Christianity.

It is Henry Adams's stoicism that permeates "Gerontion" with a pathetic futility. A crucial passage is directly out of Adams's own encounter on the Potomac with a culture he found seductive, though it seemed to him more Pagan than American, coming as he did from the stern, cold Boston milieus. It is the seductive world Adams encountered as "depraved May," among "dogwood and chestnut, flowering judas," and it speaks a sensual world as if the sensual alone were the proper end of man. (See chapter 18 of Adams's *Education*, "Free Flight.") Eliot exorcised that New England, Henry Adams stoicism, I have suggested elsewhere, in "Ash-Wednesday," a poem to read alongside "Gerontion." Lowell and his fellows could not. Nevertheless, Lowell encountered that world below the Potomac as seductive, as Adams had, finding in it a spirit quite alien to his New England heritage. It was Southern in very literal ways. It was there in a border country, through the person of John Crowe Ransom at Kenyon College. He traveled deeper into this strange South, pitching a Sears-Roebuck tent (literally doing so) on the grounds of Allen and Caroline Tate's Benfolly. But that pull between his Adams inheritance and the Southern "New Critics" was not to be reconciled by Lowell, or by his fellow aging youthful poets. A persuasive footnote to this point is Blackmur's forty-year struggle to write his *Henry Adams*, finally published posthumously.

Now it is one thing for Lowell to have misunderstood his Southern teachers. That misunderstanding becomes a part of the poetry he has given us, a poignant and haunting presence in it I believe. But it is a serious critical error not to understand better just what it was that he misunderstood. The misunderstanding led him to try to reinvent himself at considerable cost. This is the point missed by Miss Perloff's remarks on Lowell's seduction by the New Criticism. Most certainly Ransom, Tate, Brooks, Warren did not teach him that poetry is "wholly unrelated to life." That is more nearly a residual presence in him from Henry Adams. One should read Tate's essay contemporary to his supposed teaching of Lowell and those other displaced poets, his "The New Provincialism." What these critics taught—these "New Critics" of a Southern anchor (and what Eliot taught as well, beginning with *The Waste Land*)—is precisely that art is intimately related to life. That lesson unlearned is what underscores the pathetic confusions in the lives of Lowell, Berryman, Jarrell, and their kindred. It is worth reflecting, then, that Flannery O'Connor directly shared with these poets the same teachers, but she came to a very different understanding of what those teachers were saying about life's relation to art. The fault that Miss Perloff (and I have chosen her essay as example of a more general attitude toward these particular New Critics) lays at the teachers' door lies rather at the poets', and especially insofar as the "brooksandwarren" influence is concerned. We need only look at the "Letter to Teachers" that Brooks and Warren supply to that most influential New Critic book, *Understanding Poetry*, to take the point.

In the "Letter" the argument is that, if poetry is to be studied as literature, "one must grasp the poem as a literary construct *before it can offer any real illumination as a document*" (my italics). It must be read as human artifact of mind before one can safely see its possible correspondences as a document of that mind's engagement of life. Thus the three principles governing the selection of poems in the anthology:

1. Emphasis should be kept on the poem as poem. [That is, the poem is not a philosophical, theological, sociological treatise, nor a historical document.]
2. The treatment should be concrete and inductive. [Otherwise, emotional feeling about a poem and not intellectual understanding of it distorts the poem. It must be seen first in itself, according to its nature in the order of art, as Maritain had already cautioned in *Art and Scholasticism*, out of Saint Thomas.]
3. A poem should always be treated as an organic system of relationships, and the poetic quality should never be understood as inhering in one or more factors taken in isolation. [Again, in respect to the order of art as Maritain (and Saint Thomas) would put it: the poem is a made thing, and as such it is a thing of parts more or less suited to its body, the parts members thereof.]

This "Letter to Teachers" closes by quoting with approval remarks by Louis

Cazmian: "More important [to the student of literature as opposed to the historian], and much more fruitful than the problems of origins and development [the *history* of the poem], are those of content and significance. What is the human matter, what the artistic value of the work?" These matters grow out of history, including the particular history of the poet himself, no less than from immediate human experiences taken generally, in recognition of which one may not overlook such poems in this revolutionary text as Donald Davidson's "Lee in the Mountains" or Tate's "Ode to the Confederate Dead." Whatever art's relation to life, immediate or remote to a reader's experience, life is not separated from art. It is rather that Brooks and Warren require as the beginning of our discovery of such a relationship an understanding of the poem as a thing in itself, properly true to itself in the order of art as opposed to the order of history. Theirs is, in fact, a very Aristotelian and Thomistic position, hardly revolutionary as it was taken by some. Even the celebrated concern in the text with paradox is one manner of their homage to the mystery of life as it impinges upon art, lest the work of art be reduced to a "document" whereby life itself is reduced to literal history.

That our latest generation of lost poets misunderstood their teachers on this point is rather conspicuously demonstrated by their lives and haunts their poetry. Indeed, their common problem is a failure to separate life from art in a way significant to the demands of art itself. They are not, then, able to use reason in the making of poems (as Saint Thomas advises as necessary), becoming instead waylaid by *private* agonies as both the cause of and the end of their making. Remembering Santayana, another of the sons of Henry Adams, we may say that they are the remnants of the Genteel Tradition. They reduce both art and life to the circumference of the private, occasionally erupting into the larger world as if to escape the private but continuing removed nevertheless from the larger mysteries of life as shared by discrete persons. The *private* confounds the *personal* in such art. For when the personal, which is appropriate to art and to life in community, becomes excessively determined by private agonies of a dissociation of the person from both art and life, the *person* becomes excluded in subtle ways from persons. Increasingly, these poets were unable to distinguish their own lives from their art, and the anguish of alienation becomes the only object of art. The illusion they come to suffer, which gives their poetry an energy of pathos, is of the self as vortex, the art bubbling with the private. The reality they suffer, however, is that of the maelstrom, in which the ego is self-consumed. There is a religious intensity of testimony in them, but it is that of the lost soul crying out in the desert of the self.

Their prophecy, which has been widely responded to, is of the abyss. But their work has the force of entropy at last. Freud as their priest (such is their attempt to anchor the private life and art together) combines with New England Puritanism collapsed into a stoic defeat. In Henry Adams, the principal figure of this collapse, they puzzle a spiritual predicament. Theirs then, is a sense of doom, which becomes too often a wailing self-justification, though the poetry often engages one through its sardonic wit. Flannery O'Connor to the contrary sees in the New Criticism a rediscovering of artistic principles articulated by Saint Thomas; confirmation she finds in Gilson and Maritain, particularly as we have said in Maritain's *Art and Scholasticism*. She finds it also in that very "Southern" writer, Caroline Gordon, in *How to Read a Novel*. These recovered principles are conspicuously present in the wise and generous-spirited book by Mr. Brooks with which we began our tribute to him. (In her letters to would-be writers, Miss O'Connor repeatedly recommends Brooks and Warren's *Understanding Fiction*, sending her copy to one correspondent and remarking that it is "full of my juvenile notes.")

Now the heart of this matter is at last the distinction between man as creator and God as Creator, between man as Artist and God as "artist." If art is not carefully distinguished from life in the light of this distinction—*distinguished* not *removed*—it becomes inevitable that the poet confuse himself with God. But, in that event, since he cannot create ex nihilo, he can but feed upon himself. The consequence of such confusion is our general decline into the new gnosticism about which Eric Voegelin (one of Miss O'Connor's authors and Mr. Brooks's longtime friend) warns us. For man's assumption of himself as the god of being touches not only poets but scholars and politicians and theologians as well. The consequence of the error in the poet is that pathetic self-consumption toward nothingness, reflected in sad wayward, and sometimes arresting, poets like Lowell and Berryman. It may be their fate as poets to survive as epitaphs of our age, more than as abiding poets. That they themselves recognized this likelihood is revealed in their lives and letters again and again, but nowhere more conspicuously than by that sardonic (not tragic) irony of their poetry, the last refuge of pathos in art.

That sort of sad incompleteness is why it is important to value art as praised and practiced by Cleanth Brooks and Flannery O'Connor. Reading them, like reading Faulkner, is to experience as a gift recovered a moment of life freed from time. It is like sitting on the front porch in the always-gathering dark, before bedtime and before the pressing necessity of tomorrow's life, in a civil moment. It is a community moment, larger than the history of the particular evening itself with its enveloping geography—because it is larger than the particular persons forgathered in that moment. One shares communion with humanity in a grace of understanding, in the highest literature, a communion without which life itself has no meaning. In short, one recovers in such moments and in company with such minds the ordinate relation of art to life. One comes alive refreshed, beginning to understand that it is possible to become a person anew. Or, as Saint Paul puts it with good effect upon Eliot in his Adams-like dilemma, become a "new man."

IV. Robert Frost
One Who Shrewdly Pretends

I have it in me so much nearer home To scare myself with my own desert places.

—Robert Frost

William Carlos Williams (in *In the American Grain*) praises Edgar Allan Poe as the first American writer in whom place is decisive. Poe is "a genius intimately shaped by his locality and time." In him is "a *new locality* . . . ; it is America, the first great burst through to expression of a re-awakened genius of place." And again, "What he says, being thoroughly local in origin, has some chance of being universal in application. . . . Made to fit a *place* it will have that actual quality of things anti-metaphysical"; "The language of his essays is a remarkable HISTORY of the locality he springs from." Williams's use of *place* and *locality* is confusing to say the least, given Poe's actual work, and his praise might seem better suited to a poet like Robert Frost. But then one sees that he is giving a special twist to the terms, which in his usage point, I think, to a fundamental if unexpected kinship between Poe and that New England poet of the local, Frost. It is a kinship beneath Frost's surface of local images and Poe's surface which deliberately excludes the local. And it is precisely in the metaphysical ground of each that we find the kinship in spite of Williams's attempt to rescue Poe from the onus of a position, metaphysical or other. For the burden of this praise of Poe is on Poe's independence—his rejection of the traditions of language and, in the final analysis, of place itself. Poe dares to be "original." He does so "in that he turned his back and faced inland, to originality, with the identical gesture of Boone."

Poe faces not inland but inward; he does not address himself to that vague "America" realizing slowly westward, about which Frost speaks, in a poem made famous by his reading of it at the inauguration of President John F. Kennedy. Poe's country is that vague modern country without national bound, the self. In that cosmological poem he calls *Eureka* there is a concern with the origin and end of *thing*, but most particularly a concern with that thing of all things, the individual consciousness. And he anticipated for it an ultimate annihilation. In his own words, "*In the Original Unity of the First Thing Lies the Secondary Cause of All Things, with the Germ of their Inevitable Annihilation.*" His best

52

poems and tales, his prose poems and criticism, engage the struggle to escape annihilation, to arrest a moment of consciousness as a stay against the confusion of a world outside consciousness. That world seems always to be attempting to break into the consciousness through the senses, like a thief intent on plundering thought, and so must be kept at bay. The body is too willing an accomplice, an "insider" *almost*, who is not to be trusted at all. Consciousness, then, is in constant danger of betrayal by what should be its dependable buttress against the invading sensual world. Poe's attempt through art is to stay consciousness against the threat of the insistent particularities from an outer world, particularities whose tentacles touch consciousness through the body's porous walls.

Those particularities, in the larger Western tradition, incarnate our words with resonances of being at the most local level of our existence. Poe, in order to protect consciousness, rejects this tradition of the local, which is most conspicuously anchored in the mother tongue as it in turn is anchored in the motherland, the world of our senses, from which is fed (in Eliot's phrase) "the dialect of the tribe." That language itself is historically anchored in what Hawthorne called "our old home," our European (and specifically our English) origins. Poe is notorious for antipathy to European influences on American letters, but his disdain is not simply explained as an "American" rejection of old world origins in the interest of an original American literature such as William Carlos Williams himself champions in his essay. Poe can be scathing about an American inclination to praise whatever book comes to it as a foreign imprint. But the real antagonist to Poe is the existing world itself as it invades consciousness at the most local level, his own body. The long Western literary tradition has dramatized for the most part the mind's attempt through the body to come to terms with the existential reality of the world in which mind finds itself a pilgrim. Poe's attempt is to deny the possibility of ever doing so. That attempt is revealed in the imagistic language he uses. His works carry on their imagistic surface no significant marks of place, of the local, the traditional significant of language. It is not that his words are made "to fit a *place*," as Williams has it emphatically. It is rather that he intends by words to keep *any* place in which consciousness finds itself trapped at a safe distance. The deepest terror in Poe nevertheless lies in the loss thereby of any end toward which consciousness may move in its desire. It is doomed to a perpetual rejection of existence as the only cause, finally, of its own existence, and so its end is the agony of being haunted by itself.

Williams admits as much. "What he wanted was connected with no particular place; therefore it *must* be where he *was*." But where Poe was as a writer was not Philadelphia or Boston or Virginia. If "American literature is anchored, in him alone, on solid ground," Williams's words are metaphorical, Poe's "solid ground" being the vague, rootless homesickness that is common to much American literature sprung out of a disappointment with this new Eden we call wistfully America, the Eden we have been "vaguely realizing westward" against the frontier. Frost is himself in this tradition, though he is much more cautious about his own homesickness and hides it from us skillfully through the concrete particular that speaks its New England locale.

One is not surprised to find Williams setting Poe above another New Englander who, like Frost, uses the local; who, like Frost, is heavily dependent upon traditional forms. Williams says, "What Hawthorne *loses* by his willing closeness to the life of his locality in the vague humors; his lifelike copying of the New England melancholy; his reposeful closeness to the town pump—Poe *gains* by abhorring, flying to the ends of the earth for 'original' material." What Williams's argument boils down to finally, after one gets through the mimicry of Poe's rhetoric and typography, is that Poe is our first great genius, the founding father of American literature, because he chooses originality over all else and has the courage to reject both the past and the particularity of the local so that he may assert the absolute independence of the Self. Such an independence proves grievous to us at this juncture of our history, its cost being isolation, alienation. It was the same for Poe, despite Williams's celebration of him as if he were as "American" as Whitman. The separation from both the past and the present local is of such a degree that Poe often feels he writes only for himself. Reading *Marginalia* is like reading the notebooks of Stephen Dedalus, in spite of the fact that Poe sent those paragraphs abroad into the proliferating periodicals to woo a popular audience, for which he hungered. That is one of the added ironies, which explains his constant quarrel with the reader, for whom he nurtures a generous contempt.

Now such a reading of Poe makes him appear diametrically opposed to our popular understanding of Robert Frost. What poet of the new world has a closer, more careful concern for the particulars of the local, or more assiduously cultivates a closeness to the town pump? What sharper eye for a white feather in the tail of a frantic bird, a smoldering woodpile, cobwebs, hay stubble? Who knows hired men better, or the loneliness of isolated women? But if Poe has made his address to the dangers of the abyss, to the threat of the absurdity of existence, by divesting poem and tale of the local particular to lean upon tone and rhetoric to court horror—which he sometimes calls Beauty—we need not conclude prematurely that Frost's address to the secret of existence through his explicit images of the local sets him a pole apart. Insofar as the ground—the metaphysical ground—of his work goes, he is a hemisphere closer to Poe than to Hawthorne.

One is advised to remember that Frost is in large part a wily Odysseus, one who believes that in the interest of survival in strange seas it pays to be shifty and secretive. One may on some occasions admit to being acquainted with the night or speak of those desert places near home, closer even than snow-filled stubble. But for the most part, the strong are saying nothing about the vague homesickness that leads to uncomfortable conclusions about annihilation. Hints of spring are not evidence of immortality. The strong may say nothing, or they may tell a lie with metaphor, just for fun. And it is the poet who is best equipped to tell the lie, as Plato complained long ago. But the poet's danger comes when he *believes* the lie. When the strong talk, they do so in the subjunctive mood. The "extravagance" Frost allows himself as poet is to play the game called "it sometimes seems as if."[1] He adds, "politics is an extravagance . . . about *grievances*" (which he enjoys at times, as in "New Hampshire"). But "Poetry is an extravagance about *grief*." At his best, grief is his occasion, in "Home Burial," for instance, and in "After Apple-Picking." But it is an extravagance; one must never forget the deliberateness of the excess. To do so may result in one's being pulled into the game of poetry over one's head—lost in higher agonies of the self through illusions about metaphysical ultimates of a Platonic cast. That is, one must stay on guard by remembering that poetry is a game one plays, like restoring a wall or clearing a patch on the face of the natural world. The figure a poem makes is a momentary entertainment of the consciousness for its own protection, lest its self-universe be shaken to its foundations. Because that threat is a constant, one must be prepared to take one step backward if necessary. "The play's the thing," Frost says in the introduction to E. A. Robinson's *King Jasper*. "Play's the thing. All virtue in 'as if' . . . As if, as if!"

There are poems other than these introduced by allusion in which Frost is threatened. "For Once, Then, Something" is one. Here he recovers through playfulness, a pattern repeated to the point that some of his best poems are weakened. He will retreat into the coy or sentimental, neither of which pose is to be taken too seriously, as the threat itself must not be taken too seriously lest the beauty of the game turn toward horror and despair or even hope for a transcendent. And in this ruse he is most unlike Poe, who courts despair. Frost's retreat is a sign of a deliberate recovery of equilibrium, the step backward taken. "What was that whiteness? / Truth? A pebble of quartz? For once, then, something?" So too ends *The Narrative of Arthur Gordon Pym*, with the image of the vague figure of man standing over the abyss. But Poe's novel ends with no question mark. Frost reduces the terror and awe that creep in about the edges of his playfulness by the juxtaposition of inordinates—quartz and truth—to maintain (to borrow from another New England poet) a quartz contentment. So too at the end of "After Apple-Picking" in the juxtaposition of a woodchuck's "sleep" to "just" some human sleep. The effect is to undermine, to reduce, the seriousness of that encounter that borders upon vision and reduce it to an illusion from which the speaker has recovered.

1. "On Extravagance: A Talk," in *Robert Frost: Poetry and Prose*, ed. Edward C. Lathem and Lawrence Thompson (New York: Holt, Rinehart and Winston, 1972), 449.

Allen Tate, in his "Robert Frost as Metaphysical Poet," complains of "Birches" that the trees "seem too frail to bear such a portentous allegory." And he objects as well to the concluding line: "'Marse Robert' might have spared us the sententious meiosis of the last line."[2] But Frost isn't simply playing devices of prosody out of Quintilian. He might have spared us, but to do so would have required his going beyond the game of poetry, beyond playacting the role of poet as wise man, even cracker-barrel wise man. He would have needed to *become* the wise man, perhaps as Socrates was, whose wisdom lies in his knowing that he knows nothing. Socrates's is a movement of consciousness such as requires a surrender to something other than its own devices. But as long as we dance in a circle and suppose, so long as we play *as if*, we can distract ourselves in the dance and set aside the threat of the secret in the middle. Truth? Quartz? The "matter of fact" about ice storms, which is a delightful dance of fancy on ice rather than fact's matter?

Not that Frost hasn't pretty well decided about that secret. He speaks of it directly in a letter to the *Amherst Student*: "The background in hugeness and confusion shading away from where we stand into black and utter chaos" (March 25, 1935). That is what remains when the dancer and the dance are separated out. Chaos is the antagonist of mind, and chaos will prove victorious if mind, through self-delusion, supposes that form resides in chaos or beyond chaos or anywhere except in the action of the mind where we stand. For Frost as for Poe, in Williams's words, place is "where he *was*." There is more of Sartre in both poets than usually noted, though it is less grimly and humorlessly present in Frost.

We note Frost's opposition to "many of the world's greatest—maybe all of them" who are "ranged on that romantic side" called Platonism, as Frost remarks in contrasting himself to Robinson.[3] Plato's Idea is transcendent and requires an action of the individual consciousness for which the consciousness may take no credit. There is, one discovers, something of the New England trader about Frost in this respect. ("The Road Not Taken" is still "told" by the words, Frost's deposit in the world. He is flirting with immortality in the poem as Shakespeare does in Sonnet 18. And he is good enough, one adds, that his account is still solvent.) His mean words about Robinson, a poorer poet and greater soul than Frost, are out of the same ambition in Frost to be seen as the one great American poet of his generation. One sees that hunger for acclaim in the sharp jealousy toward Edgar Lee Masters, who seemed to threaten Frost as *the* American poet after *Spoon River Anthology*. It is also in his public, playful

2. *Memoirs and Opinions: 1926–1974* (Chicago: Swallow Press, 1975), 104.

3. Quoted in Cleanth Brooks and Robert Penn Warren, eds. *Understanding Poetry* (New York: Holt, Rinehart and Winston, 1960), 370.

encounter with Sandburg over the question of form in poetry—kitten play, but
with his claws not quite sheathed. One prefers Frost's advancement of the Self as
gamester in the poems, of course.

It is in the poems that Frost makes the best of his anti-Platonism, rather than
in unfortunate remarks to Louis Untermeyer or in his occasional prose statements and prefaces. One doesn't need to be told apart from the poems that Frost
takes mankind to be, as he says in his letter to the Amherst students, "thrust
forward out of the suggestions of form in the rolling clouds of nature" or that
what really signifies is "any small man-made figure of order and concentration"
cast against "the background in hugeness and confusion shading away from
where we stand into black and utter chaos." And one knows, reading his poems
"in the light of all the other poems ever written" as he suggests, that "so many of
[the poems] have literary criticism in them—*in* them." He adds, typically, "And
yet I wouldn't admit it. I try to hide it." How skillfully and effectively hidden is
revealed by reading "Birches" or "After Apple-Picking" against Keats's "Ode to
a Nightingale," through which reading one sees Frost's criticism of the dangers
of Platonic illusion. The same may be done with "A Boundless Moment," a more
playful reading of the Platonic inclination. And Wordsworth's wooing of "something deeply interfused in nature" in "Tintern Abbey" receives a rather more
caustic commentary in Frost's "Mending Wall." Wordsworth is attracted to hedgerows that have become "little lines of sportive wood run wild," thus violating the
poet's mind through illusion, as they violate hedgerows' responsibility to con-
strain nature. Something in nature doesn't love a wall. But it isn't elves: it is
inrolling clouds of chaos, with which one may play the game of personification
if he will, so long as he doesn't succumb to the belief that something in nature
binds consciousness in a larger order than of its own devising. (It is at such
points that one finds Frost aligned with Wallace Stevens, incidentally.)

Allen Tate, in his remarks on Frost as metaphysical poet, remarks of "Mending Wall" that "good neighbors are good to have, but good fences do not make
them good neighbors. Here we have Frost's perilous teetering upon the brink of
sentimentality. Fences good or bad make nothing; but upon the rhetorical trick
that attributes causation to them the poem depends." Mr. Tate finds the poem
subject to the same weakness in its conclusion that I have suggested one finds in
"For Once, Then, Something" and "After Apple-Picking." But I do not think
sentimentality threatens "Mending Wall" as it does "Birches." There is rescue
possible, which requires first a more extensive quotation from Mr. Tate. He
continues: "I could wish that this fine poet had drawn upon his classical learning
and had alluded to the first thing that the Romans did when they were making a
settlement: they built a low wall that would enclose a forum and in the middle
set an altar. The wall around the altar shut out the infinite . . . as if they might
have foreseen the disorderly love of infinity that Walt Whitman would bring into

the world."[4] I could wish the same, but I recognize that Frost's position opposes both Walt Whitman and the Romans. For all his celebration as public poet and in spite of his classical training, Frost is not a poet of community, any more than he is a poet who will allow consciousness to bleed freely into the world as Whitman does. "Mending Wall" precisely reflects Frost's position. The act of building walls does indeed preserve *one* (not the community) from both the encroachment of infinity and the dissipation of the self in infinity where all walls are down (as with Whitman). There stands the figure of chaos in the shape of a man, the neighbor hulking beyond the wall "like an old-stone savage armed."

The poem, given such an antagonist, becomes finally a game like that of swinging birches—one that the narrator must play alone, since the "neighbor" will not go behind the scripture on walls. That neighbor might possibly agree to "elves" as the culprit, but that reduces the game to a rather primitive level not worth the wit expended. The suggestion isn't even made aloud. For there has been no response to the suggestion that "My apple trees will never get across / And eat the cones under his pines." A response is possible: pines invade and take over ordered trees—apple orchards. Even that domesticated cow can be affected by disorder in fallen fermented apples and go wild, as the neighbor well might know. But he moves in darkness himself, a darkness of the mind that doesn't know the game of the mind with chaos, which game depends upon the mind's cleverness with walls, one of which walls is the language itself. The *why* of walls is left the sole interest of the narrator, who plays with words against himself. The interruption of the game by the repeated "saying" from a New England almanac that concludes the poem is ironically deceptive. One proof that it is so is that one has so often to point out, even to bright readers, that the narrator initiates the repair, that the narrator is not opposed to walls at all.

More often than we notice, Frost is playing a private game in his poetry, a poetry disguised as public through its particulars. In this respect, once more, we find him akin to Poe and to that direct descendant of Poe, Wallace Stevens. The game in Frost is typically between fact and fancy, as in "Birches," where the reality of the ice storm is adorned metaphorically till fact is hardly extricable from fancy and is indeed of very minor interest. The more interesting game is in the dissolving of the point of view so that the remembering man becomes the boy and returns to being the man—a modulation of awareness such as one finds less skillfully done in Whitman's "Out of the Cradle Endlessly Rocking."·The game under way in "After Apple-Picking" lies in the dissolving of sense images into faint dream images veiled from the senses' actions in the world in order to please a weary body and yet not surrender the world. The body drifts toward sleep, but the "feelings" still reach toward the outer world. The mind won't

4. *Memoirs and Opinions*, 105.

surrender its images to oblivion, and so dream is the compromise it makes with the tired body. The "I" holds an impression of the world through the instep arch that "keeps the pressure of the ladder-round." And it keeps the body's larger feeling for the ambiguous outer world in the kinetic image of that line in which meter and sense (taken doubly) complement each other so effectively as to gently stir the body back to the world: "I feel the ladder sway as the boughs bend." The lover of that ambiguous outer world has had as much love as the body can take, but is reluctant to let go. The internal game that teases chaos is somewhat obscured for us by the very concreteness of Frost's images from the world adjacent to the senses. We too have seen stones like loaves, have filled cups up to the brim and over, have seen dirt on a spade. But what I suggest is that the surface virtues of Frost's poetry, for which he is generously praised, are in part a crafty disguise of that internal game. If Poe's rescue of his independence takes the form of rejecting the local, Frost's may be said to take the form of hiding it deeply in the local.

Strategically, insofar as Frost's poems are deliberately dramatic, his celebration of the Self lies in his pitting heart against mind in their conjunction with consciousness. The dramatic game aims toward balance. One may take a poem that is not among his best, "On the Heart's Beginning to Cloud the Mind," as a paradigm—as a key to the bulk of Frost's poetry. The speaker sees a light in the darkness, through "wreaths of engine smoke," against which to play heart and mind. The light is seen first sentimentally with the heart, then realistically with the mind. The poem comes to rest in a balance, falling rather neatly into halves. This playful struggle between heart and mind carries the implicit message that the one is required for the pleasure of life and the other to prevent the pleasure from consuming the speaker in illusion. The one is a "feminine" impulse, the other "masculine." If the "feminine" is victorious, it draws the consciousness off to "lady-land," a victim of chaos, however soothing the images of that chaos may be, as in woods filling up with snow. If the "masculine" overwhelms, it so isolates the consciousness from the threatening chaos that no game at all is possible. The game is most engaging on the precipice, so long as one has the option of taking one step backward.

When Frost's poems are most dramatically successful, the impulse of heart and the requirements of mind find embodiment in human figures, usually husband and wife. The drama is nicely balanced (in the old sense of *nicely*) in "Two Look at Two." The conflict is resolved in a softening of Warren in "The Death of the Hired Man," the turning point Warren's concession through his use of the familiar "Si." The conflict is left suspended in "Home Burial." It is played out but not resolved in "The Runaway," the feminine having the last word, the snow still falling. It is mischievously and playfully suspended in "Stopping by Woods on a Snowy Evening" by a reversal of roles through which the horse speaks horse sense, with the repetition of words in the final line leaving an afterglow of feminine irresolution. One might be tempted, reading these poems, to see as the dramatic center in Frost the battle of the sexes. But that would be a mistake. For he is fundamentally an allegorist of the alienated Self. One need only turn to those lyrics in which there is but the one character, the awareness of the poem, to correct the inclination: "Acquainted with the Night," "Desert Places," "Design," "For Once, Then, Something." The dramatic game between heart and head finds its dramatic form when played against the rolling clouds of nature, which when seen from the perspective of the consciousness behind the poems includes horses and woodchucks and woodland clearings and farmers and their wives and dead and dying children. It is a game which for itself alone might find few players, and that is one reason for its prudent disguise in the poems. For Frost, like Poe, seeing no meaning in existence beyond the individual present moment of the consciousness, is nevertheless and contradictorily hungry for audience. Like the drumlin woodchuck who knows the variety of his escapes, Frost through the game of verse can write, pretending to be the woodchuck:

> I can sit forth exposed to attack,
> As one who shrewdly pretends
> That he and the world are friends.

Such is the secret side of Frost's lover's quarrel with the world.

Frost, is, then, in his understanding of the mind's relation to existences separate from mind, closer to Poe than the obvious differences in their strategies with image at first suggests. What we discover, when we plumb the images of both, is that Frost's solution to Poe's dilemma of the alienated mind, besieged by the existent world and cut off from transcendence, is to become a wily tactician. I mentioned by analogy the wily Odysseus, that great hero in the Western tradition, a man for any encounter. But with Frost at last I come to be reminded also of another Greek, one bearing a suspect gift. Sinon (as Aeneas laments) maneuvers the famous horse into Troy through a very clever fiction. It is a fiction of "as if," accepted by the wise men of Troy (with occasional objection, as by Cassandra) as actual and not illusional. One might say that a subjunctive taken as indicative proves Troy's downfall. I suspect that one may at last discover that Frost's uses of the local, his uses of place that are so very persuasive in the superb gift of image and music that is his, prove no more a recovery of the local to anxious listeners than do Poe's. For at the level of each poet's vision of man in the world lies a terror. Frost, in a famous sentence we have already alluded to, says that a poem is "a momentary stay against confusion." For him, the origin of that confusion is the threat to his own consciousness of an invasion by the world, against which the senses are uncertain ambassador at best. Frost in this respect is very much the modern autonomous and alienated mind. His tactic is to overcome the world through its own tactics, by reducing its reality to the subjunctive "as if" and thus undermining its intolerable actuality.

As prosodist and rhetor, Frost reminds one of John Donne. He is a most "metaphysical" poet, though his metaphysics is that of the alienated, secular mind when all is said and done. If his were a vision of human existence allowing no alternative vision, we should have to celebrate him with less reservation than I have. Given his vision, his uses of that vision in art are superb. A Frost poem at his best, taken at the level of art, is an arresting fiction. One honors the gift. It is only that we must be reminded that the virtue of art and the virtue of prudence have in the end a relationship that can be ignored only at risk to the good health of mind itself. One must be cautioned, I believe, not to embrace the implicit vision in Frost's art through an easy faith in that vision as the one true way of seeing man in his own nature and in nature. The warning is less necessary with Poe, because his very placelessness (William Carlos Williams to the contrary) is an ever-present caution to us. Frost's poetry is so palpable through his strategy that his position as autonomous mind and his advocacy of that position as the only tenable one are very easily overlooked.

V. Ezra Pound
The Quest for Paradise

i

For an old bitch gone in the teeth,
For a botched civilization. . . .

I ought to set out my own position as I begin this essay on Ezra Pound.[1] His understanding of the nature of man and of man's relation to existence differs so widely from my own that the reader needs to know that a basic argument, as ancient as Plato and Aristotle, is at issue. To know my position in the argument will protect the reader, since I intend to call in question Pound's, while nevertheless paying tribute to him. One acquainted with his life and work will know already that he called for "the collapse of Xtianity" early in his attempt to become a vatic poet rescuing Western civilization. I myself find Christianity, if not in collapse, certainly in considerable disarray, in a condition that troubles me. On the other hand, I observe that the secular civilization that would replace it is in even greater danger of chaos, and I believe as well that it is Christianity that may call us back to a way lost in the dark wood of history since Dante's day. Not that I intend to press that point: I intend only to alert my reader to my position, so that he may judge my praise of Pound in the light of that commitment.

My position, then, is that man is individually and collectively incapable of overcoming, through his powers alone, the inherent inadequacy of his fallen nature. He is tempted therefore to a cowardly despair on the one hand or to a tragic arrogance on the other; only through that miracle whereby time and place were overcome, the Resurrection, I contend, may man's desire for order, for right-mindedness, find ultimate significance. One sees immediately that in my terms neither Pound nor Eliot is finally identified with Prufrock's great refusal—his cowardly despair. But one sees as well that Pound's address to the world is that of one who would transform the present and future through his

---

1. I am indebted to Pound's publishers for the quotations from his poetry as follows: Ezra Pound, *Personae*, copyright 1926 by Ezra Pound, reprinted by permission of New Directions Publishing Corp., and Faber & Faber, Ltd. Ezra Pound, *The Cantos*, copyright 1934, 1948 by Ezra Pound, reprinted by permission of New Directions Publishing Corp. and Faber & Faber, Ltd.

own will, whereas Eliot takes history to have been once and for all transformed two thousand years ago. It is on this point that Eliot and Pound diverge, being otherwise so often in agreement in their pursuit of beauty and order.

Allied in my thinking with Eliot, I must as critic necessarily approach my subject from a committed position. But in consequence I need not set aside achievements of such non-Christians as Pound on the grounds that they must of necessity bring forth unpalatable fruits; nor need I find a means whereby obviously appealing fruits may be rationalized as in some vague way consecrated by the rationalization itself. The devil, we know, has a gift for song, even as have the angelic hosts. But one were arrogantly brave indeed who presumed to know too easily which is which, as one were foolishly vain to turn the uses of either to his own ends. As for the songs of men, their sources are not so purely demonic nor angelic as to allow our anthologizing in one book the praises of Christ and in another songs to the Antichrist. The complexity of man's will and the mystery of Grace affect all the gestures of the mind toward truth, the formal gestures of words no less than any other.

Given the controversial nature of our subject, we might note that Eliot views Pound with far more tolerance of his humanity and understanding of his art than are exhibited by some of the severe, strident critics who rose in such righteousness against Pound's person and poetry subsequent to World War II. The point I underline is that, given the Christian perspective, a charity is possible which is not consequently permissive. One is certainly not encouraged by that position to assume the role of Dante's Minos. On the other hand, it is rather characteristic of our un-Christian times that Pound was in effect condemned without a trial and for a time his poetry dropped from the anthologies. There was an attempt by some, professing a dedication to liberty and justice, to relegate the man and his art to outer darkness, an attempt that met courageous opposition from men like Allen Tate, Conrad Aiken, and Eliot. A confrontation with the man and his work was for a time expediently avoided through declaring Pound insane. His devotion to literature, and particularly to the works of others at the expense of his own economic well-being, was offered in evidence. Pound was then committed to thirteen years' confinement in St. Elizabeths Hospital for the Insane. (A minimum sentence of five years imprisonment and a fine was a possibility had he been tried and convicted.) Pound was in effect found guilty and imprisoned without trial, and I know of none of his enemies who is not embarrassed by that fact, save perhaps Robert Graves.

As we move further from the events of World War II and its aftermath, we shall investigate more calmly a relation between Pound's sanity hearing in a federal court and our legal stance at the Nuremberg trials. Certainly the recent agonies of civil disobedience, the questions of order raised by our H. Rap Browns and Eldridge Cleavers, make the question of Pound's incarceration all the more complicated. Pound's letters from Italy to Attorney General Francis Biddle in July 1943 may prove prophetic. On learning of his indictment for treason, he wrote: "The assumption of the right to punish and take vengeance regardless of the area of jurisdiction is dangerous. I do not mean in a small way; but for the nation." Draft-card burners give an emphasis to Pound's words, though they cite not Pound but the Nuremberg trials.

When we reach a position from which to survey these circumstances more dispassionately, we may conclude what was concluded of old: that intolerance springs most intolerably into voice and deed whenever the fundamental Christian position is abandoned for the prospect of man's making the present and future in his own image. When a worldly utopia is being pursued, any means become sanctified by desire, the means becoming increasingly cataclysmic as that utopia more and more fails. The smoke that lingers over Auschwitz signals a failure, but so does the smoke over Detroit, Chicago, and Washington, a point to be observed in the degeneration of dissent into anarchy. In Pound's America the degeneration is to be observed historically in that confused decline of Puritanism which fascinated Hawthorne, worried James, and angered Pound. It is a degeneration reflected in the abuse of the world's body by the forces of pragmatic conservatism on the one hand and pragmatic liberalism on the other, whether the current banner be Fascism, Communism, or the Great Society. Given a secular world, we tend not to see in it any witch burning if there is not in fact either a literal destruction of the body or a widely publicized persecution. We become highly incensed by the spectacle of Joseph McCarthy, but we cannot conceive of having abused Ezra Pound. It is at least ironically disproportionate to condemn Pound's attacks upon Franklin Roosevelt as treason and be amused by a *MacBird*.[2]

I shall be concerned with Pound's poetry in the following pages. But his political, social, and economic affairs are inextricably woven into the literary concerns. Pound has insisted from the beginning on risking both his person and his art on what he considered fundamental issues, an insistence that, in an age largely concerned with self-preservation and material well-being, has made him appear indeed insane. As uncommitted as Pound is to the basic Christian position of the Fall and Redemption, the basic point to be kept in mind in this essay is that he is in many respects a figure like God's fools, who always appear both

2. Though sensational at the time, Barbara Garson's *MacBird* (Berkeley: Grassy Knoll Press, 1966) is now largely forgotten. Dwight Macdonald in a lengthy review of the play (*New York Review of Books*, February 9, 1967) declared it the "funniest, toughest-minded political satire I've read in years." He did caution against our taking too seriously the implications, established even in the name of the publishing house now as passe as the play, that even as Shakespeare's Macbeth is the moving cause of Duncan's death, so too was LBJ in John Kennedy's.

ludicrous and dangerous. This likeness alone is sufficient to give one pause, in the interval of which these observations on Pound and his work.

ii

seeing he had been born
in a half savage country, out of data. . . .

Ezra Loomis Pound was born October 30, 1885, in Hailey, Idaho, where his father had gone to open a land office and act as assayer. His parents themselves were recent migrants, having made the move apparently as a practical convenience to Ezra's grandfather, Thaddeus Coleman Pound, who had acquired silver mines in the region. When Pound was eighteen months old, his parents moved to New York City, and thence to Wisconsin, where the grandfather was established as a minor lumber baron. From Wisconsin they moved to Philadelphia, where Pound's father, Homer Loomis, became assistant assayer of the U.S. Mint. The family lived in Wyncote until Homer Pound's retirement, at which time both mother and father joined Ezra in Italy.

Pound is very much aware of the history of his family, a witty account of which he gives in "Indiscretions, or Une Revue de Deux Mondes," in which he acknowledges a descent on his mother's side from New York horse thieves. But it is his grandfather Thaddeus who was most immediately relevant to Pound's career. The old man's influence upon Pound's ideas is acknowledged in the *Cantos* and in Pound's political and economic prose as well. Thaddeus rose to some eminence, establishing the Union Lumber Company, building a railroad, serving in Congress and as lieutenant governor of Wisconsin. Apparently he accomplished his ends by immediate, practical actions. For instance, he issued company scrip, in competition with the U.S. Treasury, redeemable in merchandise or lumber, until the federal government intervened.

It should be remarked that Thaddeus differed from the nineteenth-century barons more famous or infamous than he in that he seems not to have been intent on founding a dynasty in which the family exercised political and economic control of a domain. Nor did philanthropic foundations ensue, through which patronage of the arts might follow in the spirit of Renaissance Italy. The old man kept money in circulation and did not bind his son close to him. It is difficult to be certain, given our distance, but Thaddeus seems to have lacked that kind of warmth for his children that is everywhere apparent between Homer and his son Ezra, especially in the warm affection of Pound's letters to his parents.

Pound's affection for his parents and for his wife and children is in rather significant contrast to the attitude in his poetry concerning the family as a social institution. With respect to this attitude one might also contrast him with his contemporary William Faulkner, who shares a fascination with the history and destiny of America. Faulkner's own grandfather was a southern version of Thaddeus Pound. Faulkner seems possessed by the continuing presence of the past, dramatized by appropriations from local history and through such figures as the Sartorises, as if the past is an infection of the blood. His concern is reflected dramatically in the family relationships that give an epic dimension to his work. Violations of that past borne in one's blood, misunderstandings of it, bring grief, whether these violations reduce themselves to an abuse of persons or an abuse of the soil, both abuses reflected in the decay of manners, customs, responsibilities.

Pound believes otherwise, insisting that "the earth belongs to the living." It is a similar attitude in Thaddeus that appeals to him, while at the same time Pound is full of indignation over the inevitable abuses of the earth. He attacks perpetual property rights through inheritance, as well as those salvings of conscience, public philanthropies, for the desecrations of nature that have been so much a part of America's social and cultural life in the twentieth century. On this point William Carlos Williams says: "Pound's 'faults' as a poet all center around his rancor against the malignant stupidity of a generation which polluted our rivers and would then, brightly, give ten or twenty or any imaginable number of millions of dollars toward the perpetuation of *Beauty*—in the form of a bequest to the New York Metropolitan Museum of Art."

What Pound demands is a responsible use of nature, by which he does not mean the quiet tenantship of Faulkner's Ike McCaslin. He is interested in a civilization's rising through the application of human skill to nature, an application which achieves responsibility as it achieves an orderly society. Pound's attention is largely focused upon value gained through the workman, whether the workman be laborer or poet, whether the result be a building or a remaking of Propertius. Order is the result of an acceptance by society of the relative contributions of the individual to society, "each in his nature," as he puts it in Canto XIII.

Pound's respect for nature is markedly different from Faulkner's. When Pound invokes "Mercury god of thieves" as a particular muse in his poetry, he is revealing his attitude toward the world and its past: the world belongs to the living. "Nothing counts save the quality of the affections," he says in the very moving *Pisan Cantos*. But affection is finally a personal, self-made quality, an addition by the will, rather than through the bonds of nature that Dante makes so much of. Nor does a man found a line extending into the future, built by his own presence as a point on a line of points out of history. One rather lives as ex-emplum of affections; one orders the mind and actions toward nature and man, being otherwise an accident of time. In that ordering of mind and action, one appropriates whatever comes under the examination of mind—Confucius, Ovid, Villon, Sigismondo Malatesta, Jefferson, Adams being equally fathers of that mind.

A man of no fortune may then come to have a name, given bravery in addi-tion to a good mind. Where Faulkner sees such an approach to the world as implicitly arrogant, leading inevitably to tragedy, as in the history of that self-made man Thomas Sutpen, Pound is himself too actively engaged in that mak-ing to dwell on its tragic possibilities. Horatio Alger as an American hero is extended by Pound beyond the materialistic implications usual to that myth. The self-made mind defines the responsible uses of nature, material and intel-lectual, toward civilization. And with its inexhaustible energy (since it is Pound's mind) it sets about becoming father to a world. Pound's devotions are not only to the making of poems but to the making of poets and statesmen alike, albeit with the most generous of intentions and with personal sacrifices. Pound's view of tradition and the possibilities of family as made by the self-made mind is implicit in his cry to poets to "make it new," as it is a part of his insistence that local gods are more important than the more substantial patriarchs. The posi-tion is reflected more largely in his poetry, particularly the *Cantos*, by the center of that work, the mind of Ezra Pound, which is busy assimilating and building out of assimilation. The poet is the local god to his work. Sartoris and Sutpen are centers separate from William Faulkner; but we are always aware of the immediacy of Uncle Ez despite the marvels of his masks. Nor is the difference in genre sufficient to explain the difference between Pound and Faulkner. Both men are set upon an epic dimension to their art. The difference lies rather in the men's views of tradition and family, which views affect the role each assumes in his own work. I think Faulkner's a sounder view, for with it he sees, as Pound cannot, that the successors to the Sutpens and the Mussolinis of the world are very likely to be kinsmen of Flem Snopes and not heirs of Confucius. Through Flem's odyssey, Faulkner indicts those evils in the modern world that Pound opposes, but far more tellingly than Pound does in his crying out against usury.

Pound's view of tradition is that one may elect his ancestors. It is a view of importance to any reading of his work. It is, in part, his solution to the problem that haunted Hawthorne, James, and many other Americans who set out to be artists but thought themselves either in a traditionless society or alien to a Puritan tradition set too firmly upon a pragmatic road. How can culture flour-ish in a rootless society increasingly devoted to things, but not seeing the beauty of things? With a sensibility akin to that of James, Pound turns to Whitman for an answer. The poet becomes all men, appropriating all conditions and states unto himself. Thus it is that a poet becomes father to his age. Considering this the bard's role, Pound becomes quite other than the singer of the first *Odyssey* or the poet of the *Metamorphosis*, those works nevertheless considerable influences on the *Cantos*. I suggest that Pound's particular devotion to the troubadours, though in part an attraction to their skill (the absence of which in Whitman embarrassed him), is in large part an appreciation of their kindred rootlessness in a society undergoing rapid changes with no clear center by which to measure the change. Despite his debt to Dante, Pound is more at home with the more secular poets—Cavalcanti, Bertrand de Born, Arnaut. The emergence of merchant princes at the time of poetry's great flowering in Europe was suggestive to Pound of possibilities in America itself. He sought a practical way of harnessing some of that energy toward art, pursuing patrons for promising sculptors, musicians, poets, novelists.

The possibilities of a renaissance led Pound to act out the poet's role as he thought most effective. For the poet must sing into being a culture; he cannot lament the past or dwell too long upon the future. Pound, the wandering troubadour of our century, seized from the past for immediate use whatever he considered economically, politically, or poetically viable, attempting through the qualities of his own voice to "make it new." A liveliness, a spontaneity results in his work. One notices also in considering the large body of his poetry that he more often sings joyfully, confidently, than do most of his contemporaries. In an age when the dominant note of our poetry and fiction has been a lament for the decline of the West, Pound has been predominantly optimistic. Not, of course, that he doesn't write lament. But his lamentation turns quickly to an indictment of particular people and principles, followed by a program for recovery, however vague that program. He is quick to illustrate, whether through "Homage to Sextus Propertius" or by sharing scant money with a hungry fellow poet.

In *Patria Mia* (written in 1912) he builds a program: "The first duty of a nation is to conserve its human resources. I believe this sentence contains the future greatness of America. I believe that because of this perception we shall supersede any nation that attempts to conserve first its material resources." This is to set about a rescue of the world on a very large scale indeed. Such a rescue requires very large programs, administered on a large scale: in the light of our nation's midcentury programs, Pound's are less startling now than they were before World War I. One should, of course, keep in mind that Pound's program was to be evolved out of natural resources, not out of wealth decreed into existence through the fiction of deficit spending, a major difference that led Pound to oppose Franklin Roosevelt so intensely as to be formally charged with treason.

One of the proposals in *Patria Mia* is that a publicly supported academy of artists be established, toward the evolution of a cultural capital to set a pattern for natural cultural development. Environment was to be radically affected. When Pound presently looks into Confucius, he finds there principles he has already accepted. Canto XIII presents the position:

> If a man have not order within him
> He can not spread order about him;
> And if a man have not order within him
> His family will not act with due order . . .

A man sets stability in his family, rather than the other way around. He begins as "a man of no fortune with a name to come," an American frontier formula, though the phrase is out of the *Odyssey*. "The French morale," says Pound in *Patria Mia*, "starts with the belief in the familial unit. . . . We in America are horrified at the French matriarchate, at the tyranny of the family, but hardly as much I think, as at the English 'chattel' system." And in the same work, "Our family bond is so light that we collect another family, not bound by blood, but by temperament." This is the frontier spirit, the migrant spirit which must find community as it shifts and moves. Where there are family ties, such as those commonly attributed to the more settled southern culture, danger lies: "The worst element, from the intellectual point of view, are the 'good families' in the small 'lost' towns! They own property. They are the most important factor in the places." Again, "There are in the south quaint remnants of the feudal system, of the plantation. Neither of these relics need be much considered in forecasting America of the Future." Pound proposes the establishment of family lines based on the "quality of the affection." Why not an annuity to the promising artist, which that artist passes on when he no longer needs it "to the man who, in his opinion was most likely to use his time for the greatest benefit of the art." If he needs that annuity all life long, supplied by the government, he could leave it by his will "to his heir in art."

Pound is clearly set upon a most radical change in the nature of the family, at once discounting the natural affections that give rise to those comforts and protections that family continuity has given its members, whether blessed by many or few talents. The family has historically proved itself a check upon the excesses that rise to destroy society itself, utopian abstractions usually being the immediate weapon. In his arguments, Pound is very much what one must call, with our contemporary political vocabulary, a liberal, believing in the desirability of government's adjusting the society through its power and potential wealth, toward a flowering. And very positively he is concerned for the little man, the oppressed; poverty is generally the dragon he pursued in the late 1920s and the 1930s in arguments that led him toward St. Elizabeths.

Within a decade following Pound's writing of *Patria Mia*, "a man of no fortune with a name to come" began his rise to a position of power under Pound's eyes, putting into operation expeditious programs that turned his society upside down, but bringing out of the turmoil a momentary order such as his country had not enjoyed for a long time, largely through turmoils he had himself deliberately fomented toward his own ascendancy. His display of effective leadership in the world won public praise from such men as Winston Churchill and Franklin Delano Roosevelt no less than from Pound. That man was, of course, Benito Mussolini. The point repeatedly insisted upon by Pound in the years preceding World War II was that Mussolini, like Jefferson, was an individual who saw possible solutions to large problems and went about implementing them efficiently to the cultural and economic advantage of society. That the solutions were also ruthless is always easy to overlook if one looks only to the larger effects, a secret Pound kept from himself for some time.

One finds in Pound, as revealed by his approach to his ideal family and nation and art, a very strong pragmatic bent. In this respect he is a child of nineteenth-century America. He isn't transcendental along with his pragmatism, and thus he escapes to some extent that tearing of the self one finds in such sons of Puritanism as Hawthorne and James. But his position is not compatible with Christian orthodoxy, as Eliot's is. Kung, according to Pound, said "nothing of the life after death." What Pound insists upon, with Confucius as authority, is concrete action here and now, resulting in a strong order and stable economy, out of which he expects beauty to flow. He overlooks the possibility that art may be the child of disorder, nowhere better illustrated than in Pound's own struggles as a lyric poet in pursuit of the epic.

What art doesn't touch at some tangent the question of life after death? Even Pound cannot refrain from introducing that tangent by negating it. In a very real way the theme of death haunts Pound, whether expressed in angry denunciations of Christianity or in a Keatsian attempt at beauty against chaos. Canto XIII ends with such an attempt, those very beautiful lines reminding us how closely Pound associates the concepts of beauty and order, terms sometimes interchangeable in his art:

> The blossoms of the apricot
>> blow from the east to the west,
> And I have tried to keep them from falling.

Pound says with Heraclitus, accepting the inevitable, "All things are a flowing." What sets his teeth on edge is the "tawdry cheapness" of our age that disguises that flowing, thereby denying both chaos and order. But ignorance is the enemy, and education—not salvation—the weapon.

iii

> He strove to resuscitate the dead art
> Of poetry; to maintain "the sublime"
> In the old sense.

Patria Mia is an angry love letter to America, to which Pound wished to play Pygmalion. The resuscitation he practiced was shock treatment (one of the reasons he was attracted to H. L. Mencken) and the mouth-to-mouth respiration of poetry through his singing of old poetry made new. In anger he castigated intellectual slovenliness, particularly as he saw it settled into the academy; cultural poverty as he saw it reflected in the respected journals and publishing houses; and political duplicity as he saw it rewarded at the national level by high office in executive and legislative branches of government. Through sheer force of mind, and out of that love that has seemed hate to many, he did finally establish a kingship in our literature.

Pound gives himself to action. Viewing the late nineteenth-century political, social, artistic life characterized by the disease of usury, he joined battle with America and on America's behalf and did not relent. To him the most basic meaning of that important word *usury* is the abasement of the mind and of nature for the private ends of lust, gluttony, and avarice.

There is a poignant recognition of failure near the end of his life, remembered by Allen Ginsberg from a visit to Pound in Italy. Ginsberg was attempting to reassure Pound of his accomplishment as poet in the *Cantos*. Pound responds, "The Paradise is in the desire, not in the imperfection of accomplishment." But he goes on, thinking of himself as poet, "The intention was bad . . . any good has been spoiled by my intentions—the preoccupation with irrelevant and stupid things." And near the end of his life he wrote: "Re USURY. I was out of focus, taking a symptom for a cause. The cause is AVARICE." That is a distinction he should have learned from Dante much earlier. For as Dante, and Ezra's friend Eliot, believes, what is at most desperate risk is not society eroded by usury but the particular soul of the usurer eroded by willfulness. The social evils of usury obscured the personal evil of avarice. But there is a more basic personal evil involved.

As Parson Eliot (or Dante) points out, avarice has its own root cause in pride. The sins of incontinence (lust, gluttony, avarice) are therefore not conditions of the soul sufficient to heroic or tragic scope, though pride has proved to be. That is the point finally of Eliot's criticism of Pound's Hell Cantos (XIV-XV). In his constant pursuit of a definition of money, Pound strove to establish a basis for an equitable relationship of citizen to wealth within the governance of the political state. In his early career, he spent a disproportionate amount of time writing on the theories of C. H. Douglas and, later (in the 1930s and 1940s), on those of Silvio Gesell. In the early thirties, having tried for fifteen years to influence economists, statesmen, poets, and artisans, he was insisting as strongly as ever that "the scientific price of any article to the consumer is the cost of production." The evils of the depression could be cured by issuing scrip to consumers determined by the cost in labor of unconsumed goods for which there existed no money for purchasing. Dante, too, argued against the inflation of usury, considering man's relation to nature that of temporal reeve. But the emphasis is upon usury's preventing the sinner's final union with God.

In his monetary arguments, Pound replaces Douglas with Gesell's arguments for a "shrinking money." As Pound explains it, he would have "a paper-money system by which everyone was obliged, on the first of the month, to affix a stamp on every note he possessed equal to one per cent of the note's face value. . . . in 100 months, the issue will be valueless . . . thus bringing to the treasury a sum equal to the original issue," since no notes of that issue would be outstanding against the treasury's gold or silver. As Charles Norman points out, the argument comes ultimately from Marx's Das Kapital, though Pound thinks of Gesell and Douglas as ending the Marxist era. Pound's economic theories are an outgrowth of his older argument that the earth belongs to the living. They reduce finally to a worldly concern. Pound seems to believe that, with the correction of appetite within the state, through economic measures, order will descend upon the state. In spite of the constant individual encounters that are momentary evidence to the contrary, Pound seems to believe that man is perfectible, but within the city of Dioce, the earthly city of the Cantos, and not by grace in the City of God. Like Socrates, or Pound's Confucius, he would make the mind clear, each mind in its own nature. Evil is ignorance and not perverseness. Pound will have none of the concept of man's fallen nature implied in original sin.

His position may seem strange in the light of his argument against Rothschildian conspiracy, which he strives to make satanic in the Cantos. Yet reduced to its essence, his hell is contemporary indeed. Evil is anti-progressive.

And when we look at that positive picturing of the good city of Dioce, we are amazed at how progressive and modern it is. For Pound's is an attempt to persuasively define the "Great Society." Indeed, near the end of World War I, Pound called for a "New Deal," the phrase he uses. But the implementation of Pound's practical programs would of course involve a bureaucracy as unwieldy as that he opposed. How many federal managers would be necessary to a system of "shrinking money"?

The bulk of Pound's own paper work—letters, endless monetary pamphlets and articles, portions of the *Cantos*—ought not make us overlook his valid insight into the disintegration of civilization, or a larger principle that cannot be ignored by the Christian mind as it attempts to do justice to Ezra Pound. Pound holds basically that money is a symbolic representation of work *done*. As with Dante, money is one of the daughters of art. Money representing valid work is the only legitimate money. Money out of money is the great economic heresy in Pound's economic thinking. Hence his excoriation of private banks, dramatized by reference to the Rothschilds. Hence his desire that the state act as referee of money value. It is with scorching anger that he attacks the argument that "the man who buys a plough commits the same act as the buyer of mortgages." His convictions concerning work and its fruits led to that desperate attempt to reconcile western powers before World War II, *Jefferson and/or Mussolini*. Jefferson is praised for opposing national deficits while Franklin Roosevelt is attacked for creating money ex nihilo to call forth work. Roosevelt's is a false work in Pound's view, analogous to pumping the Atlantic into the Pacific.

In Mussolini, Pound was taken in by the greatest journalist-propogandist in this century. He thought Mussolini was dedicated to an "equality in respect to work and to the nation." He understood Mussolini to insist upon "difference only in the grade and fullness of individual responsibility" ("each in his own nature"). Having moved to Italy in 1924 and having seen Mussolini's effect upon Italy in restoring order and establishing a version of the New Deal, Pound sought to exemplify his own metaphysics by referring his arguments for order in the state to Mussolini's accomplishments. Here one sees Pound bringing together his conception of the poet as the supreme priest of words and his belief in the poet as the supreme man of action. He describes Mussolini as having a poetic mind capable of seeing the *Cantos* as New Rome's *Aeneid*. Rome held much promise for the world, as Washington, New York, London, Paris did not.

In the 1930s Pound found the poet-king the culmination of a dream he had long pursued. It is a concept out of his attempt to see his country as a whole, one spirit, with one head, the fruition of that anthropomorphic inclination in him which makes him elevate the state at last above the local gods. In his earliest writings he laments that the United States has no true capital. In calling from London for a "College of Arts," he says: "It has been noted by certain authors that London is the capital of the world, and 'art is a matter of capitals.'" Really, he insists to Harriet Monroe (from London in 1916), "geography is not the source of inspiration." And again, "The gods do not care about the lines of political geography." His immediate dream is that such a capital of art might be created in America. In the interest of cultural renaissance, he called for a College of Arts in New York or San Francisco or Chicago: "a college of one hundred members, chosen from all the arts, sculptors, painters, dramatists, musical composers, architects, scholars of the art of verse, engravers, etc., and they should be fed there during the impossible years of the artist's life—i.e., the beginning of the creative period." Denying the relevance of geography to art, he sought to "find or found" a city in time and place.

But we may at this distance see that the city Pound sought in his journey was not the million-peopled metropolis free of the provinces, as he at first thought it to be. It was in his own mind, as he discovered so shatteringly in the cage at Pisa. When Virgil brought his country virtues to town, the city he announced in the *Aeneid* was as modern and immediate as yesterday's devious maneuver by Augustus Caesar. He wrote under the comfortable wings of Maecenas. Pound speaks with the voice of an impoverished Maecenas. In desperation, his voice tends to become as authoritarian as Caesar's, as in this January 1915 letter to Harriet Monroe: "My problem is to keep alive a certain group of advancing poets, to set the arts in their rightful place as the acknowledged guide and lamp of civilization. The arts must be supported in preference to the church and scholarship. Artists first, then, if necessary, professors and parsons." To Mencken he wrote, "The *country* U.S.A. [as opposed to the *cities*] is hopeless and may as well go to hell its own way."

Given our world's inclination to embrace whatever is large and in itself all embracing, it seems curious that Pound didn't receive wider support. His work is full of statements that have become clichés in social and political rhetoric. But Pound received little support. He struck many people as a wild man, in part because he insisted on a hierarchy of values within his system. For each in his own nature implies difference: some minds are better than others as some poems are better than others. Also, the very energy of Pound's dedication made many uneasy. Eliot recalls that he "was ready to lay out the whole of life for anyone in whose work he was interested." Many a beneficiary wondered what his game was in such unselfishness, a point that also baffled the four psychiatrists who examined his record and declared him insane.

Perhaps the Caesar in him was the most significant handicap to his pursuit of the golden city of Dioce. He was, in Eliot's phrase, "a dominating director." Devoted to order (*to kalon* is already a key phrase in *Patria Mia*), he would direct not only what was produced but also what would be preserved from the past. To prepare the way for Dioce, Pound sets out to educate readers. Chaucer is, culturally, an internationalist, the man in English letters Pound most often sees himself analogous to. For Chaucer lived at a point in England's history parallel to Pound and America. Each country, in the analogy, was emerging from its countriness. Pound cites with approval the Japanese emperor who selected Noh plays and then consigned the rest to oblivion. Chaucer in effect practiced a similar office in his appropriations from continental literature. Pound practices that office deliberately in his poetry, anthologies, and critical works.

In those early London years in particular, Pound appeared to be a John Brown let loose upon the world of art and politics. Those who were still comfortable in their inherited Victorian tastes, reading the Georgian poets with mild pleasure but not noticing D. H. Lawrence included among them, were horrified by Pound, if moved at all. It is at this point that one must remember and applaud Pound's sensibility. Not many men in the history of letters have been so remarkably perceptive as he has in recognizing artists worthy of encouragement, nor so tenacious in bringing their work to the attention of a reluctant audience. When Conrad Aiken was unsuccessful in persuading editors of Eliot's virtues, he turned to Pound. Pound insisted that Harriet Monroe publish "The Lovesong of J. Alfred Prufrock"; when she took its closing lines to be too pessimistic, he responded: "No, emphatically I will not ask Eliot to write down to any audience whatever." Again, "Neither will I send you Eliot's address in order that he may be insulted." He insisted that she publish Frost, and himself reviewed those first two books Frost couldn't get published in America. Pound got financial support for Joyce and promoted the *Dubliners* and *Ulysses* (though he was cool toward *Finnegans Wake*). That Joyce had leisure to finish his great works was in large part due to Pound's seeking patronage for him. He also attempted to lead Yeats out of the Celtic Twilight by serving him as secretary, in the belief, as he wrote his parents, that it was a duty he owed to the future at the expense of his own work. While not enthusiastic, he thought that something might well come of helping Carl Sandburg, and perhaps Edgar Lee Masters also. He established a foundation in Paris whose principal purpose was to get Eliot out of a London bank to write. Because he praised Edgar Lee Masters's vers libre in *New Age*, which was editorially opposed to that innovation in this century's poetry, he was cut off in the middle of a series of articles on which he was depending for money. But Pound was unrelenting. He wrote Harriet Monroe: "Isn't it worth while having one critic left who won't say a thing is *good* until he is ready to stake his whole position on that decision? I've got a right to be severe. For one man I strike there are ten to strike back at me. I stand exposed. It hits me in my dinner invitations, in my weekends, in reviews of my own work." He was talking about survival, not social acceptability. Those early words are very like his remarks when he was arrested for treason:

"If a man isn't willing to take some risk for his opinions, either his opinions are no good or he's no good." His risks from the beginning were out of what he described as his "persistent and . . . inconvenient belief that America has the chance for a great age if she can be kicked into taking it."

iv

> His true Penelope was Flaubert.
> He fished by obstinate isles

Pound announced in an editorial in the short-lived but impressive *Exile*, which he edited out of Italy: "Quite simply: I want a new civilization." This was in 1928, as Eliot was proclaiming his homage to Lancelot Andrewes. It was no less Pound's position in 1908 or 1948. We have seen something of his feelings about the "old bitch gone in the teeth" which he had been busy kicking in the ribs. If we look at American poetry at the turn of the century, as represented in those mediators of our culture at the turn of the century, *Harper's Magazine* and *Atlantic Monthly*, we can appreciate Pound's violence. One Julia C. R. Door, in the January 1908 issue of the *Atlantic*, addressed incredible, interminable lines to "One Who Went to Carcassonne":

> I can scarce believe the tale
> Borne to me on every gale!
> You have been to Carcassonne?
> Looked its stately towers upon?

Miss Door concludes with the vague desire to

> Learn its language, pray its prayer,
> Linger there till dreams are done—
> Yet—few go to Carcassonne!

Pound had gone, and so was intent on learning its language, praying its prayer. Living on the edge of poverty, he attacked with vigor such "dryrot, magazitis," but found few listeners in America.

What sets Pound aside from his contemporaries also engaged in a revolution in poetry—William Carlos Williams, Eliot, and the Vanderbilt Fugitives—is his public devotion to his elected duty, his obsession with a responsibility to poetry on society's behalf. The obsession is out of his conviction that he was the one man on the scene sufficiently equipped by talent and training to effect a revolution. Out of this conviction came an energy such as one finds self-generated in the religious fanatic, which is what Pound was. For he saw himself late and soon as Apollo's Moses, Saint Paul, Aquinas, and Milton all in one.

A case can be made that his devotions to other artists, musicians, and writers affected his own production adversely. Particularly so if we consider the dominating influence economics came to have. Certainly, judging from western literature in general, Helen and Maude Gonne are more effective as correlatives in art than is grain control in the straits off Troy or political maneuvers in Ireland. Flaubert may have been true Penelope to Pound in respect to *le mot juste*; but perhaps Douglas and Gesell were his false Calypso in respect to *l'idée exacte*. For in spite of his enlivening of fragments from Confucius, from the founding fathers such as Jefferson and Adams, and from the general history of international finance, he does not evolve in his work a metaphysical vision of money that convinces with the force of myth. When he attacks usury, as in Canto XLV, he writes movingly, but the effectiveness here lies in the enumerations of the rewards of pursuing one's daily bread, free of abusing nature or one's own mind. Those elements of the good common life attracted his nineteenth-century literary adversaries no less than Pound.

Among his many commandments, Pound is particularly emphatic about the mind's abuse of language, whether by poet or by politician. In *Patria Mia* he insists that "bad technique" is "bearing false witness"; it is a sentiment many times repeated. He sets an example by learning prosody from true poets, as a farmer or wheelwright learns of his fathers. He goes to Homer and Sappho, Horace and Ovid, the Anglo-Saxons, the troubadours and Dante, Browning and Swinburne. But of special interest to him as poet are those Englishmen who are still close enough to European literature to have not yet been overcome by the serpent in the garden of English prosody, accentuation. The Eden from which English poetry is fallen lies with those English lyricists between Chaucer and Shakespeare. In the *ABC of Reading*, he sets the following lesson:

Contrast

Chaucer	Shakespeare
the European	the Englishman

And he adds, "Steadily in the wake of the sonneteers came the dull poets." Even the continental sonnet "by 1300 . . . was becoming . . . declamatory, first because of its having all its lines the same length, which was itself a result of divorce from song." Transported into English, equal lines hardened under the dominance of accentuation as the determinant of meter, so that the freedoms still to be observed in Sidney soon gave way to the absoluteness of pentameter in the seventeenth century. In "A Retrospect" (1918) Pound advises, "Let the candidate fill his mind with the finest cadences he can discover, preferably in a foreign language." This for the sake of "rhythm," in the interest of infusing the English line with music. He quotes again that third Imagist principle he enunciated in *Poetry* in 1913: "As regarding rhythm, to compose in the sequence of the musical phrase, not in sequence of a metronome."

In the *Pisan Cantos* Pound recalls a first labor on behalf of poetry as song: "To break the pentameter, that was the first heave." One wishing to see the arguments of his struggle to rescue the English line from the metronome will read *The Spirit of Romance*, the *ABC of Reading*, and *Guide to Kulchur*, as well as those critical pieces conveniently available as edited by Eliot in *The Literary Essays of Ezra Pound*. But there is a more direct way, recommended by Eliot: reading Pound's poetry. For Pound is nowhere so persuasive a teacher as in his practice. His essay attack upon nineteenth-century sad prettiness, "Mr. Housman at Little Bethel," is carried out more effectively in verse mimicry, through which he heightens those weaknesses:

> The bird sits on the hawthorn tree
> But he dies also, presently,
> Some lads get hung, and some get shot.
> Woeful is this human lot.
> Woe! woe, etcetera . . .

"Mr. Housman's Message" in three stanzas shows the intrusion of the message by burlesquing Housman's rhyme, meter, and diction. In his attempt to lead Yeats into a new poetry, Pound proceeds more indirectly, attacking the sentimentality of the man he calls the "greatest minor poet who ever lived." Under Yeats's title, "Lake Isle," he writes:

> O God, O Venus, O Mercury, patron of thieves,
> Give me in due time, I beseech you, a little tobacco shop,
> . . . .
> And a pair of scales not too greasy,
> And the whores dropping in for a word or two in passing. . . .

The tone shifts in the closing lines, as the poet's voice turns from mimicking prayer to attack Yeats's bearing of false witness:

> or install me in a profession
> Save this damn'd profession of writing,
>   where one needs one's brains all the time.

Using one's brains, and talents, one can produce good music; that is, one can produce poetry in which the music does not sentimentally dominate as in Yeats's "Lake Isle of Innisfree," or which does not mechanically weld music to words as in Housman. "The Seafarer" carries an appropriate music; so does the lovely "A Virginal." But they are not the same music, the one recollecting hardship in adventure, the other maintaining the sweet languor of love. "The Seafarer" we are expected to read as much against Tennyson's "Ulysses" as against its Anglo-Saxon source:

> Bitter breast-cares have I abided,
> Known on my keel many a care's hold,
> And dire sea-surge. . . .

And "A Virginal" shines marvelously through its sonnet form so that one does not feel the dictation of pentameter or quatrain. As if adding the virtues of Lawes to Shakespeare, he begins:

> No, no! Go from me. I have left her lately.
> I will not spoil my sheath with lesser brightness,
> For my surrounding air hath a new lightness;
> Slight are her arms, yet they have bound me straitly
> And left me cloaked as with a gauze of aether. . . .

In another sonnet, which might be called "Mr. Shakespeare's Message," Pound comments on that hyperbolic love poetry Shakespeare himself satirizes in "My Mistress' Eyes":

> When I behold how black, immortal ink
> Drips from my deathless pen—ah, well-away!

> Why should we stop at all for what I think?
> There is enough in what I chance to say.

Pound set out not only to "break the pentameter" but to enliven the established stanza forms. Early and late his advice to aspiring poets was to write in strict form until form is mastered. He himself did just that, not by slavish imitation but by rescuing the abstract form through the particular exercise of his own voice. He demonstrates innovation from within strict form, calling attention to the necessity of making even a hoary form burst out in newness. Thus his "Sestina: Altaforte." Where most users of the sestina wrestle with repetitions in pale, timid redundancy, Pound rings out a call to action, and rings changes on that initial outburst throughout in such a manner as to imbue the form with some of the vigor one more nearly expects in the freer blank-verse monologue. Form allows, it does not dictate; that is, one hears the music of the thing in relation to its words and not in relation to the formula of its verses.

> Damn it all! All this our South stinks peace.
> You whoreson dog, Papiols, come! Let's to music!
> I have no life save when the swords clash.
> But ah! when I see the standards gold, vair, purple, opposing
> And the broad fields beneath them turn crimson,
> Then howl I my heart nigh mad with rejoicing.

One turns then to the quiet, subtle words and music of that voice named "The River-Merchant's Wife," whose letter borders on the sentimental, but never quite crosses over. One goes on to that strong expression of wonder that hovers between compliment and satire, "Portrait d'une Femme." In reading through the early poems of *Personae*, we see Pound the teacher, showing what is wrong with modern verse, showing what might be done about it, and exploring the reaches of his own knowledge, as much as of his talent. His own rigorous apprenticeship, full of marvelous occasional effects, comes to the test in that long poem he undertook to clear the air of the "schools"—Imagism having degenerated into unformed, unmusical sentiment, and Vorticism having given way to the absurd. About some of his early work, he wrote in 1918, "It has been complained, with some justice, that I dumped my note-books on the public." But for two reasons, he says. One, to train an audience toward accepting the best. And second, to survive while learning to produce the best. "It is tremendously important that the great poetry be written, it makes no jot of difference who writes it." But "when a man is not doing this highest thing . . . he had much better be making the sorts of experiment which may be of use to him in his later work, or to his successors." Pound's own first "highest thing" came two years later in *Hugh Selwyn Mauberley*.

The persona of this sequence is very close to the Pound who began to despair of London as Culture's hope at about the time of World War I. The poem embodies a varied form and music, controlled and ordered. Here is variety ordered by a will that is not overwhelmed by its experiences in the world. It is as if the poet himself dominates through a force of personality which transcends the varied inflections of that voice one finds displayed in a sequence of poems which are separate in form, diction, syntax. As the poems preceding *Hugh Selwyn Mauberley* are a preparation for that poem, so too the poems within the sequence itself are a preparation for the "Envoi," which stands as the climax and resolution, though followed by the five poems of "Mauberley." There is, in the "Envoi," such a giving of the will—the personality that dominates the rest of the poem—to the expression of the "Envoi" that the poem becomes both climax and resolution, the "Mauberley" section striking me, at least, as anticlimactic. It is as if Pound intends a structure to the poem comparable to James's ideal of the novel, in which the rising action and the falling action are equal, the climax coming precisely in the middle: one recalls his words in his "Credo" (1918) that "only after a long struggle will poetry attain such a degree of development . . . that it will vitally concern people who are accustomed . . . to Henry James." *Hugh Selwyn Mauberley* is such masterful handling of line, rhythm, rhyme, allusion, employed to sustain a moving voice, that one may take it as the high point of Pound's lyrical talents, one of the finest displays of the qualities of Pound's art and affections.

In his efforts to liberate the English line from the constrictions of pentameter, Pound emphasizes the rhythms of the singing voice, insisting that poetry decays as it moves away from music. A parallel concern is with the characteristics of the individual word, through which he seeks a firmness that he makes analogous to sculpture. (*Section: Rock-Drill, 85–95 de los Cantares* takes its title from an Epstein sculpture.) He wants a hard, precise diction that uses "absolutely no word that does not contribute to the presentation." We have heard this argument from Poe in relation to the art of the short story. But Pound has a more complex concern. In the Fenollosa manuscripts on the Chinese written character, which came into his hands in 1913, he found a key to the concreteness of the word as image which he was seeking. Subsequently, the Chinese written character comes to signify his ideal of action; it represents to him a dream of Imagism to which Amy Lowell never aspired, as if indeed the word were made flesh through the art of the Chinese brush. The written character represents a condensation that Pound finds the most economical and efficient and beautiful means of wedding mind to object so that an active, inclusive state of being—the ordered awareness—results.

The poet paints language, escaping the abstractness of a discursive, ana-lytical structuring of words. Through this approach to the elements of dis-course, language gains a precision, a solidness, which any intellect has diffi-culty distorting. Pound's poetry concentrates upon the precise noun, while connectives, adjectives, and articles are at a minimum. Greek and Latin phrases appear along with Chinese characters, used almost as if they too were painted. (Pound almost always translates or paraphrases the foreign element in the vicin-ity of its appearance.) Thus the pentameter is overthrown by the line as image as much as by the line as musical phrase, by the weight of each word upon the page as much as by its sound in the ear. In the *Cantos*, for example, one's eye must move slowly, while verse fragment as image follows verse fragment as image. Pound argues, in *Gaudier-Brzeska*: "The image is not an idea. It is a radiant node or cluster; it is what I can, and must perforce, call a VORTEX, from which and through which, and into which, ideas are constantly rushing." Its proper analogy in his argument is to a formula of analytic geometry. Against distortions by imagists like Amy Lowell, he says, "The point of Imagisme is that it does not use images *as ornaments*. The image is itself the speech. The image is the word beyond formulated language."

But, pursuing precision and tolerating only the essential language elements in the attempt to concentrate essence, Pound's language ultimately tends to remove distinction, the opposite of his intention. Pound's conception of lan-guage's relation to the mind becomes virtually a superstition. For he sees in language an intuitive communication of mind to mind rather than a discursive one. In Milton's distinction, Pound would have the image be an angelic mode rather than a human one; it is "the word beyond formulated language." That is why Pound is increasingly fearful of metaphor, since in metaphor each term is distorted from its imagistic essence by an emphasis upon "likeness." Beauty is in each *thing*, but to call attention to a likeness in unlike things is to remove words from the particular realities they embody. Not that Pound does not use metaphor in his poetry. But when it is used it must heighten an awareness of beauty in each term, in each image. To make the point, he analyzes a metaphor:

The pine-tree in mist upon the far hill looks like a fragment of Japanese armour.

The beauty of the pine-tree in the mist is not caused by its resemblance to the plates of the armour.

The armour, if it be beautiful at all, is not beautiful *because* of its resemblance to the pine in mist.

In either case the beauty, in so far as it is a beauty of form, is the result of "planes in relation."

The tree and the armour are beautiful because their diverse planes overlie in a certain manner.

. . . The Poet, whatever his "figure of speech," will not arrive by doubling or confusing an image.

What Pound is in pursuit of is an ordering of the world by the mind in which, in respect to poetry, images are directly, simultaneously present in the mind so that their mutual presence constitutes "planes of relation." Pound is surely right in his conclusion. What one may wonder, however, is whether Pound's understanding of the mind's operation is so certain as to allow a removal of the discursive elements of language. That bad poets use images as ornaments or make bad metaphors with *like* or *as* or verb connectives does not indict the language so much as the poets.

The difficulty one has in reading Pound's poetry lies in his conception of the image's relation to the mind. When that difficulty is overcome, one sees the greatness of some of his poetry. On the other hand, the weakness of his poetry lies here also. For, though Pound would avoid identifying image with idea, his images tend to become ideas, the referents of which, because of the absence of transition, a reader must seek in the history of Pound's mind. To confront *all* of Pound's images, one must know all of Pound's prose works, plus the writings he has read, plus the encounters with other minds in his personal life. From these one must reconstruct the "planes of relation" Pound intends. Not that such pursuit is unrewarding, up to a point. It is rather that those ideas which are "constantly rushing" through the vortex of image, as Pound calls it, are often out of his mind, rather than out of the images themselves. They are neither common to other minds nor easily discoverable to those minds that proceed discursively.

Pound strives to write images, whether his medium is verse or prose, an attempt that makes his work unmistakably his. He also came more and more to speak images. And when one is not initiated into his mode of discourse, it seems strange in the extreme. In fact, it was this strangeness that contributed heavily to his being declared insane. Repeatedly, the testimony of the four psychiatrists who so pronounced Pound expresses bafflement over his mode of conversation. Though the doctors had brief access to a section of Canto LXXX and other of his works, they were apparently content to take the word of "experts" that he was a great poet and not themselves examine that poetry in relation to the man whose mind they were judging. Thus Dr. Overholser of St. Elizabeths, admitting no familiarity with his "great" poetry, testified as evidence of an unsound mind, "He speaks in bunches of ideas." Pound's attorney, questioning a Dr. Muncie, his own appointee to the board of examiners established by the court, elicited from him confirmation that Pound "has a system of reasoning which is embedded in his mentality so that it is impossible for him to think outside of that system." The assumption was that Pound's "private" system, to which much critical attention had already been directed by readers of his poetry, was inaccessible. One has descriptions of Pound from the doctors: he would sit unable to speak to their questions, as if words would not come, which state the psychiatrists took to be evidence of an unsound mind. It might better have been taken as Pound's attempt to recover a mode of expression he had long since abandoned, the discursive mode, to replace his speaking in "bunches of ideas." Discursive language, including metaphor that does not eschew "likeness," is the means of communicating unperceived relationships to another mind. It is possible to conclude Pound mistaken for abandoning discursiveness and not insane, as indeed some of the younger staff of St. Elizabeths did conclude.

Pound's mistake as to the nature of language's relation to the mind—if it is a mistake, as I believe it to be—is a concomitant of his understanding of man's relation to the world. Rejecting any reference to an afterlife, he nevertheless seems to assume a supernatural power in that ideal language he pursues. And to him, as to Socrates or Confucius, goodness is knowledge—the perfection of the intellect, a perfection that results when knowledge is so ordered that one lives in harmony with an external world made intelligible by the ordered mind. To Pound the evangelist, language in its relation to that orderly state of awareness is not so much a tool of knowledge as it is an infallible medium that transubstantiates external existence in such a way that the mind is powerless to disgorge it. Or in another metaphor, language is an umbilical cord, allowing mutual subsistence of perceiver and perceived. It is this faith in the infallibility of an ideal language that makes him misjudge the perversity of the individual's will. His address to a reader, in his prose and poetry alike, assumes again and again that an acceptance of his version of the proper political, economic, cultural action follows the right word spoken. Because it is the right word, it ministers inevitably to the needs and demands of the intellect. Accompanying his faith in the perfectibility of the intellect by the beautiful and orderly (whose image for Pound is *to kalon*) is a blindness to his own appeals to the emotions rather than to the logical mind. Without quite realizing it, he requires a sophisticated sentimentality—a point of kinship between him and some nineteenth-century poets he castigates for Boeotian sentimentality, "ole shepe" Wordsworth for instance.

To hear the right words in the right order or to see the image they make is not necessarily to be changed. In his experience in the world, Pound recognized this. When his arguments did not strike his reader as self-evident, he reacted with a shrillness that contradicts his certainty as seer and prophet. And while he has, on the one hand, an unquenchable belief in a particular man's gift of intellect, his deportment often spoke despair of mankind as unsalvageable fool. Pound's desperation over the failure of his language to perform the miracle of reformation led him more and more to that shrillness of the 1930s that culminated in the broadcasts from Italy for which he was charged with treason. There developed a stronger insistence upon state centralization and upon the image of the poet as dictator, the supreme priest of words. Mussolini became an image out of whom Pound thought ideas constantly rushing. But once more, the radiance of Mussolini as image was out of Pound's own mind. Into that image Pound's ideas rush uncritically. Il Duce was not the acceptable substitute for the Second Coming that Pound wanted to believe him.

V

"Daphne with her thighs in bark
Stretches toward me her leafy hands"—
Subjectively.

Let me here be concerned with an initial difficulty many have in reading Pound. His friend William Carlos Williams, and many others, finds in him an almost intolerable arrogance that makes any suspension of disbelief difficult. That is, Pound the man seems always intruding, particularly in the *Cantos*. Particularly so if one is close to him, as Williams is, or if one brings newspaper accounts and literary gossip to the reading of the poems. It is finally necessary to bring the man Pound into his work; his deliberate intrusion into his work is a reaction to what he takes to be cowardice in other poets, who refuse to take a stand from which to risk their song or themselves.

The poet, to sustain song beyond the brief lyric cry, must have a place to stand, from which he may see himself in relation to the world. But to Pound, the nineteenth-century decay of art into sentimentality, into a mechanical version of man in the world, hardly left the poet any ground common to his audience. The poet might enliven an old vision, as Eliot does, or attempt to conjure a new one, as Lawrence does in pursuit of his "blood knowledge" or as Yeats does with his *Vision*. Pound, hungering for the beauty of order, chose rather to become poet to what he judged a more concrete world. His pursuit of imagism out of Confucian ideas is a pragmatic search, but not in the mode of the philosopher. For he would sing it into existence so immediately that it must be granted as self-evident. Pound confronted an elementary problem: that of a personal address to the universe which must be larger than personal, the election of an attitude and a voice appropriate to the poet as seer. It was a serious concern whose solution colors our own image of Pound from the beginning, making him seem not only arrogant, but an arrogant buffoon.

Nathaniel Weyl, writing in the heated circumstances of the Bollingen award, cartooned that public image, out of various recollections by Pound's contemporaries: "The young Pound of London and the Latin Quarter was the very model of a Bohemian. His beard was bright red and stiletto pointed. His hair was a lion's mane, his collars Byronic and his cape long and flowing." But given this as Pound's presence, it is mistaken to conclude him either unaware of his shocking appearance or merely playacting for publicity's sake. Some thirty years after this impression of Pound as bohemian was established, the psychiatrists adjudging him insane cited his bohemianism to support their judgment, concluding, "He has long been recognized as eccentric, querulous, and egocentric." They, no less than many of Pound's intimates, were baffled by Pound's "poor judgment as to his situation, its seriousness and the manner in which the charges are to be met," whether charges of bohemianism or of treason. But to an age dominated by Prufrock and Sweeney, Pound declares, from his cage at Pisa:

> I surrender neither the empire nor the temples plural
> nor the constitution nor yet the city of Dioce
> (Canto LXXIV)

His is certainly not the error of a "diffidence that faltered." And he sees sharply the complications we are uncomfortably aware of since the Nuremberg trials. At Pisa he reflects:

> the problem after any revolution is what to do with
> your gunman.
> (Canto LXXX)

Defiant instead of contrite, feeling himself more loyal than many who served in Washington in high places during the war (an opinion borne out by history, as the Alger Hiss entanglements show), he sends Eliot a message:

> . . . say this to the Possum: a bang, not a whimper,
> with a bang not with a whimper,

> To build the city of Dioce whose
> terraces are the colour of stars.

As Pound was recollecting the past and apprising himself of his situation in the *Pisan Cantos*, "the Possum" too was looking back. In the September 1946 issue of *Poetry*, Eliot wrote about poets "who could have been of use to a beginner in 1908," the year of Pound's first volume. Such a beginner had to go to the poetry of another age and to other languages, Eliot argues. Browning "was more a hindrance than a help. . . . Poe and Whitman had to be seen through French eyes. The question was still: where do we go from Swinburne? and the answer seemed to be nowhere." Yet in 1908 Pound was imitating Swinburne. Furthermore, he was more fascinated by one "Master Bob Browning," as he called him, than Eliot was. One poem borrows a title from a Browning poem on a subject very much at the center of Pound's concern for finding his voice as poet: "Mesmerism." He attacks Browning with praise:

> You wheeze as a head-cold long-tonsilled Calliope,
> But God! what a sight you ha' got o' our innards. . . .

He concludes that Browning, "old Hippety-hop o' the accents," is "True to the Truth's sake" through being a "crafty dissector." Browning's experiments with point of view and with masks are what interest Pound, an interest perhaps memorialized in his title to the collected shorter poems as they have been varied and enlarged since a first edition in 1909, *Personae*.

From the beginning, Pound tries to assume other voices: "Scriptor Ignotus" he dates Ferrare 1715; translations and adaptations alike speak his concern. But Pound's powers are unlike Browning's: Pound's are primarily a gift of music. Music enchants the object out of time and place. Through music the poet becomes mesmerist. One sees Pound presenting "Plotinus" not as Browning would have in monologue, but in lyric. None of the rough calliope. Nor is there the dramatic character independent of the poet's voice, or pretended voice, as when the narrator of *Sordello* separates himself apologetically from his poet-hero. At this stage in his development, represented by *Personae*, Pound tries to draw his characters into himself. His approach is as if he were refining and polishing Whitman, the Whitman who would have it that he is everyman. The impulse of mind in each is alike. As Pound acknowledges in his "Pact" with Whitman, the "Yawp" and he are closely akin. His early revulsion from Whitman was out of an embarrassment over Whitman's failure to achieve what he,

Pound, was to attempt in the *Cantos*—a concert of lyrics constituting a poem of epic proportions.

Whitman is naive if one looks at him from the sophisticated position of the comparativist such as Pound. For the poet who would attempt to embody the world and sing as if he were everyman requires an intellect on the order of Sophocles' or Dante's or Milton's. Whitman doesn't have that kind of mind, and in consequence tends to emote through catalog, with an assumed rather than an established tone:

> To get the final lilt of songs,
> To penetrate the inmost lore of poets—to know the mighty
>   ones,
> Job, Homer, Aeschylus, Dante, Shakespeare, Tennyson, Emerson;
> To diagnose the shifting-delicate tints of love and pride and
>   doubt. . . .

Whitman's is the voice of the outsider talking about poetry, and not a very discriminating outsider. Is Tennyson to be placed alongside Aeschylus and Dante, or is Whitman flattering current taste, including that for Emerson? Whitman's stance as poet is to feed whatever can be named from the world through the "I" which speaks his one poem, wooing all readers rather than the discriminating. No wonder such a poet as Pound, intensely American as he is, felt embarrassed by this "pig-headed father."

Clearly it is necessary to "penetrate the inmost lore of poets," but not through talk of doing so. The necessity is particularly pressing, given Pound's belief that a journey into the cultural past was the proper preliminary to a significant American poetry. Given the disadvantage of his "half-savage country," Pound felt that his journey in search of his Dioce required the kind of rashness one remarks in his deportment and appearance in order that he might escape private bucolics or the sentimental decay into sociological poetry. Neither Frost's way nor Carl Sandburg's was suitable to Pound. Pound's insistence that there was a way out of the dark wilderness in which American culture found itself at the middle of its journey and that he was the Virgil called forth to lead toward Dioce took him east out of Idaho and Pennsylvania, and ultimately to Italy; it took him back through our literary heritage. In his poetry he attempts to see with eyes freed of time and place, freed of the provincialism of the present, thus to rescue and present the "shifting-delicate tints of love and pride and doubt."

In an early poem called "Masks," he reflects both his intention and his awareness of a world hostile to such attempts:

> These tales of old disguisings, are they not
> Strange myths of souls that found themselves among
> Unwonted folk that spake an hostile tongue. . . .

As poet, through masks, he may rescue "Old singers . . . painters . . . poets . . . wizards,"

> All they that with strange sadness in their eyes
> Ponder in silence o'er earth's queynt devyse. . . .

Pound's lines imply ancient masters aware of their failures but aware of possibilities in the midst of hostilities as well, in contrast to his own age, in which the masters seem equally unaware of failure and of possibilities, intimidated by hostility from "Unwonted folk." How does one "make it new" to enliven one's day? One way is by turning "Historian," not only as in *The Spirit of Romance*, but in one's own poetry:

> Thus am I Dante for a space and am
> One François Villon, ballad-lord and thief,
> Or am such holy ones I may not write
> Lest blasphemy be writ against my name;
> This for an instant and the flame is gone.

It is in the context of this pronouncement upon the poet as historian that one reads "The River-Merchant's Wife," "The Ballad of the Goodly Fere," and "The Seafarer." And one remembers it as well in trying to appreciate the magnitude of the task Pound elects in the *Cantos*. For the problem there is to find a technique that will support a talent whose powers do not sustain long flights: the enchanting of oneself into an assumed persona, Sigismondo or Odysseus or John Adams, is "for an instant," and then "the flame is gone."

Pound attempts to resing an earthly eternal that is temporarily neglected by the world. The attempt is through a metamorphosis in which the poet retains his own powers of intellect while becoming some other. Thus the poet's "personality" is a kaleidoscopic medium in Pound, in contrast to Dante's orderly development of a single persona on a journey of transcendent ends, a difference that occasions much debate over form and meaning in the *Cantos*. In the first two of Pound's cantos there is a gliding in and out through the voices of Odysseus, Dionysus, and Pound, accompanied by a rich imagery of changing sea and growing things. Canto III begins in Venice at the time of Pound's first volume, *A Lume Spento*, with a recollection of that time when, through the poet's mesmeristic powers, "Gods float in the azure air." The canto takes us back not only to the methods of the first two cantos but back as well to the short poems of that Venice residence, in one of which he wrote,

> . . . I have been a tree amid the wood
> And many new things understood
> That were rank folly to my head before.

In another, "Aube of the West: Venetian June," there is such a forgetting of self into the natural world that, except for the music of the poem, one might take it to be Wordsworth speaking of sensations from a vernal wood. Pound appends a note to the poem: "I think from such perceptions as this arose the ancient myths of the demi-gods; as from such as that in 'The Tree', the myth of metamorphosis." In the *ABC of Reading* he recalls a time when one had "Platonism believed. The decadence of trying to make pretty speeches and of hunting for something to say, temporarily checked." It is just such a period of faith in his own mind that allows him to attempt in Canto III that world of the floating gods:

> Panisks, and from the oak, dryas,
> And from the apple, maelid,
> Through all the wood, and the leaves are full of voices. . . .

But such making of poems, new flowers of these prayers of earth, as he calls them, raises a haunting question. Pound is determined more and more to comprehend the world's possibilities through his sensibilities, but he does not build of that comprehension such edifices as Sophocles' or Dante's. What is the star by which he or we may measure the wind's veering in his poetry, except his own sensibilities? Such questions lead him later to write "from the wreckage of Europe," feeling himself "A lone ant from a broken ant-hill."

Pound's arrogance, I come now to suggest, is an accident out of a high, intense concern for his integrity as a poet. He defends himself against those who argue that "This fellow mak'th his might seem over strong" by defining his faithfulness to his calling as poet. The integrity he pursues is that which the literary man of this century has been much concerned with: not a mere following to the letter of one's principles, but an explicit definition of those principles that have to do with wholeness. The question of the Complete Man has been the literary theme of our age, out of the cultural decay since the Renaissance. Its documents are extensive, including *Lord Jim*, *The Brothers Karamazov*, *Sons and Lovers*, *Antic Hay*, *The Waste Land*, *The Sun Also Rises*, *The Tall Men*, and "Ode to the Confederate Dead." Pound assumes in himself an integrity as an act of faith in his own powers, in the interest of action, the germ of which lies in his berating Browning at the beginning of Canto II:

> Hang it all Robert Browning,
> there can be but the one "Sordello."

Sordello, rather than Odysseus or Sigismondo Malatesta or Dante, might have been a point of departure and a reference better suited to Pound's pursuit of Dioce, Sordello being the poet out of Dante's world most reminiscent of Pound.

Pound is doing two things in declaring "there can be but the one 'Sordello.'" First, he is differing with Browning on the uncommitted position Browning's narrator assumes. That knotty and least penetrable portion of Browning's poem, book 1, is the poet's careful dissociation from his character through playful argument about point of view. Browning's narrator insists that he cannot get inside Sordello, and so must tell the story imperfectly from outside. Thus there is the fallible narrator as buffer between the poet himself and the poem. It isn't so much a "queynt devyse" in Pound's view as Browning's refusal to risk his imagination. A second thing follows from this. There can be but the one Browning, or Sordello, or Pound if there is to be a wholeness. The Sordello of Browning's poem, seeking integrity as man and poet, does so with an attitude that some would call humility, but that Pound would likely consider timidity. The result is that there are various Sordellos, from recluse to activist. The absence of a consuming boldness may be taken as the cause of Sordello's ineffectiveness in his world. His late, minor gesture in sacrificing himself is not sufficient to Pound. One must be bold from the beginning, as assertive as the pope or emperor. There can be but the one Sordello if he is to be powerfully whole.

It may be true that one mind is incapable of such powers as to justify the boldness, but it must assume itself capable. Pound makes of his life a bold fiction and a sacrifice. He is ready all along to accept the consequences of his presumption. He chooses Villon for emulation, "ballad-lord and thief," and invokes as his muse Mercury, "Patron of thieves," in his assault upon the present and past to make a new poetry and a new culture. It is not enough simply to recover fragments, as he takes Eliot to be doing. They must be enlivened, even if not structured in some grand design of "Dantesean rising." Thus his early rebuke to Eliot, in Canto VIII:

> These fragments you have shelved (shored)
> "Slut!" "Bitch!" Truth and Calliope
> Slanging each other sous les lauriers. . . .

He seems here to suggest that Eliot fails as does Browning by a separation of himself, through which the viable truths are shelved, sandbagged against an intruding world.

One considering Pound's arrogance in relation to his life and work begins to see a deliberate exaggeration which risks a tragic or comic resolution. In 1913 Pound anticipates the treason charge in an attack upon American complacency in "Pax Saturni":

> Say that I am a traitor and cynic,
> Say that the art is well served by the ignorant pretenders:
> You will not lack your reward.

Such a risk, such an act of being as he was embarking upon, proved not unlike that which the Greeks (whom Pound comes finally to admire) recognized not only as the cause of woes to individual men but as the cause of greatness in them as well. Without the violation of whatever fates, through strong acts, there can be no grand reprisal that elevates the offender. Agamemnon's and Oedipus' worlds end not with a whimper but with a bang. But Pound saw also the possibilities of the comic in his exaggerated stance; during World War I he wrote, in "Monumentum Aere":

> You say I take a good deal upon myself
> That I stint in robes of assumption.

He concludes, "In a few years no one will remember the *buffo*." Though the comic detail lingered to haunt him in the Washington hearings, it is the tragic outline that has more and more emerged to elevate him in our respect. For accepting the consequences of his attempt to be the complete man, he insists upon an enlarged figure of man in a nonheroic age:

> yet say this to the Possum: a bang, not a whimper,
> with a bang not with a whimper,

To build the city of Dioce whose
terraces are the colour of stars.

vi

Till change hath broken down
All things save beauty alone.

In seeking a language that would order the mind and allow it to exert order upon the world adjacent to it, Pound argued, "Language has improved; . . . Latin is better than Greek and French than Latin for everything save certain melodic effects." Latin, the instrument of the Empire which made the Empire possible, whose latest blossom is Flaubert's French, turned Pound upon that voyage which sets out from Ovid and Homer and "forth on the godly sea." By an act of the imagination, the mind enchants a timeless world of *now* which may be to the elect a new Koran, a new Bible, but whose ends are more nearly those of the *Aeneid*. Thus is established the city of the mind, whose extension must inevitably be that earthly metropolis Pound sought. By an act of will and art, he attempts to become, to absorb, various spirits. His isn't a fictional device, such as the one Eliot uses through *The Waste Land*, the disembodied consciousness afloat. Pound's is a voice set upon affirming, entering, informing, withdrawing. Eliot, with justification, protests Pound's uses of material so far removed from even the elect's experience that the necessary key is missing. The poetry becomes too dependent upon an intermediary researcher or critical explicator: "In the *Cantos* there is an increasing defect of communication not apparent when he is concerned with Sigismondo Malatesta, or with Chinese dynasties, but, for instance, whenever he mentions Martin Van Buren. Such passages are opaque: they read as if the author was so irritated with his readers for not knowing all about anybody so important as Van Buren that he refuses to enlighten them."

Noel Stock, sympathetic to Pound in his *Reading the Cantos*, documents that opaqueness, even in the *Chinese Cantos*. His conclusion is that Pound's uses of history are vague and uncritical "because while supposedly writing a poem, Pound is also trying to compile an anthology in which the quotations retain something like their original identity and meaning, and at the same time to annotate and use them for his own historical, religious and anthropological purposes."

Pound's faith that connections exist between the varieties of fragments he draws into the *Cantos* does give the work a kind of unity. But it is the force of his will that gives whatever unity there is, rather than an intellectual comprehension, such as that in Dante's greater poem. Many critics have wished for a large, whole, reassuring poem as a stay, longer than momentary, against our age's confusion and decay. The temptation is to complete the poem through our own willfulness, to overlay with heavy pencil marks the illusion of dotted lines or the illusion of an orderly confusion of numbered dots that the *Cantos* represent to us individually. The difficulty, fundamentally, is that the *Cantos* are a vehicle for recording Pound's intense and fallible mind on a journey that has a willfully anticipated end, unjustified because self-generated by the desire for that end. Desire mistakes itself for pattern and meaning. That is what Pound realizes as he talks to Ginsberg, the *Cantos* behind him. For indeed "Paradise is in the desire" when desire is rightly taken. Or as Eliot or Dante or Saint Thomas would say, Paradise is that fulfilling of a proper and final, not a mediate, end; thus desire comes to rest in the perfection of one's gift of being. Intention throws one off the mark when willed to mediate ends as if they were final ends. Pound is on the verge of realizing that point when he says to Ginsberg, speaking of the imperfection of the *Cantos*, "The intention was bad . . . any good has been spoiled by my intentions."

Before the observations of Eliot and Stock, before the complications of the Chinese and Adams *Cantos* or of *Thrones* or *Rock-Drill*, Yeats observed of Pound's poetry: "Even where the style is sustained throughout one gets an impression, especially when he is writing *vers libre*, that he has not got all the wine into the bowl, that he is a brilliant improvisator translating at sight an unknown Greek masterpiece." Perhaps Yeats is essentially right. Perhaps, in a more appropriate figure, suited to Pound as heir of Whitman, what we have in the *Cantos* is an intricate web anchored in dark, uncertain regions of art and history, upon which a marvelously "queynt devyse" glistens light illusively like that invoked in Canto III: "Light: the first light, before even dew was fallen." In that light Pound would be first creator, giving voices to the leaves, where "clouds bowe over the lake, with gods upon them." It is Pound's way of singing Eden.

But the web of song, by its very sparkling, shows how empty are the courts of the sun. For an uneasy moment, the spider is held waiting at the center, in a restless peace, at a point central to the web: the *Pisan Cantos*. For the spiderweb strikes our eye as we inhabit a world where there is sunlight on a broken column, where personal bravery in the name of self and of beauty is not finally sufficient. Anchor lines, out of the intellect, drawn to a center from the dark regions of history and art, the "star-span acres of a former lot," are gridded by graceful lyric lacings of emotion. All this in an effort to rescue and justify the mind. My figure of Pound as spider and his work as web gives us a perspective upon his worldly Dioce, within which we may see its beauty without concluding it the final truth. For though Pound is hardly noiseless, and seldom patient, his procedure from the beginning is what Whitman describes as the spider's exploring "the vacant vast surrounding" by launching forth "filament, filament, filament, out of itself." As with the spider, according to Whitman, so with the soul. But it is not enough for the web to find anchor upon time's broken columns, the furthest reach possible to the self. The soul's anchor is in a city not made by the finite self, rather than in a Dioce of the fallible mind. While Confucius gives the words *order* and *brotherly deference*, he says nothing of "the life after death."

Eliot came to a disaffection with Pound's commitment in *After Strange Gods*: "Le monde moderne avilit. It also provencialises, and it can also corrupt." But the solution is not so simple as reordering it into another human version of the world. On this point, Eliot speaks of the *Cantos* as they struggle with the decaying, temporal world: "If you do away with this struggle and maintain that by tolerance, benevolence, inoffensiveness and redistribution or increase of purchasing power, combined with a devotion on the part of an elite, to Art, the world will be as good as one could require, then you must expect human beings to become more and more vaporous. This is exactly what we find of the society which Mr. Pound puts in Hell." Eliot, orthodox in his religion, is charging Pound with utopianism, the inevitable substitute religion following a rejection of the concept of original sin. That rejection undercuts the necessity of an intense moral struggle on the personal level, placing its ends in knowledge and systems, a repetition of man's first disobedience whose modern fruits we label Communism and Fascism, in which systems the individual becomes vague and vaporous.

One might object at this point that the human beings of Pound's *Cantos* are vaporous because of the technique of the mask, rather than because of what Eliot calls Pound's "theological twist." But Pound develops this technique out of his utopian position. (He protests against the label *utopian* as early as *Patria Mia*, but what utopian ever yet allowed the derogatory sense of the word as appropriate to himself?) The secular utopian inevitably obliterates distinctions, the last thing Pound ever wanted: he insists again and again that we "call things by their right name." Yet in his uses of historical people, in his juxtaposition of Chinese emperor to John Adams, or Mussolini to Jefferson, the names become confused with the complexities of persons and ideas; the distinctions that discursive metaphor makes possible are obliterated. The details are firm enough— the word-hardness that William Carlos Williams praises and Pound headnotes as "Rock-Drill." But our language is finally analogous to web rather than rock. Pound's sensitive web begins to vibrate with the capture of pitiful flies.

Eliot detects three principles at work in the spinning of Pound's web upon the world: "the aesthetic . . . the humanitarian . . . the Protestant." Pound announced in a prospectus of the College of Art he wanted to found in London: "We aim at an intellectual status no lower than that attained by the courts of the Italian Renaissance." The humanitarianism is that of Gesell's and Douglas's economics. The Protestantism in Pound, who on occasion sounds like a Jonathan Edwards preaching a second coming of the Renaissance, is the acceptable Protestantism of the late nineteenth century, not Billy Sunday's or Eliot's, but William James's. Confucian aesthetics is the true mover of the state. Its violation warrants Pound's hell. As Eliot objects, Pound's hell is really anti-hell, implying that his heaven is anti-heaven: "If you do not distinguish between essential Evil and social accidents, then the Heaven (if any) implied will be equally trivial and accidental. Mr. Pound's Hell, for all its horrors, is a perfectly comfortable one for the modern mind to contemplate . . . it is a Hell for the *other people* . . . not oneself or one's friends." Given the Confucian insistence upon "brotherly deference," with its social and political implications, there still remain the elect, those whose intellectual status can be the equal of that attained by the courts of the Italian Renaissance. These elect relate to Pound's city as agent angels, creating Pound's version of heaven.

Pound's vision finally lacks an appropriation of individuality, in spite of his strong insistence upon concreteness. He is caught up by an abstract dream in the very attempt to avoid the dangers of abstraction. Responsible Platonism distinguishes between idea and its shadow, thus paying its respects to the insufficiency of analogy between shadow and reality. It respects metaphor's "likeness" as less than identity. Heaven's streets are not literally of gold. Pound too often overlooks the metaphorical, analogical aspect of names, mistaking the abstract as radiantly present in concrete language. It is a confusion in him which makes him misjudge men, while judging well of their poetry, as in his equating Mussolini's aphorisms to Mussolini himself.

It is the judgment of Noel Stock that the *Pisan Cantos* are the most effective unit of the Cantos, largely because they sustain tone through Pound's remembering of the past in relation to the present. I believe the effectiveness of these cantos lies more immediately in Pound's coming to realize weaknesses in his intellectual position. One notices it in his recollections of individuals, here less vaporous than in other sections. Even G. K. Chesterton is recalled with sympathy in contrast to an early dislike. And Wilfrid Scawen Blunt, severe critic of the British empire as it existed in the nineteenth century, is recalled, but not for his intellectual position:

> To have, with decency, knocked
> That a Blunt should open
>   To have gathered from the air a live tradition

or from a fine old eye the unconquered flame
This is not vanity.
  Here error is all in the not done,
  all in the diffidence that faltered.

The tradition that impresses Pound emanates from Blunt's eye, the gateway to the person, and not from a vaporous imagining of local gods as in Canto III.

Pound's pursuit of the true and lively word, which began so intensely at the University of Pennsylvania with his study of Romance languages, reached a shocking arrest in the cage at Pisa. Incarcerated in less than humane manner and circumstance, he began composing those cantos that reveal him at his most human and humane. It is not that Pound abandons any of his large principles: he does not forsake Dioce. It is rather that he is brought into a relationship with the seasons and weathers of nature, and with subtle aspects of human character such as he had scarcely time to observe in their actuality. Indeed, in those cantos there is something like Wordsworth's lament for having lived at a distance from the kind.

In contrast, we recall Pound's pursuit of knowledge in the *Fifth Decad* of the *Cantos*, a pursuit of an abstract ideal of being whose abstraction is camouflaged by the particularity of the knowledge acquired from specific works of literature and history. The abstractness leads to the large and easy solutions proposed to our monetary problems (on this subject he wrote more than four hundred articles and letters to the editor in the four years preceding publication of the *Fifth Decad* in 1937). Quotations from the multitude of historians, economists, politicians, presented as if direct colloquy, seem concrete argument; they are rather a sequence of allusions to complicated speculation in tomes not easily available to the reader. As if aware of the abstractedness of his projected world, Pound states that one would find in it "Grass nowhere out of place." In the Nuevo Mundo gathering, the ideal he establishes would move on "Towards producing that wide expanse of clean lawn." On the other hand, current economics destroy. For, as he says in the famous Canto XLV:

                    usura
        blunteth the needle in the maid's hand
        and stoppeth the spinner's cunning.

But Pound is using the concrete emblematically; the images carry in them something of the feeling of that pastoral imagery of the Old Testament, an imagery the prophets found daily renewed by nature. Pound is not here "making it new" in terms of current circumstances and language. He is the poet of the city, borrowing bucolic clichés.

On the other hand, the *Pisan Cantos* reflect Pound's awareness of his immediate circumstances, as a context to reflections on his own history rather than on the history of the world. His special gift for song emerges, giving a tone maintained through a convincing use of the concrete world at his fingertips. He records gratefully the Negro soldier's words on giving him a desk made of old packing crates, a far cry from the furniture Pound made in Paris in the early years of his pursuit of the courts of the Renaissance: "doan yu tell no one I made it." He sees birds on telegraph wires beyond the compound as constantly changing notes on a musical stave. The mountains and clouds and sky are firmer, more real than in Venice in 1908, when through a conjuring act nature was asserted to be transformed into myth. For the metamorphosis that occurs in the *Pisan Cantos* is not through Pound's becoming Daphne or Dionysus. It is through his becoming more fundamentally himself. Now he affirms in very moving poetry that "nothing matters but the quality of the affection." The minor act of charity by the soldier is valued not for the beauty of the packing crate; it is an act by a man who would never have reached into the upper courts of Pound's Dioce.

And Aubrey Beardsley's old words that "beauty is difficult," carrying still a hint of cowardliness and fin-de-siècle decay, take on complexity nevertheless. Pound sees beauty as involving more than the mind's order:

> Beauty is difficult . . . the plain ground
> precedes the colours
> and this grass or whatever here under the tentflaps
> is indubitably, bambooniform
> representative brush strokes wd/ be similar

But the brush strokes would not be flatly "the grass or whatever," but rather a touching through art of a mystery that a name or brush stroke cannot fully solve. It is as if Pound for the first time bends to count the lily's stipules. His seeing is not only through the senses but also in the quality of his affections. Robert Allen, who visited Pound in his cage at Pisa, reports, "He told me of spending hours watching wasps construct a nest and of his fascination with the work of an ant colony." The simple tasks of existence assume a new importance and new dignity, since the poet is forced to see as with the "caged panther's eyes." Arachne means more now that he sees a spider spin a web in his cage than when he approaches her with his literary myth as a magnifying glass. The guard towers at the corners of the compound and the guards at the gate hold his attention with more reality than the circumstances of Hercules or Odysseus:

> 4 giants at the 4 corners
> three young men at the door
> and they digged a ditch round about me
> lest the damp gnaw through my bones

Let us recall an earlier way in which Pound sees the world. In correspondence with Iris Barry at the time of World War I, Pound undertook to educate her. There is a noticeable depreciation of the Greeks, Sophocles receiving particular attack: "I think it would be easier to fake a play by Sophokles than a novel by Stendhal, apart from the versification." Again he wrote, "Certainly the whole Oedipus story is a darn silly lot of Buncombe—used as a peg for some very magnificent phrases." But at St. Elizabeths he translated the *Women of Trachis*. Though his version makes the play something closer to the Japanese Noh than to the Greek tragedy, it is nevertheless a tribute to Sophocles. And in a message through his editors, introducing *Confucius to Cummings* (1964), he affirms Sophocles more profound than a maker of "magnificent phrases": "the emendation of his proportionate estimate of authors in world literature accessible to him can be summarized . . . in his phrase, as 'dress (in the military sense) on Sophokles.'" One of the causes of that emendation is Pound's discovery that knowledge is not sufficient to human existence, individually or collectively, as Virgil made clear to Dante on leaving him in Beatrice's hands.

At Pisa, Pound is reduced to the human as he had never been before, and his greatness is proved by it. He emerges with a new dignity one hardly sees reflected in those hearings on his sanity. The experience in the cage blinds him, but it does not destroy him. He achieves that classical mind such as Eliot calls for. The romantic, Eliot said, "is deficient or undeveloped in his ability to distinguish between fact and fancy, whereas the classicist, or adult mind is thoroughly realist—without illusions, without daydreams, without hope, without bitterness, and with an abundance of resignation." And is not Oedipus' history that of the romantic like Pound? Oedipus moves from romantic to classicist as he moves from Thebes to Colonus. The mature, adult mind (Eliot means the Christian mind) sees its own history from the beginning, weighs it with a firm affection freed of illusion and daydream. It is inevitable to Pound, since he is a brave and honest and honorable man, that he discover a new measure of the worth of Sophocles, if not of Christ.

So much for the change evident in Pound's position at Pisa. Our responsibility in attempting to come to terms with him from a Christian perspective is to see him at that point with an understanding of ourselves. In general his contemporaries have avoided coming to terms with him, dropping his poetry from anthologies, condemning man and work out of hand. But next to our picture of that young dandy in London—earbob flashing in one ear, nineteenth-century Byronic dress—let us set a later description of Pound as buffoon, in the cage. The source is again Robert Allen: "During the first week or so in the Medical Compound he kept to himself in his tent. His food, eaten from an army mess kit, was handed to him through the . . . fence. He soon stripped off his Army fatigue clothes and spent the warm summer days comfortably attired only in Army olive drab underwear, a fatigue cap, G. I. shoes and socks." And we see Pound emerge: "He found an old broom handle that became a tennis racket, a billiard cue, a rapier, a baseball bat to hit small stones and a stick which he swung out smartly to match his long stride. His constitutionals wore a circular path in the compound grass."

If we put aside any anger we may husband toward Pound or toward his prosecutors and defenders, and put aside as well any sentimentality we're prone to confuse with the quality of the affections, we may introduce one more comparison, one that summarizes fairly, I think, the modern confusions that have prevented our dealing effectively with our revolutionaries. Pound in his youth said cutting things about G. K. Chesterton, but he wrote sympathetically at Pisa of "Chesterton's England of has-been and why-not." As Pound sought heroes in Confucius, Adams, Jefferson, and Mussolini, so Chesterton in his "Lepanto" praises Don Juan of Austria, who stood against the Turks when Elizabeth and Philip chose rather more private wars. John, bastard brother to King Philip, answered the Pope's frantic call to arms:

> The last knight of Europe takes weapons from the wall,
> The last and lingering troubadour to whom the bird has sung.

In the battle, Cervantes distinguishes himself under John, carrying with him on his return to Spain not only crippling wounds but also, as Chesterton has it, a memory of John transformed toward art:

> He sees across a weary land a straggling road in Spain,
> Up which a lean and foolish knight for ever rides in vain.

Not poetry to win Pound's admiration; but a glimmer of heroics worth more than "has-been." There is a marvelous adventure befalling the "Knight of the Sad Countenance," a man of wit but little humor, as is Pound. His friends devise a stratagem to bring him home: "they made a sort of cage of criss-crossed poles, sufficiently large to hold Don Quixote comfortably. . . . The issue was that they dragged him to the cage and shut him in, nailing the bars." Then the barber (for whom we may read psychiatrists in our analogy), with his face masked, says to the caged knight: "be not grieved at your confinement. It is needful for the speedier conclusion of the adventure to which your great courage has committed you." Quixote protests but concludes, "Perhaps chivalry and magic in our day must follow a different course from that pursued by the men of old." Then he turns to reassure the "ladies" who pretend to weep at his departure: "Do not weep good ladies, for all these mischances are incidental to the calling I profess. . . . For such things never happen to knights of small name and fame."

Instead of focusing on the reality of Pound's situation and trying him on a charge of treason, we may have confirmed him in his old belief that such mischances as his are incidental rather than consequential. And we excuse ourselves the strict necessities of examining Pound's arguments and art. Both he and we are the losers.

The romantic such as Don Quixote makes a gesture he does not fully understand. But in making the gesture he may come to understand it somewhat. Though it involve him in destruction, as the world takes destruction, it may involve him in salvation as well. He may emerge a knowing Oedipus, or continue as innocent as Quixote. Either state, surely, is preferable to that of a Prufrock or a Sweeney. Eliot comments in "Little Gidding" on the possibility that such attempts may lead to the classical, adult mind:

> We shall not cease from exploration
> And the end of all our exploring
> Will be to arrive where we started
> And know the place for the first time

Only after an attempt to find, or found, oneself or Dioce, is one ready for the possibility of an everlasting City. That Pound moves in such a direction is at least hinted at by the attention to the ant, the wasp, the spider, an attention colored by an affection that Saint Francis held.

> When the mind swings by a grass-blade
> an ant's forefoot shall save you

the clover leaf smells and tastes as its flower

And Brother Wasp is building a very neat house
Of four rooms, one shaped like a squat Indian bottle.

In the end of our exploring, we trust, is our beginning, for which we may be truly thankful. As Pound says, out of that literal Fall experienced in the open cage:

If the hoar frost grip thy tent
Thou wilt give thanks when night is spent.

Don Quixote is something deeper than a clown, as Oedipus is something more profound than an arrogant king. If either is wrong in quixotic ventures, the attempt is not itself wrong—the attempt to assume a role sufficient to define the possibilities of human dignity and heroism that hopefully lead to salvation. The degenerate romances that Quixote fills his head with and the assumption of intellectual prowess that Oedipus makes are equally dangerous. But there is something true about the old gentleman that cardboard armor merely emphasizes; and there is something just and seemly in Oedipus' conduct that Jocasta's fears underline for us. Pound's attempt to live as the complete man is doomed, I believe, because the Christian dimension of wholeness is rejected. But for all its false show, his life speaks strongly for him, particularly as we look more closely at his age and its few heroes. We are left wondering finally—in proportion as we have learned from Aeschylus that in our own despite comes wisdom—whether it is Pound or Quixote or Oedipus who is caged or blinded. Or Jocasta, the Barber and Priest, the four psychiatrists in a district court—or perhaps ourselves.

VI. Richard Weaver against the Establishment
The Southern Tradition at Bay

i

In the late 1920s T. S. Eliot wrote, "There is no such thing as a Lost Cause because there is no such thing as Gained Cause. We fight for lost causes because we know that our defeat and dismay may be the preface to our successors' victory, though that victory itself will be temporary; we fight rather to keep something alive than in the expectation that anything will triumph." At that time Richard Weaver was a very young man, generally ignorant of causes lost or gained. In 1932 he joined the American Socialist party, caught up in the general sweep of sympathy for abstract social good that was growing out of grave economic realities. He thus embarked upon a disillusionment that led him to a revolt against the "establishment," at that juncture of our history called the New Deal. Within the decade he set about his own reeducation because of disillusionment—"at the age of thirty," an age considered terminal by our young revolutionaries, though that is the age celebrated by poets and philosophers as the beginning of wisdom out of youth's illusions. In the middle of our life, we often come to ourselves in a dark wood—as do Dante, Milton, Wordsworth, Eliot, Weaver.

Richard Weaver's revolt was not in consort, not spectacular (in Aristotle's sense of the term so appropriate to the modern scene, even though the modernist mind confuses spectacle with essence). On the surface his revolt was highly mobile. Having graduated from the University of Kentucky, studied at Vanderbilt, taught in Texas, he entered graduate school at Louisiana State University, spending summers at the Sorbonne, Harvard, and the University of Virginia before settling more or less permanently at the University of Chicago. He was engaged in rooting out what he calls (in *Ideas Have Consequences*) those vague influences on his education stemming from the "stultifying 'Whig' theory of history, with its bland assumption that every cause which has won deserved to win." It led him to see that his chief adversary was the American educational system, which failed to train the intellect to make fundamental distinctions. That is, he committed himself to the principle that ideas do have consequences in the affairs of man and that, consequently, bad ideas have bad consequences. He entered the academic world. In this sense he joined battle against a triumphant educational system on its own grounds, maintaining that system is (in the modern jargon) "irrelevant" to fundamental principles of humanity. His choice is a comment on his courage and sets him in contrast to some of his contemporaries who shared his conviction that many causes of the failure of American civilization may be laid at the door of the American academy. One thinks particularly of Ezra Pound, who conducted his guerrilla warfare against the academy from the continent, and of T. S. Eliot, who joined battle from the removed cliffs of London.

Weaver's belated education led him to conclude that to study a lost cause has "some effect of turning history into philosophy." It is a point central to Jack Burden's similar pursuit, which Robert Penn Warren was expanding at approximately the same time Weaver undertook his formal study, and with Louisiana State University as a point of departure also. The result for Weaver was not that he narrated the influence of history in a novel, nor rescued and revitalized history with the immediacy Pound sometimes manages in the *Cantos*, nor dramatized the tragedy of loss and the mystery of spiritual recovery as Eliot does in the body of his poetry. He analyzed, rationalized (in the oldest sense of the word), and expounded a tradition he considered of vital consequence to the survival of Western civilization. That is, he wrote *The Southern Tradition at Bay*, the foundation upon which the larger and better-known body of his work rests. It is a study that illuminates the Southern Literary Renaissance as very few have managed to do, but it also makes understandable, from home grounds, the Americanism of such concerned minds as Eliot and Pound.

Specifically, *The Southern Tradition at Bay* grows out of Weaver's prodigious reading of "first-hand accounts by those who had actually borne the brunt as soldiers and civilians" in the South between Appomattox and the year of Weaver's birth, 1910. The book therefore reaches back into time and place, emphasizing the importance of what Weaver calls "particularism"—that concrete multiplicity of the world of mind and nature requiring careful distinction as vital to the pleasures of abstraction. Weaver, in his study, discovered principles out of the individual's involvement in the local scene that Pound discovered codified in Confucianism, that great learning "rooted in watching with affection the way people grow," as Confucius put it, the completion of which knowledge is "rooted in sorting things into organic categories." Weaver's procedure in recovering the principles affecting the mind and the blood, the body and soul, is more arduous, finally, than Pound's, but more organic as well. For one thing, it required his reading with attention a great deal of poor writing—aesthetically, polemically, philosophically inferior. But there is compensation. His understanding is more inclusive as a result, for his idea of the traditional does not isolate the desirable;

the desirable is highlighted in contrast to the undesirable that is always a part of time and place, however much we come to love any particular place at any time. Weaver is constantly aware that tradition is a continuous presence of both the desirable and the undesirable. His mind, rooted in organic categories, is finally closer metaphorically to Yeats's great-rooted blossomer than to Pound's mind with its selected fruits, the anthologist aspect of Pound's work that so troubles one's reading of him.

The distinction is of such fundamental importance that it is worth further pursuit. It seems to me that Weaver understood more fully than such a traditionalist as Pound that the organic metaphor for the continuity of society depends more heavily upon the limitations of time and place than Pound was able to admit. It allows Weaver to be aware continuously, but not hysterically, of both old dead feeder roots and today's dying leaves, of both the healthy and the erratic buds and blossoms. For instance, it makes Weaver capable of seeing the distorted truth in the position of the whole school of poets, sociologists, and politicians for which William Carlos Williams affirmed a doctrine when he asserted "No ideas but in things." Yet he is not so late in coming to terms with nature—the natural world and human nature—as is Eliot. Neither do we have in Weaver the pathos of Pound's final fragments:

> From time's wreckage shored,
> these fragments shored against ruin.

There Pound's insistence of wholeness—"I, one thing, as relation to one thing"— is uncomfortably stated as if the wholeness is feared an illusion out of Whitman. The Confucian still point not realized, Pound is left with that old nineteenth-century romantic malady of knowing "beauty and death and despair," thinking "that what has been shall be, / flowing, ever unstill" for "The Gods have not returned."

Weaver sensed, and finally understood and accepted as fundamental to society, a principle likewise sensed and accepted, but not sufficiently understood and acted upon, in the South generally. A Confucian teaching from the *Great Digest* says it succinctly: "the real man perfects the nation's culture without leaving his fireside." He also was aware that the mind as an agent of being, operating from that fireside, is severely limited, as poets quite often fail to acknowledge sufficiently. For while the discursive intellect probes being, it cannot finally encompass it. The process is illusional if one fails to admit that the mind's process is a discontinuous probing of being whose analogy (simplified for clarifying my point) may be the film. A succession of frames will give the illusion of continuous motion, all aspects of which the viewer seems to have grasped; a succession of ideas and images gives the mind an illusion of having grasped being. But being is always leaking out of the jointures of syllogism or analogy or metaphor. One defines essence, but definition does not comprehend. Mystery leaks in where being leaks out, which is why to poet and philosopher alike the ancient mystery of man's being created in the image of God (Perfect Being) has become of such importance in this century. To insist that there are no ideas but in things is ultimately to deny the mind's existence, to deny also all distinction; and to lament the failure of the Gods to return is to acknowledge hollowness and hunger of the mind. To invite the mystery of Grace into the mind, as Eliot does in the *Four Quartets*, is to reject denial and despair in a gesture, "a condition of complete simplicity / (Costing not less than everything)" as Eliot says. In a word, then, Weaver out of his hard-mindedness insists upon the old virtue of humility, which recognizes the mind's limitations. It is inevitable as well that in the details of his historical particulars there is much attention to Southern arrogance as well as a special emphasis upon the religious inclination of the Southerner as an influence upon his developing history.

The ideas Weaver pursues in his book finally ally him with such eminent contemporaries as Eric Voegelin and Leo Strauss, and with those other minds pursuing the timeless, the poets. But the book speaks more immediately. One reads it in conjunction with George M. Fredrickson's *The Inner Civil War: Northern Intellectuals and the Crisis of the Union*. One reads it with profit along with such a variety of alarms and excursions as Ralph E. Lapp's *The New Priesthood: The Scientific Elite and the Uses of Power*; Robert Ardrey's *African Genesis* and *Territorial Imperative*; Lionel Tiger's *Men in Groups*; Rachel Carson's *Silent Spring*; Eric Hoffer's engaging and disturbing reflections on the state of American civilization; Gore Vidal's happy, ignorant welcoming of 1984, *Reflections on a Sinking Ship*. The list can be extended. But it is upon the immediate relevance of Weaver's book that I wish to concentrate.

ii

With the proper distinctions, and with that sense of irony always appropriate to principles seen in their historical manifestations, one may discover in Weaver's book something of the kinship between his personal concerns as a young Southerner and the impulses of some of the more militant of our disaffected youth, those in particular who, alas, swell the crowds under the leadership of the doctrinaire anarchists and related cadres of chaos. Indeed, the sentiments expressed by some of those caught up in the Chicago embranglement of the summer of 1968 seemed to me at the time to indicate an affinity with Agrarian arguments of forty years ago which Weaver is sympathetic to. Compare, for instance, Morris Kight's words explaining why he showed up for the happening. He had sold his seven hotels to take up a new life, arguing at Chicago that the machinery of industrialism must be made "to work for man, not against him. Let them make it possible for man to return to the soil. Make them clear the air, rather than foul it."[1]

Shades of *I'll Take My Stand*. And if only someone could have handed out copies of Donald Davidson's *Attack on Leviathan* at the time, along with at least Weaver's *Ideas Have Consequences*. For what many of our young protesters lack is not a cause, as their antagonists rather desperately acknowledge in public confessions of guilt that would make a Southern evangelist envious of the young radicals. They lack a knowledge of its particulars—most importantly the principles that must ultimately justify or condemn causes. It is that absence of knowledge in them which makes them sacrifices in a lost cause, struggling against what Weaver calls our monolithic state become "rigid with fear that it has lost control of its destiny."

Those of our separated youth who finally refuse to abandon the gift of mind will come to consider whether Richard Weaver does not express arguments more relevant to their sentiments than those of Thoreau or Bob Dylan. For Weaver is bent upon rescuing and maintaining the eminence of *being* over *doing*, a distinction ancient but neglected and one that goes to the heart of our century's troubles. Sadly enough, neither church nor state—of old constructed upon such distinctions—addresses the distinction persuasively. "Literalism," Weaver says, "is the materialism of religion." It is an inevitable stance of the modern public mind, developed out of a climate of thought in which *doing* assumes precedence, whether church or government program or massed opposition to those programs. And since *doing* is necessarily prescribed by the temporal world, when it is given precedence the things of the world inevitably define the essence of human existence. Human virtues become anchored in a materialistic climate of thought. Thus solutions are in terms of moneyed programs on the one hand, in terms of destroyed property on the other. Surely our nation's continuing chaos may be understood to some extent within this context. For what we are experiencing is the acceleration of a trend centuries old: a continuous schism in the secular world over its basic doctrine of *doing*. In our country one can trace it in the decay of Puritanism and Transcendentalism into Pragmatism. The intellectual history of Emerson is informative on this point, as well as the disturbing fiction of Hawthorne. More broadly, one can discover the lines of its descent into Sartrean *doing* for the sake of existence. (It is of interest

1. *National Review*, September 24, 1969, p. 499.

that the straight-faced clown and first-called saint of existentialism, Jean Genet, covered the Chicago convention as an activist reporter.) A more immediately dangerous manifestation is the struggle of Herbert Marcuse and his followers with the "establishment" as they define it. In that blind struggle, the attempt is to control the sources of power that reside in human numbers and natural and industrial resources. Here literalism is the one-dimensional measure of human existence, whether it speak on the one side about social rehabilitation in terms of material identity or on the other of ABM protection for the things of the world, including population. For literalism is not only what Weaver says of it, the materialism of religion, but the source of a false secular piety, though the intellectual community may think literalism applies only to fundamentalist readings of the Bible. Literalism inevitably means the death of the imagination and vision, the rejection of wonder and mystery. The consequence is a suspicion of the created world either as evil and to be rejected (a religious gnosticism) or as a property to be possessed and exploited (secular gnosticism).

A symptom of our ignorant condition that makes my point is the general absence of humor in the New Left Marcusian, in Sartre, in their precursors, no less than in the minions of the state and church they confront. The Absurd each posits is not the modern discovery it is taken to be. In the West its presence is celebrated as anciently as the humor of Homer and the tragedy of Euripides and his fathers. The civilized man, who possesses what Eliot calls the classical mind, carries a knowledge of the complexities of human existence and expresses it through a sense of humor and its complement, a sense of tragedy. In his essay "Aspects of the Southern Philosophy" Weaver, in defining a difference between the Southerner with his historical awareness of the human comedy and his Northern counterpart who generally lacks it, says the Southerner "has had to face what the existentialists call 'ultimate situations' and has come through." He brings with him a "belief in tragedy [that is] . . . essentially un-American; it is in fact one of the heresies against Americanism." His inability to respond effectively, because overwhelmed by force, leads him to humor's saving virtues. Weaver has specifically in mind both the Civil War and Reconstruction. Of the war itself he says, in *The Southern Tradition at Bay*, in speaking of the policy of Sherman and Sheridan, "There remains considerable foundation for the assertion that the United States is the first government in modern times to commit itself to the policy of unlimited aggression." Andrew Lytle expands this argument in his introduction to the second edition of his biography of Nathan Bedford Forrest. And see also Lytle's "A Hero and the Doctrinaires of Defeat."[2]

It is a statement about our government generally popular out of the South

2. *Bedford Forrest and His Critter Company* (New York: McDowell, Oblensky, [1960?]). The essay is in the *Georgia Review*, 10:4 (Winter 1956): 453–67.

since the Vietnam War. Yet one will find more Southerners defending our role in that war on principle than not. They do so for reasons Weaver makes understandable: the South is still committed in large to the premise that communism, being atheistic, is demonic. The triumph of what the South believed a materialistic and irreligious enemy in 1865 made it more unwavering in its opposition to that enemy, whatever form he assumed, even in defeat, as the postwar apologists make clear. The epithets against such an aggressor, whether simplified to *Yankee* or *Puritan* in those postbellum days or to *liberal* or *leftist* in our day, have source in the Old Southerners' old commitment as God's custodians of society and nature, a commitment far greater than the clownish antics of their position, so easily cartooned, allow an external public to recognize. The typical Southerner, for instance, worries less about the economic cost of the war than about its righteous cause. (He is more angry about the economics of domestic policy.) He feels more strongly that victory is a moral imperative, that political compromise is dangerous. For to compromise with "communism" is to him in some wise to bargain with the devil. As Weaver points out in his essay "Aspects of the Southern Philosophy," the South, out of a memory of the possibilities of defeat, "has remained the most militarily inclined of the sections." (Thus it was the South, through its congressmen, that "swung the vote for renewal of conscription in 1941.")

Weaver contends, persuasively, that it is the South which has managed to preserve certain dimensions of human existence for which our world is blindly hungry. For the South, he says emphatically, was *"the last non-materialist civilization in the Western World."* His book is no encomium. He concludes finally that the South failed its highest responsibility, though it still "possesses an inheritance which it has imperfectly understood and little used. It is in the curious position of having been right without realizing the grounds of its rightness." Its most catastrophic failure, Weaver believes, was in not studying its position "until it arrived at metaphysical foundations." The weaknesses of righteous arrogance and complacency, along with a failure to encourage the development of the mind except through training in law, preceded the exigencies of those years between 1840 and 1865 and accompanied the Southerner to Appomattox. The defeat of a righteous cause by force of arms proved so traumatic as to focus attention upon the loss, with the cause itself defended vigorously and eloquently, but still without the necessary metaphysical basis from which alone, in Weaver's view and my own, a defense could have been effectively persuasive. Energies spent in justifying actions, energy spent in surviving the aftermath of defeat, wasted slowly into the province of nostalgia and romance, so that by the turn of the century the South's "people suffered from intellectual stagnation." A generation gap at that point of its history was particularly obvious, as Weaver shows, with the young in pursuit of a new world opened by science and technology. "The ultraconservative Southerner, who worshipped the South in its crystallized form, was as much at fault [for the stagnation] as the devotee of 'progress,' who turned his back upon history and thinks of the past as so much error." The inevitable effects of the mutual failure were predicted by some lingering members of the old order, speaking to their own disaffected sons, as we shall presently see, sons who seemingly heard not a word. We observe that, ironically enough, those sons are the fathers of our world, against whom we witness the revolt of our own sons today.

In pointing to the eminence of *being* over *doing* as manifest in the early history of the South, Weaver argues this inheritance as being implicitly out of Aristotle and Aquinas, though rarely articulated from its intellectual sources in Southern literature. Law, not philosophy, was the calling of the gentleman, and Cicero's orations were venerated while the *Ethics* and *Summa theologiae* were neglected. Still, the general assumption of the preeminence of being is evidenced, and so ordered by Weaver's presentation that it cannot be ignored as an attribute of the influential minds in the early South. The timeliness of one of his conclusions is evident also: "Unlike the technician of the present day, the typical Southerner did not feel that he must do a thing because he found he could do it." The phrase "do a thing" anticipates the current shibboleth on everyone's lips since Weaver's death in 1963; for one to "do one's thing" is for one to deliberately distort technological specialization, its vocabulary in particular, in the interest of *being* over *doing*.

iii

Where Weaver would seem to part company with our unhappy youth, and where the South itself appears repulsive to them and they generally to it, is on the question of the meaning of and necessity for order in society. But it does not follow that Weaver, in the name of order, accepts the "establishment." He sees rather that the necessity for order is not finally obviated by the perversions of order, whether manifest in bureaucratic machinery or in the personal abuses of power. Weaver argues the necessity of order in the affairs of man, an order he finds undercut by the modern world's denial of those natural bounds that impose hierarchy upon society willy-nilly by the fact of existence itself. That is, he moves away from that insistence on absolute freedom which grew out of a secular reading of nature when social science came to dominate society after New England theology prepared the way. "A classless society," Weaver says, "is invertebrate." Indeed, the experiments out of Lenin down to the current turmoils in China and the Soviet bloc countries, added to the general history of society—primitive and civilized—rather suggest class as a presumption of that earthbound organism called society. The argument over hierarchy reduces finally, not to whether there shall be class distinctions, but to the principles upon which procedures and precedence are to be established. When all is said, the struggle between the Marcusians and the technologists of the establishment is over the definition of the elite. The question is how shall power be organized. For the organism called society has power (which is not in itself evil) to the extent that it has moved analogically from jellyfish toward vertebrate existence.

Weaver's concern for class in society is out of the tradition of Aristotle and Aquinas. He sees a desirable unity in the undeniable diversity as possible only where diversity is both recognized and cherished. But more important, he sees diversity as a legitimate determinant of place in civilized society, whose necessary referent is not efficiency (the technological concern whether capitalist or communist in politics) nor inheritance (the assumed prerogatives of whatever species of decayed aristocracy). The determinant is *being* itself. Weaver's version of order in society, then, is divorced from the several versions that deny spiritual dimensions or pay only rhetorical homage to them, since he does not confuse temporal ends with ultimate ends. He does not, that is, confuse the ultimate value of the individual being with the social or sociological position the individual occupies by accident, grace, or industry. Weaver's argument for social order is one discoverable in a logical projection in Aquinas and in an imaginative one in Dante. (See, on this specific point, Canto XIII of the *Paradise*.) It is therefore not surprising to hear him say of its possible recovery to the world, after the South's failure to establish a defensible metaphysical justification, that "barring the advent of an illumination by some fateful personality, the task falls upon poets, artists, intellectuals, upon workers in the timeless."

Order, one concludes from Weaver's arguments, is fundamentally personal and humane; it sees individual differences in character, temperament, talent, and intellect as necessitating community, in which individual limitations are complemented by individual strengths to the common good. He is interested in the possibility of civilization as influenced by the hierarchy within the family, within the community, within town, borough, or county—those political entities born of a conjunction of families in community. The sense of social and political place in community is, to Weaver, properly allied to one's sense of geographic place, in which there is a mystical relationship of man to that natural world lying immediately at hand, a matter of paramount importance to the Southern mind that Weaver adumbrates. Place, such a Southerner believes, feeds a hunger in every man, regardless of social or political estate, a point Weaver illustrates profusely from the literature of the South before 1910. One may demonstrate the same point out of much greater Southern literature than

Weaver uses in his limited span, and in literature that the South finds congenial. For place is of fundamental moral importance, from Odysseus' concern for Ithaca to Sutpen's concern for his One Hundred. Its aesthetic and moral importance troubled Hawthorne, James, Pound, Joyce. Conrad expresses envy of Hardy's advantage over him in being grounded in the English shire rather than tossed drifting about the oceans of the world as he himself had been. Ezra Pound fulminates against geography as having little literary importance, but he also insists upon the necessity of local gods to literature. Such restless souls juxtaposed to Weaver's raise two interesting points of comparison. First, we may contrast Weaver's concern for the local as the point from which civilization is to be rebuilt with Herbert Marcuse's concern for the local as the point where the last vestiges of Western civilization are to be destroyed. The militant nihilists to whom Marcuse speaks are urged to "envisage . . . some kind of diffuse and dispersed disintegration of the system, in which interest, emphasis and activity are shifted to local and regional areas."[3] Second, in spite of the close parallels in Pound's Confucian sense of order, it is the ultimate effect of self-order through ordered family to the well-ordered state that commands Pound's attention. Pound would make Confucius spokesman to the modern statesman as Machiavelli was to the Renaissance statesman. Pound's teleological concern is the ordered state constituted of ordered individuals. "The men of old wanting to clarify and diffuse through the empire that light which comes from looking straight into the heart and then acting, first set up good government," says Confucius. Pound, defending Confucianism against the charge that it has no metaphysics, summarizes: "metaphysics: Only the most absolute sincerity under heaven can effect any change." Pound, finally, has an innocent faith in the perfectibility of man through the perfectibility of a few men who perfect the state. It is not only perfection in nature, but natural perfection of man's mind, an ideal the obverse of D. H. Lawrence's "blood knowledge."

The saving sense of place, Weaver argues, imposes upon a man a "sense of trusteeship" that ultimately leads to moral engagement, whether that engagement be limited to cabin or plantation. Place is, indeed, a corollary to community for the individual person. For as the soul is related to the body, so community to place. The inverted Platonism of the modern world (in a word, Manichaean) is precisely that its materialistic desires require a dissociation from the particulars of the natural world. Materialism is in its worst form a technological abstraction of nature in which nature is coldly violated. Streams mean ergs and trees translate to board feet. The inordinate and grotesque result as manifest to us is the City of Man, whose problems are multiplied by the attempt to deal with them on the same principles that created them in the first

3. *IT/54*, April 11–24, 1964.

place. A nation whose population is overwhelmingly concentrated on less than 10 percent of its land is at last asking whether *rural* development may not be more beneficial to our soul sickness than urban development, whose principal effect seems so far to have been to make the slum mobile within the metropolis, at prodigious economic and social cost.

The world being always with us, a particular place in that world inevitably carries dangers: in maintaining a responsibility as trustee in nature, man tends to develop "arbitrary, self-willed, and dictatorial" traits. The quoted phrase was specifically applied to Mississippi planters by an observer in the nineteenth century. But when one reflects upon the revolt of the 1960s—our own civil war divorced of place and directed against system as represented by parent, college, and all institutions of government—he finds current vitality in the old epithets, though their form be comparatively mild. The conclusion is that the evil is not a necessary consequence of place, since it has flourished when society and government are largely divorced of place. The suspicion arises that evil may be in man, which to Weaver's Southerner is not a suspicion but a fact of human nature.

Parent, college, congress: symbols of familial, intellectual, political hierarchy. To our revolutionaries, symbols of false institutions. But their feeling of betrayal, their charges of hypocrisy directed against the "establishment" in its several manifestations, one might have expected. Southern apologists very soon after 1865 began to predict just the sort of turmoil we currently try to enjoy, since we cannot understand it. For many of them believed that, when egalitarianism is elevated to the status of a secular religion but with the hidden object on the part of the elevators of consolidating political power, a hidden hierarchy must inevitably, if slowly, reveal itself. Between that new power structure's real nature and its public sentiments the gulf would widen. The credibility gap of recent notoriety is an illustration of the disparity anticipated. Hypocrisy appears even in such secular religions as egalitarianism, but then so does self-deception when sentimentality overwhelms thought. Thus it was predictable that the inevitable effect of the stratagem of absolute equality would be number replacing name. The machine dictates a sequential relationship of number to number: the abstract configuration of person—his voting or technical value—becomes the hierarchy. Marcuse argues that the mass power base, the workers, is no longer made up simply of the exploited, for which reason the anarchists can hardly depend upon them (except in France, where ironically the *tradition* of anarchy is venerable). Affluent, the working class incorporates "highly qualified salaried employees, technicians, specialists." They occupy "a decisive position in the material process of production." One may attempt to argue them exploited, as Marcuse does, but limited as he is to materialist concepts, he will hardly convince them. When in the interest of continuing that system we elevate gluttony, avarice, and envy to virtues in order to move consumer goods or shift political power, the corrosions of spirit are eventually self-revealing. Consider the catechisms, exemplums, testimonials of the advertising world alongside their counterparts in the political and social world now in the ascendancy. In "Aspects of the Southern Philosophy," Weaver attributes to the Southern people a "comparative absence of that modern spirit of envy." This absence is traditional, in part accounting for "the fact that three fourths of the soldiers of the Confederate armies owned no slaves and never expected to own any." Not, says Weaver, that the Southerner will not take a better job or pass up a chance to make a quick fortune or

> will not admire material success. . . . What I do affirm is that it is not in his character to hate another man because that man has a great deal more of the world's goods. . . . He is not now and never has been a leveler. . . . The modern impulse which elevates envy into a principle of social action . . . is . . . completely foreign to his tradition, though now and then he has struck back politically when he felt that he was the victim of sectional political exploitation.

Life threshes for survival, but it is increasingly apparent that it is a spiritual life that struggles in unexpected ways and in strange places in our placeless society. In the midst of and out of material affluence, there is a desperate attempt by some of the young to reject materialism, a clutching at such straws as Zen Buddhism or drugs. These signs an older generation tends to read poorly, missing for instance the possible relevance of the studied physical dirtiness to the advertising pitch on the moral plane that tries to sell soap and deodorants as the first step toward salvation. As I write there is in the local news a confrontation of the South. Elements of the local "establishment" and the disaffected young are involved as if in a spontaneous allegorical masque. In a Georgia county adjacent to Athens—"Advancing Athens" the promotion says—a sheriff raided what he and the newspapers called a "'Hippie' Haven." The landlady is none other than ex-congresswoman Jeanette Rankin, who opposed entry into both world wars on pacifist grounds. The sheriff seized marijuana, but it was the "collection of weird things" that fascinated him, including strange posters that read ". . . is alive and well inside himself" and "Only four more voting days till 1984." There were psychedelic colors on walls. An assortment of deodorants, auto parts, guitars, Bob Dylan records, a book by Eldridge Cleaver. The newspaper reporter who covered the raid, and whose paper publishes embarrassingly sophomoric front-page cartoons to cheer on the football team, reacts to that collection of weird things: "Outlandish, way-out posters and stickers plastered the walls," psychedelic colors "prevailed in virtually every room." The sheriff sees no pattern in the queer collection of persons and things. The reporter cannot distinguish between the violation of federal drug statutes and poor taste in decor. A long-haired youth, driving an "expensive motorcycle," appeared on the scene, explaining, "I use this place to sort of get away." The newspaper's editorial attacks these outsiders for their moral degeneracy in an issue that carries movie ads promising a display of several kinds of sodomy, while an earlier issue praises Gore Vidal's essays advocating test-tube reproduction and homosexuality as the new religion. None of the principals recognizes in the emaciated young the suggestions that he is the prodigal son, not the outsider, the foreigner to the South that the newspaper wishes to believe him. The life he struggles to save isn't the one he recklessly risks on his expensive motorcycle in defiance of public-safety-commission slogans. It is more likely the life of the spirit seeking a still point in the flux, something to which Mrs. Rankin's pacifism, Marcuse's anarchism, and the "establishment's" version of order do not speak in their formulations of man. Nor does the sheriff or the trained newspaperman sense aught but threat in the young man, judging from their indiscriminate uneasiness. This paradigm's appearance in the South, near the oldest state-chartered university and involving some of its students, is richly ironic. But then consider with what innocent irony a recent American Nobel laureate in literature has romanticized a materialistic, rootless society in *Travels with Charlie*, the affluent society's version of *The Grapes of Wrath*. It is neither accidental nor irrelevant that Steinbeck toured America in company with a poodle.

iv

Weaver observes that "every established order writes its great apologia only after it has been fatally stricken." Although he makes specific application to the defense of the Southern position that followed immediately upon Appomattox, he is very much aware that the agonies of a dying civilization are to be observed in a span of decades and in scope larger than the South. Certainly we are as heavily engaged with a tradition at bay in 1970 as Alexander Stephens, Albert Taylor Bledsoe, or Robert Lewis Dabney was in 1870. It is one of the misfortunes of their lost cause, on a level as decisive as the South's failure to make clear a metaphysical position, that those defenders of Western civilization outside the South have not recognized the South as ally and so have not helped it clarify its true cause before the world. One is painfully amused to notice in the reviews of Weaver's book by Northern traditionalists, for instance, a late recognition of kinships never before seen (as in John Chamberlain's review in *The Freeman* of April 1969). And so one is tempted to venture that some of these gentlemen have been misled by political spectacle, rather than guided by metaphysical principle: they did not understand Stark Young's words in 1930, "We defend certain qualities not because they belong to the South, but because the South belongs to them." Taking appearance for reality, the spectacle as revelation of the obscure essential, one may fail to see the typical Southern governor or senator as a pragmatist between whose rhetorical stance and operative principles there lies a widening fault. Politically and economically, the Southern politician of this century is almost invariably more socialist in domestic policy than capitalist, despite the rhetorical camouflage with which he hides in the hustings. One need only review the general record of Southern congressmen from New Deal days to the present to place their typical member in the camp of the political left in home affairs—except as the politically expedient issue of race may be introduced. For the typical Southern politician has a New South, not an Old South, heritage, as Weaver's book points out: he has learned from the experiences of such men as North Carolina's pioneer governor after the Civil War, Charles Brantley Aycock, who was elected on a platform of white supremacy, universal education, and progressivism.

The curious political aspect of the South that so puzzles other regions, one ventures, is its vestigial emotional responses to its cavalier past, from which heritage principle is long since decayed; to these are added the appetites accentuated by the economic and political deprivations of Reconstruction. Hence perverse racism supplied energy to the South's progressivism—its own brand of materialism evolving therefrom. Its leaders, avowed states' rights advocates who enjoy a talent for political maneuverability, could funnel federal monies into the states over the years as if no strings were attached. But since the mid-twentieth century the South has had to pay increasingly for those abandoned principles and its political duplicity. An educated, articulate spokesman for Western civilization in its Southern manifestation, such as Robert Lewis Dabney, who wrote a hundred years ago, would be appalled that such modern versions of the scalawag as we tend to elect governor or send to congress are acclaimed with righteous zeal by the Southerner. He would view with irony local battles with the modern version of the carpetbagger, disguised as missionary humanitarian, in the light of state and federal economic policies so closely in accord with those of the local enemy. For the epithets *pinko* on the one hand and *fascist* on the other but cloud political kinships.

The circus of Southern political and social gymnastics may be closely and appropriately related to what goes on in the next ring, the conflict between the New Left and the "Establishment," which one will hardly distort by calling it the "Old Left." That is why Weaver's book is so richly appropriate to our moment of national history. From the foundations of this country, as Weaver shows, Southern leadership was suspicious of that pervasive influence upon our destiny out of the French Revolution, which the South (in spite of Jefferson) found antipathetic because it represented "a sort of political humanism which had the effect of deifying an abstract concept of man." By the 1890s "under 'progress' the generations were becoming estranged" in the South. The young Southerner who literally built the foundation for France's famous gift, the Statue of Liberty, could also create a cartoon image of the Southern Colonel (in *Colonel Carter of Cartersville*) still dear to the Herblocks of the editorial pages and the sentimentalists of the comic strips and TV series. The belated attempt of the Southern apologists to withstand both industrialism's exploitation of body and soul and secularism's triumphant creed of avarice had failed, leaving largely an emotional residue.

But emotions are respirations of spirit in the world. If their function is erratic, the diagnosis is not necessarily a failure of their vital sources. Perhaps there is an allergic reaction, and the suffering subject, if it does not succumb, becomes acutely aware of an unhealthy state. This is to say that the human spirit may be violated, but not indefinitely. It cannot abide hypocrisy, even when it cannot say the word in all its particulars. The Democratic party, which threw the South a life raft in the 1870s, is shocked to see the South vote for Goldwater, a Republican. It is subsequently shocked, after appropriations of public money for public property in the name of Lincoln's "of . . . by . . . for the people," to see some of those people entrench themselves on national malls or burn public buildings with the defense that these belong to a free people who may, because they are free, do with their own property what they please.

Weaver's examination of the Southern apologia is most instructive on the causes out of which such recent emotional disorders develop. That Southern defense, after the fact of military and political defeat, concentrated on principles considered valid in spite of their having been overcome by force. A faith in the validity of those principles would not allow the apologist to accept it as decided that God was on the side of cannon or votes, which between 1865 and the ratification of the Fourteenth Amendment were synonymous. He, helpless to all effect, looked to a vindication by history. Such spokesmen as Bledsoe, Stephens, and Dabney enunciated those principles as the South's legacy to the future, the legacy of a character larger than regional. The vice-president of the Confederacy, for instance, anticipated eventual vindication as a result of the general subjection of a whole people to the new principle he called "Empire"— centralization—within which system both agent and subject alike were to be reduced to the abstraction of number. We observe in retrospect that, the sovereignty of locality long since overthrown, a new principle has emerged from the general revolt against the predicted "Empire": the sovereignty of the individual. The principle is a radical throwback to the beginnings of civilization out of which community slowly emerged. And perhaps this is what Hillary Rodham, 1969 valedictorian at Wellesley, was noticing when she said, "There's a very strange conservative strain that goes through a lot of New Left, collegiate protests that I find very intriguing because it harks back to a lot of old virtues, to the fulfillment of original ideas."[4] The catastrophic prospect in operation, the cause of panic, is that it makes helpless the technological sophistication of that Empire which the South held suspect long ago. Draft-card burners and computer burners, operating as they contend upon moral principles of individual sovereignty, are difficult to debate, but only partially because they lack a metaphysics. Man deified, the logical extension is that each man is his own god. And Dabney predicted, in 1867, that the South would be sadly vindicated by "the anarchy and woe" which the "disorganizing heresies" of the victorious North were imposing upon the South. A son of the New South, Woodrow Wilson, in abandoning the South, observed: "It is evident that empire is an affair of strong government, and not of the nice and somewhat artificial poise or of the delicate compromises of structure and authority characteristic of a mere federal partnership."[5] He was to go on from there to a further enlargement in his battle for the League of Nations, unable finally to make it an instrument of empire, even in the name of peace.

What the estranged younger generation managed to forget in the South by the turn of the century was an old knowledge, obscured by such spectacles as Joe Wheeler at San Juan Hill shouting, "The Yankees are running! Damn it! I mean the Spaniards!" What they forgot was the effect of empire upon the individual. But all had not forgotten. In *The Leopard's Spots*, published the year after Wilson's arguments for "empire as an affair of strong government," Thomas Dixon has a character say: "I hate the dishwater of modern world citizenship. A shallow cosmopolitanism is the mask of death for the individual. It is the froth of civilization, as crime is its dregs. The true citizen of the world loves his country." Dixon clearly means "loves his country through its regional aspect." The wisdom from our distance is impressive if Dixon's art is not, as the themes of the greater writers who succeed him, particularly those of the "Lost Generation," show. Dixon has another character in the same work anticipate the future effect of those disorganizing heresies that flourished at the turn of the century, the "anarchy and woe" Dabney had spoken of thirty-five years earlier. The Reverend Mr. Durham, refusing an invitation to the larger, cosmopolitan world of Boston, says to a Boston deacon, who is enticing him to a higher and broader calling, "Against a possible day when a flood of foreign anarchy threatens the

4. Quoted in *Life*, June 20, 1969.
5. "Reconstruction of the Southern States," *Atlantic Monthly*, January 1901.

foundations of the Republic and men shall laugh at the faiths of your fathers, and undigested wealth beyond the dreams of avarice rots your society until it mocks at honor, love, and God—against that day we will preserve the South."

V

One of the South's legacies as a region has been a keen sense of history through which such prophecies as Dabney's or the Reverend Mr. Durham's or Richard Weaver's are made possible. It has been instinctively committed as well to a metaphysical, as opposed to an empirical, concern for cause and effect in its view of history. That is why, as Weaver points out, it could counter Locke's assertion that "man is free by nature" with the aphorism from Aristotle, "man is a tyrant by nature." It could sense, and sometimes argue, that Plato's abstract metaphysical concern for the irreconcilable One and Many occurred at a point of dissolution of the concrete Many—the Greek states. Not only ideas but also events out of ideas have consequences. The South was aware that Alexander waited in the wings. Reading Suetonius, it discerned in the elevation of Augustus to Godhead the prospect of his successors. Reading Shakespeare, it could make a distinction between the arguments for the divine right of kings and despotic abuses of office. It did not make haste to substitute the secular right "each man his own king," fearing an elected One as the greater despotism. Any elevated One as symbol of All in the political arena is a fatal illusion, as Alexander Stephens saw it, inevitably contradicted by the particularism of persons and places. If particularism is at first overcome by a superior force, as was gradually accomplished between 1830 and 1930, it will eventually burst out.

Yet, given our development toward political monism out of egalitarianism, we have continued to pay homage to particularism through metaphor. We prefer the illusion, as when we embrace an analogy of our national political arena to the New England town meeting, in spite of the unsettling events of the Chicago Democratic Convention. We might as easily, and perhaps more appropriately, consider our social and political condition analogous to the infamous plantation, given the pyramid of our national "power structure." With a decisive difference: the new plantation is magnified to include and extinguish time and place, and so destroy the old piety that was the climate of manners through which one acknowledged the influence of particularism upon abstraction.

The intimacies of person and place in the old society did not obviate those larger concerns such as the uses of economic and political power, but they were at least a brake upon the evils of the inevitable hierarchy for which no civilizing alternative has been discovered. The student confrontation with the multiversity daily evidences the point. We have moved from the professor on one end of the log, the student on the other, into a world where there is no log, where both float free. The dictates of supply and demand in the profession of teaching, where there has existed for some years a "seller's market," the easy access of portable grants, and the multiplication of fringe benefits in the fierce administrative bidding have made everything available to teacher and student, except the log—the classroom, a still place within which minds only move. On the other hand, the "plantation" or "town meeting," when magnified beyond the possibility of conception by the generality, requires a mystical devotion to an abstract political and social world. Such enlargement must create its own version of moonlight and magnolias or maple syrup and birches. A new piety is synthetically elicited to replace the old piety, which at least required an acknowledgment of the limiting effects of human nature and the natural world upon human institutions. The young, again and again, though they lack the understanding and faith of their forebears, nevertheless recognize the synthetic modification of their spirit. If in their reaction they are violent and irrational in their rejections, to the point of denying understanding and faith as appropriate except when focused on their own isolated well-being, there is still alive in them a hunger for some creature other than themselves in whom to rest faith. Meanwhile, the academic "establishment" officially robs them of the intellectual preparation whereby they might make distinctions and ask the right questions about themselves and the nature of mankind. Some of their elders recognize the problem. Daniel Moynihan, addressing the graduating class at Notre Dame in 1969, said:

> We are not especially well equipped in conceptual terms to ride out the storm ahead. . . . The stability of democracy depends very much on the people making a careful distinction between what government can do and what it cannot do. . . . It cannot provide values to persons who have none, or who have lost those they had. It cannot provide a meaning to life. It cannot provide inner peace. It can provide outlets for moral energies, but it cannot create those energies. In particular, government cannot cope with the crisis in values which is sweeping the Western world. It cannot respond to the fact that so many of our young people do not believe what those before them have believed, do not accept the authority of institutions and customs whose authority has heretofore been accepted, do not embrace or even very much like the culture that they inherit.[6]

The Union, the symbol of a political Arianism, has become the moonlight

6. Quoted in *Life*, June 20, 1969.

and magnolias to a social and political religion that assumes absolute moral imperative. But the body and blood are long absent from our secular, mobile, materialistic togetherness. The borrowed signs of an older order which were at first used to consolidate and manage collective force against any opposition to the progressive destiny of the Union in the Gilded Age—the apple pie and motherhood of particularism borrowed to give abstract nationalism an identity—have long since become stage properties for political rhetoricians. They have seemed discredited by sophist usage on the one hand and by the assault upon them by a more vigorous adversary on the other, the socialist invasion of the idea of union. "The socialist premise that patriotism is but a nickname for prejudice," as Weaver says, led to the desperate defense of patriotism by such people as populist Tom Watson, with the result that prejudices were dignified as patriotism. (The latest occurrence of that confusion centered around George Wallace in his third-party bid for the presidency.)

When advertising has abused its materials to the confusion of patrons and consumers, its final attempt upon its audience is to satirize its own position. Ennui follows a mild titillation, whether the product be cigarette or patriotism. It has been made increasingly difficult for one to love his home, his place. And the embarrassed flippancy with which one makes a stand in favor of the particulars of his devoir is strikingly pathetic, while the solemn rhetorical enumeration of them from a variety of podiums is irritating. Still, that hunger surfaces and longs for expression as honest sentiment; in a very real sense, the flower children's actions were sometimes efforts to find expression to replace apple pie and motherhood, to establish a sense of being out of elementary nature close at hand, and so more acceptable than the vague social and political transcendentalism of the twentieth century that dissolves persons into a secular political oversoul.

In relation to this point, it is interesting to notice correspondence between the Southern position as we have it represented by the Agrarians and new solutions to domestic problems currently in the ascendancy on the Left. Norman Mailer, in his candidacy for mayor of New York City, advocated a form of states' rights—neighborhood rights. He would have New York City granted statehood, then "some *real* power given to the neighborhoods." He advocated "vest-pocket campuses" built by students out of the ruins, not a condition foreign to the Southern soldier-student after 1865. "We'll have compulsory attendance at church on Sunday in those that vote for that." The neighborhood will have power "to decide about the style and quality and number of the police force they want and are willing to pay for." Perhaps Mailer will call his new state "The Thirteen Original Neighborhoods." Meanwhile Jane Jacobs, editor of *Architectural Forum*, wants to work toward restoring facsimile versions of old neighborhoods—Greenwich Village for example. She is for the advantages of "a muddle of oddments" to the city, by which she means diversity of enterprise such as advocated by the Agrarians in relation to land usage. She will come closer to success with the creation of organizations—Daughters of the New York Revolution or United Daughters of Confederated Neighborhoods. Meanwhile Abraham Ribicoff and Orville Freeman introduce Agrarian arguments as a possible solution to the urban problem. It would seem, indeed, that *I'll Take My Stand* may prove of considerable consequence in the final years of this century, and one may even live to hear Justice William O. Douglas or John Kenneth Galbraith raise questions as to the bad effects of the Tennessee Valley Authority on natural and human resources.

vi

The Southerner's attention to place and to the history of place dwells heavily upon the concrete particular, especially upon the particulars of persons. He tends to be a storyteller rather than a speculator in the abstractions of science or social theory. The Eastern joke that Mississippi has more writers than people who can read is truer than intended; but it might be more properly put that it has more bards among the unlettered than any comparable region out of the South, lettered or unlettered. The Southern bardic mind reflects upon what was, with a familiar intimacy that makes it firsthand, and its speculative interest in what will be seldom escapes into abstract systems of contingency. Family chronicle, enlarged and distorted in its accretions by the heart's desire, embodies not only a sense of what is meet and right in human relations but a sense of the perversity of human nature as well. The bardic mind maintains a sense of community out of the convergence of families, within which convergence the variety of humanity finds tolerable habitation, eccentric and common folk alike. It is a mind to which tragedy and comedy, the absurdities of human grandeur and meanness, are congenial. But seldom is it sympathetic to the modern pathos of displacement, the self-torturing spiritual masochism called pursuit of identity. The bardic mind, that is, does not take J. Alfred Prufrock seriously. It is apparent I trust that one finds the bardic mind in the South at the supper table and on the front porch of an evening before he finds it displayed in books. The Southern writer, to the extent that he may be so identified, is almost invariably fed by this anonymous bardic mind.

The Southern mind that Weaver addresses is a religious, poetic mind, in which the concrete is a center for acceptance of the mystery surrounding the concrete. Mystery is accepted, not analyzed. Indeed, Southern suspicion of abstract, analytical thought was and is a distinct liability, a point Weaver emphasizes heavily. As he shows, it made difficult any systematic defense of the Southern cause in the 1850s that might have persuasively engaged political and economic principles, a failure that allowed the grounds of the ensuing conflict to be shifted from vital principles to the indefensible incident of slavery. This was a point Lord Acton had effectively made before the yeomen farmers and mountain boys got home from Appomattox. "If, then, slavery is to be the criterion which shall determine the significance of the civil war, our verdict ought, I think to be, that by one part of the nation it was wickedly defended, and by the other as wickedly removed. Different indeed must our judgment be if we examine the value of secession as a phase in the history of political doctrine."[7]

One of Weaver's points is that we are busily repeating that failure to engage issues of principle through the instruments of logic. We thus allow a radical and political and social dissolution to carry all opposition before it under the emotionally persuasive banner of social justice, with the result that chaos is dictated. The consequence is that order will next be dictated in the name of freedom, but with the effective destruction of freedom as its result. Notice the respectful hearing given Gore Vidal's *Reflections on a Sinking Ship*, a collection of essays that ends with "A Manifesto" asserting "an Authority must be created with the power to control human population, to redistribute food . . . begin the systematic breaking up of the cities into smaller units," and so forth, but "the Authority may *not* have the power or right to regulate the private lives of citizens." One can but shake his head sadly at the illogic. Only since Weaver's death, with the emergence of black supremacy as an active force out of the confused thinking about humanitarianism, has it become possible to examine critically that generous, abstract cause in which person is destroyed. So it is that Weaver's study stands us in good stead. For, in spite of our inherent weakness, the suspicion of abstract thought has virtues that Weaver eloquently defends. Suspicion alone is not so effective as the reasoned presentation of grounds for suspicion, but in its opposition to possibly fatal contingency it is better than no opposition at all.

The Southern Tradition at Bay, then, may be said to speak to and for those of us who seek a spokesman for human dignity within the necessities of human community. Weaver is hopeful, for instance, when he remarks that the South's long persistence in "regarding science as a false messiah" led her to distrust technology, even when forced by the economics of defeat at the hands of a temporary "Gained Cause" to succumb to technology. For the South exhibited, and still to some extent exhibits, an "astonishing resistance to the insidious doctrines of relativism and empiricism." A suspicion not reflected, incidentally,

---

7. Lord Acton's words are from his "The Civil War in America: Its Place in History," a lecture given January 18, 1866.

in so august a figure of the thinker as Emerson, who out of the pressures of the new science moving into seats of power in government after 1865 abandoned transcendentalism to justify the illusive doctrine of Progress.[8]

Science of the sort Weaver means, and its stepchild technology, assumes nature and human nature an enemy to be overthrown and reconstituted. Its ascendancy is everywhere and by all observers remarked, usually with apologetic justification but without sufficient regard for its contingent consequences. Thus the power of the atom makes possible a plutonium 238 battery embedded to regulate heartbeat, while we worry over the accommodations for the aged so that they will not be a burden on family mobility. But against this progress in prolonging life an undercurrent moves, insisting upon the old dignity of death, the tribute life owes nature, as poets have always insisted, whether celebrated as pied beauty or lamented as the arrogance of Time. That undercurrent of unrest is at last more general than a Southern suspicion. The mad scientist once made respectable by his product—genetic manipulations for better beans and meatier hogs—begins to appear with a wild, wild look in his eye. The prospects for superintelligence bred in test tubes are fascinating. Naturally the breeding of a superrace, as Batman would say, is for Good and against Evil (as Hitler argued too), besides which such progress is shaded by Jeffersonian egalitarianism and hence palatable: we are used to saying "to each according to his merit, within the bounds of nature," and we are but extending the bounds of nature. Still, that Southern suspicion asks, whose are the bounds when nature is annihilated and the powers ascribed to Providence are assumed by the geneticist.

Contingent effects that are unfortunate restore some confidence in both nature and Providence; piety after all may prove a valuable principle cherished and kept alive in the South till more generally needed. The progressivist world's fascination with process, a Renaissance heritage that runs through history with childish innocence, may necessarily be tempered by a respect for both the elements of nature and a prospect of ends—old considerations out of medieval thought. With the Renaissance we turned from "simples" to "compounds," from arsenic or hemlock to the elaborate formulas of congregated poisons, which we with our technical skills now recognize as mutually nullifying. The legendary Borgia poisons, as we look back on them, seem quaint and foolish and ineffective, to speak nothing of the antidotes to them, though both were accidentally and not intentionally so. How quaint and amusing the chief scientist of his day, Giambattista della Porta of Naples, with his remedy to whiten teeth—until we compare it with our own remedies dramatized by commercials. And his Antidote to Venom, a universal protection, is the wonder drug of his day:

8. On this point see George M. Fredrickson, *The Inner Civil War: Northern Intellectuals and the Crisis of the Union* (New York: Harper and Row, 1965).

Take three pounds of old oil and two handfuls of St. John's Wort. . . . Macerate for two months in the sun. Strain off the old flowers, and add two ounces of fresh. Boil in Balneo . . . for six hours. Put in a close-stopped bottle and keep in the sun for fifteen days. During July, add three ounces of St. John's Wort seed which gently has been stamped and steeped in two glasses of white wine for three days. Add also two dracms each of gentian, tormentil, dittany, zeodary, and carline, (all of which must have been gathered in August) sandalwòod and long-aristolochie. Gently boil for six hours in Balneo Mariae. Strain in a press. Add to the expression one ounce of saffron, myrrh, aloes, spikenard, and rhubarb, allbruised. Boil for a day in Balneo Mariae. Add two ounces each of treacle and mithridate. Boil for six hours in Balneo Mariae. And set it in the sun for forty days . . . It will work wonders.[9]

Quaint and amusing, until we compare some of our own solutions to our problems. For now intention and accident are more alarmingly confusing to us. The Tennessee Valley Authority, which appropriated land for lakes to provide electrical power, displacing many settled people, soon turned to coal instead of waterpower. It contaminated the air to the extent that it has recently awarded contracts totaling several million dollars for limestone to be used in testing an air-pollution-control process to counteract the tons of sulfur dioxide released into the country air. At the moment there are mild alarms from New York and New Jersey congressmen over the prospect of their states acting as way stations for the disposal of World War I nerve gas, now obsolete but nondisposable. (The suggested throwaway cartons are two old "liberty" ships to be sunk in the Atlantic.) With some mild relief and in compensation (such are the uses of Emerson), we cite the return of inhabitants to the Bikini atolls, though noting an indefinite period before life can be supported independently there. Daily there are demonstrations against science as false messiah in its military aspect. Research projects bearing upon defenses are excoriated by the young who enjoy the pleasures of the pill without being equally disturbed by the prospects of blood clots. Only very slowly are we waking to the inherent long-range, in-clusive dangers of combination drugs, despite our occasional excitement over minor accidents such as thalidomide's role in a rash of birth defects—besides which, that was in Germany, wasn't it?

The extent to which the South has succumbed to the new messiah, as antici-pated by spokesmen for the South after Appomattox, may be symptomatically present in the complacent reception of such warnings as Rachel Carson's. After all, we have had a bad boll-weevil problem. If we overcome the screwworm more sanely than the boll weevil, very well: the main point is to get rid of the two pests. So then what is the cost factor in spraying fire ants by plane? In

9. Quoted by Frederick Baron Corve in "The Legend of the Borgia Venom," *Chronicles of the House of Borgia* (New York: Dover, 1962).

money we mean. And isn't it interesting, the control of the mosquito with DDT—but whatever happened to the shrimp and crab life along the coast? As I write a scientist of reputation testifies before a senate committee on inter-governmental relations that technology is seriously flawed because of its short-sighted violations of nature, that it may indeed destroy irreparably the natural capital of mankind—environment and people—"probably within the next 50 years." His testimony is reported in my evening paper as a human-interest story, a filler buried amid advertising of technology's good things. ("Got any bees in your trees? Call Orkin," a billboard says.) In the same paper another human-interest story: a Berkeley lecturer on architecture warns an Atlanta audience that Seattle has "wrecked the city with freeways" and insists that man's prin-cipal enemy is technology unbridled by humanity. Urban renewal is undertaken in the name of humanity, but with what contingent effects upon humanity? The same paper addresses urban renewal and the freeway problems in its editorials as if clustered apartments and four-lane highways were virtues of the city's soul without effects upon its body. It becomes increasingly exercised over symptoms, publishing devastating pictures of clogged and polluted streams while ignoring the washing machine in our basement or the burden of the throwaway bottle. Thus a metaphor for our concern over problems from pollution to student unrest.

After the reeducation which *The Southern Tradition at Bay* represents, Rich-ard Weaver went on in *Ideas Have Consequences* to characterize our chaos as the result of a conception of life as *practice* without *theory*, whose problems are met repeatedly by ad hoc policies that reject nature and history as bearing upon the present and future. The inevitable effect upon society as we know it in twentieth-century America is that we are managed by the complicated machinery of order but not by order itself. Thus the paradoxical situation: the "establish-ment" is itself the purveyor of disorder, as Dabney predicted, whether one look to its national, state, or local machinery. For the very machinery of society is the principal source of and cause of our disorder, despite its contradictory disguise. Such is the inevitable situation out of the ascendancy of a Gained Cause now decaying about us, a cause whose dominant stance has become that provin-cialism which, as Allen Tate observed, begins each day as if there were no yesterday. Such an ad hoc philosophy, the eternal unexamined principle of youth, endears the child's words and actions to us in our sentimental reminis-cent moments. But when a nation becomes as old as ours has since 1776, it must put aside the child's speech and understanding and thought. When it does not, its children will not refrain from pointing to the parading emperors *au naturel*. That is their brand of ad hoc policy, learned of their fathers; it is the "issue-oriented" reaction one expects when issues are not profoundly read as to radi-cal causes.

There are many ways of pointing the finger at naked truth. One may do so as directly as do Aristophanes or Petronius. Or by disrobing in demonstrations while shouting "obscene" words (once elements of acceptable discourse, as Chaucer and Dante demonstrate). Satire is scarcely possible as a literary mode in an age where absurdity is so vast as to prevent enlargement. Thus the most effective satire is spontaneous public action, which commandeers a public audience against its will where once the audience sought the satire. The theatrical variety of demonstrations and happenings makes my point. The obscene word or public nakedness proving insufficient, public fornication became the latest fad. Or one may effectively and carefully explicate history and art as Richard Weaver does. His finger-pointing is not spectacular; it is a logical and persuasive examination of some of the causes of our chaos. From such reflection, principles may emerge that make understandable such diverse symptoms of society's disease as polluted streams and student unrest. His work, as he is careful to say, is finally larger in its concerns than "Southern" history; it will help keep alive ideas of healthful consequence toward that day when we, young and old alike, return to careful reading and thinking. This is a point in the future, hopefully short of science's allotted fifty years. It is a point when we may, in Eliot's words, "arrive where we started / And know the place for the first time." Meanwhile it must be said as a minimum that anyone professing a serious concern with the social, political, and cultural aspects of American civilization, particularly that of the past and present South, is obligated to read *The Southern Tradition at Bay*—with his "Whig" conditioning suspended.

VII. Solzhenitsyn at Harvard

The mistake must be at the root, at the very basis of human thinking in the past centuries. It is the prevailing Western view of the world which was born during the Renaissance and found its political expression starting in . . . the Enlightenment. It became the basis for government and social sciences and could be defined as rationalistic humanism or humanistic autonomy: the proclaimed and enforced autonomy of man from any higher force above him.

—Alexander Solzhenitsyn, Harvard University, June 8, 1978

I think we all have a right to our destiny as individuals. And I have a right to choose mine and everybody else has a right to choose theirs.

—Cultist Christine Miller at Jonestown, November 1978, minutes before her death

i

A point overlooked in the general (and often angry) response to Solzhenitsyn's Harvard commencement address is that he spoke to a more limited audience than the media's sensational coverage reflected. He spoke to what he must have supposed a responsible intellectual community, and he did so undoubtedly out of what is to us that quaint nineteenth-century European tradition that openly assumes that a nation's intellectual character is established by an intellectual elite. However, the general history of that tradition might well have forewarned him. For the intellectual elite established themselves in such a favored position in large part by fostering egalitarian ideologies, a maneuver of Machiavellian necessity if they were to accumulate and command to their ends the power they recognized as latent in the general body of mankind. It was a maneuver accomplished over a span of time and by a variety of minds, measured variously from the inception of nominalism with William of Occam (Richard Weaver, *Ideas Have Consequences*) or the dislocations of thought by Machiavelli (Leo Strauss, *Thoughts on Machiavelli*) or those by Joachim of Floris or Voltaire and the succeeding philosophes (Eric Voegelin, *Science, Politics & Gnosticism* and *From Enlightenment to Revolution*; Gerhart Niemeyer, *Between Nothingness and Paradise*). But whatever the point of inception of the new idolatry examined by Weaver or Strauss or Voegelin or Niemeyer, its central requirement for success is to control that power resident in the will of the individual by dislocating that will from its proper end.

The latent power, however, tended to become atomized, following the Renaissance inclination to relocate the primary source of power from its transcendent cause. The medieval understanding had been that man's power in the world was a limited gift from the God of all nature, the Word still active within the world. But that old understanding was progressively abandoned. The origin of power, the post-Renaissance world declared, is man himself; in the new world dawning, man was increasingly celebrated as the maker of his own destiny. That is, in this new beginning is man's word, through which his reason will rule supreme. *Ratio* ceased to function as proconsul with *intellectus* in the kingdom of being; it began to insist upon an absolute authority.

Josef Pieper, in *Leisure: The Basis of Culture*, helps us understand why there was such popular support of the intelligentsia from the lower classes during the eighteenth and nineteenth centuries, when revolutionary movements generally were bent on abolishing cultural hierarchies. In the pursuit of millennial dreams, knowledge as the necessary means to power over nature is elevated over wisdom. A justification is made for it as a species of labor, as "intellectual work." Pieper cites Kant's words from 1796: "the law is that reason acquires its possessions through work." Two years later, Wordsworth in "Tintern Abbey" attempted to rescue a larger perspective of mind in nature, to justify that openness to existence which thinkers from Plato and Aristotle to Aquinas had understood as the operation of *intellectus* as complement to *ratio*. In that state of mind, said Wordsworth, one "sees into the life of things." (Pieper cites Heraclitus' description of receptive contemplation as "listening to the essence of things.")

But the popular spirit comes to suppose (in Pieper's words) that "if to know is to work, then knowledge is the fruit of our own unaided effort and activity; then knowledge includes nothing which is not due to the effort of man, and there is nothing *gratuitous* about it, nothing 'in-spired.'" Thus we lose the old distinction between *artes liberalis* and *artes serviles*, and educational institutions subsequently receive most general support when they present themselves as species under *artes serviles*. Facts and statistics have become the measure of effective production, whether one is measuring articles or autos. I have in hand a "memo" from the chief academic officer of a large state university that attempts to pattern itself after Harvard and declares its primary commitment as the pursuit of "new knowledge." The "memo" to all "Academic Deans" declares that all instructors are "to adhere to a 2500-teaching-minute requirement" for the five-hour course. Classes are to meet "the required number of contact minutes," whether elementary, junior high, grammar, or graduate-level microbiology.

A principal danger in this post-Renaissance relocation of ultimate power into nature and thence to man's mind was that such a shift would fracture and divide collective power in the world. The rising spirit of nationalism, the splintering reformations within and outside the church, became conspicuous signs in our history of the community disintegrating, a disintegration reaching downward into Western institutions until even the individual family trembles toward collapse in our day. And accompanying that disintegration, there rises a mindless acceptance of the letter, removed from reality, as in the directive that one must engage mind in pursuit of reality for the full "2500-teaching-minute requirement." Thus the wily ideologue comes to be served by mindless minions.

The ideologist, recognizing the atomizing effect of his own word upon traditional community, recognized as well that he must find a substitute for the Word that had held the old world together—a god larger than the individual, though created in man's likeness. Thus one might justify temporal actions performed by the state in the name of such a god. For the ideologist must establish a god, given that aspect of man's nature which requires him to worship *something*, if the ideologist is to control a collective power sufficient to perform the political or social or religious reformations of reality that his newly liberated reason has persuaded his own understanding to accept. A symbolic figure of man elevated to godlike stature could be collectively embraced, thus concentrating the lesser atomies of individual man as a reservoir of power. Then only might the ideologist perform the tremendous task of his alchemy, the transformation of reality.

That *alchemy* is the proper term here needs but our careful attention to the variety of transformational programs underway in the 1980s. There is a growing interest in "science" as magic such as we have not witnessed since the sixteenth and seventeenth centuries, an interest institutionalized by the academy's intense concern for research as its principal justification to the cost-bearing public. The president of a large university, intent on making his institution the "top" university in the nation (or at least in the Southeast, or, that failing, certainly the "capstone" of the thirty-odd schools within the system) urged his regents to support his "drive to excellence." For, said he to them, "we must find a way to reprogram nature." To the general applause and support of the regents, and most of the faculty and alumni, he transformed a university into an advanced institute of vocational technology, the ideal being always to be on the "cutting edge" of "new knowledge."

Such is the complexity of reality, especially as it becomes manifest in its pressures on man's intellect when intellect ignores that complexity, that this president lost his personal power in reprogramming his own university. But such also is the whim of fate that the cause of his downfall was comic in its spectacle: the administrative promotion of athletes out of remedial (sixth-grade) grammar courses they failed, protested by an instructor, became a media event that could not be controlled by his public-relations office. The case at last brought to court, the president's "Vice-President for Academic Affairs" appealed to the jury's supposed sentimental sociological ideology of egalitarianism: she had authorized the promotions because she preferred "to err on the side of making a mistake." The jury found against the university, the president fell, a new president was installed to continue the same "pursuit of excellence" as defined by his predecessor. To steady a confused and chaotic faculty, the new president reassured them of their importance as teaching faculty. Their proper role continues to be to "push back the frontiers of knowledge." Thus presumably—given the metaphor—ignorance will at last triumph in its invasion of knowledge. And (lest this trip into the provinces seem to be too far removed from Solzhenitsyn at Harvard) thus will triumph once more Charles W. Eliot's Harvard reformation of higher education, a reformation pervasive of the American academy. Such a reflection increases the irony of Solzhenitsyn's commencement address.

The *humanistic* concern in higher education, as opposed to the now dominant technological concern, is a very ancient one, the term here referring to that old devotion to the liberal arts as the necessity to intellect if intellect is to find itself viable against perversion of intellect—if mind is to come to an accommodation with the realities of its existential circumstances. *Humanity*, then, becomes a term well calculated to serve the ideological sorcerer, since there is a residual if vague aura about it out of the term's history. In addition, the term can be made to appeal to the individual's vanity, while reducing the individual to an integer in a collective power. Thus *Humanity* established as the God of nature, through gnosis, easily translates in common language to mean each human is a god, particularly in the political marketplace. It is important to give a focus for such restlessness, if the energy of restlessness is to be commanded toward reprogramming nature and human nature itself.

Still, more and more we find ourselves confronted by strange voices, insisting in the name of autonomous liberation, "I think we all have a right to our own destiny as individuals. And I have a right to choose mine and everybody else has a right to choose theirs." These words were spoken by cultist Christine Miller to Jim Jones at Jonestown, minutes before the mass suicide. He responded, "The best testimony we can make is to leave this goddamn world." A little later, in attempting to still the crying and screaming, he rebuked the multitude before him: "This is not the way for people who are socialistic Communists to die. Children it's just something to put you to rest."[1] I cite this modern instance of an ideologist's struggle to maintain power, even if it means annihilation, in order to

1. *Time*, March 26, 1979.

bracket a period of Western history. The other point to measure from is expounded by Norman Cohn in *The Pursuit of the Millennium*, a study of rising
sectarianism in the Middle Ages. In Cohn's pages one experiences a discomforting encounter with our own world, though his treatment of historical materials
concludes with sixteenth-century Anabaptist versions of Jonestown. The millenarian sects he studies, says Cohn, have in common a conception of salvation as
collective, terrestrial, imminent, total, miraculous. He concludes his 1970 edition as follows: "The old religious idiom has been replaced by a secular one, and
this tends to obscure what otherwise would be obvious. For it is the simple truth
that, stripped of their original supernatural sanction, revolutionary millenarianism and mystical anarchism are with us still."

Humanity as a vague symbolization of mankind could also appeal to those
residual inclinations of charity that lingered as a moral instinct in Western man
while the New Testament authority in that matter was being reduced to fiction.
Acts committed in the name of humanity become holy acts. In addition, this new
myth of humanity could be manipulated through the emerging "science" of historiography, that theology of modernism, which has been devastatingly reviewed
for us by Strauss and Voegelin. Through a reconstruction of history, an ultimate
reality emerged as a substitute for Saint Augustine's City of God: it lay in an
imminent world soon to blossom, as might be proved by the juxtaposing of a
cloudy version of the past as benighted to the brightening present as expounded
by the ideologue. The promise was that a new everyman would emerge, reaching consummation in perfect humanity—at some point just down the road of
time. Such was the promise, though its cost was each man's sacrificial journey in
the present—under the auspices of the state.

If the new principle is that each man's word is as absolute as his reason can
make it, that word will burn as brightly as the power it attracts and controls. Yet
with a multitude of contending words born of the multitude of individuals,
rather than of the Word, where may one locate any center about which the
whole consort of being—individuals, families, communities, nations—may re-
volve in any orderly dance? Shall one join his power to a Jimmy Carter or a
Ralph Nader? Or, on the darker side of the dilemma, to a Charles Manson or a
Jim Jones? For the old festive dance of all creation about the Word at creation's
heart, which had been the Christian vision, was long ago reduced to a race
toward the city of man, now deified in the name of Humanity. But alas, there
exist as many New Jerusalems as unstilled, passionate voices may declare, from
Anabaptist Münster in the sixteenth century to Jonestown in the twentieth,
from France in the eighteenth century to Russia and China and Iran and Ugan-
da and Cambodia and a multitude in the twentieth.

As Voegelin in particular has shown us, we see in retrospect that ideological
reformations of reality, attempted in the intoxicating name of humanity, have

proved to be deformations of reality leading into an engulfing chaos. We begin to recognize the spiritual bankruptcy and moral decay of our age as the principal legacy of the Enlightenment's manipulations of Renaissance exuberance. Solzhenitsyn's concern at Harvard was precisely with this dislocation which had been managed, not by man's reason, but by man's aberrant reason. Illusional "reality" brought us to disillusion upon disillusion, and to the threat of a spiritual despair which now infects the general body of Western civilization. In our country, the disturbing symptoms of that despair are visible in our conduct as a nation among nations—for instance, in our policy toward a murderous regime, Communist China. Our enlightened Eastern policy shadows the high moral stance we assume toward a Rhodesia or a South Africa. As Solzhenitsyn reminds us, our position on human rights appears strangely ambiguous to the larger world. It is a point shockingly registered on us by the dark spectacle of Jim Jones and the Jonestown massacre, for Jones's was an apocalyptic sacrifice of individuals gathered to him in the name of Humanity. We are confronted by gruesome detail on a cover of *Time*, evidence of the danger of power in the control of ideologists. The horrible deaths of hundreds near at hand arrests us as the deaths of millions in Asia did not.

Our Russian guest at Harvard in 1978 perhaps supposed himself addressing an intelligentsia somewhat different from that with which he had been most intimately acquainted. For certainly he is acutely aware of that spiritual strangulation in his own country which we Westerners encounter in its chilling effects as dramatized by Dostoevsky, Tolstoy, Gogol. The insidious tentacles of that European vine springing from the foreheads of *les luminaires* crept into Solzhenitsyn's country and came to flourish there in the nineteenth century with a smothering effect on the Russian spirit like that of kudzu strangling a Georgia pine. Perhaps, then, Solzhenitsyn supposed himself addressing an intellectual remnant in the West in whom spirit was still alive if apparently dormant. But then Ralph Waldo Emerson had long preceded him at Harvard. In 1837 Emerson called for the emergence of the "American Scholar," by whom he has been generously remembered ever since. What is of ironic significance in the light of Solzhenitsyn's Harvard appearance is that Emerson called for that new scholar to rise out of fundamentally Enlightenment ground, and the degree of his success in conjuring such intellectuals helps account for our continuing veneration of Emerson and our outrage with Solzhenitsyn. The lengthened shadow of Emerson rests more darkly upon our intellectual institutions than our Russian guest could know. The lengthened shadow of the individual man is history, Emerson confidently asserted, his faith reduced to the temporal and vested in the future.

See as an example the fourth paragraph of Emerson's address. Here he secularizes Saint Paul's crucial metaphor of the Christian Church (Romans 12:4), each person's membership in that body whose head is Christ. Emerson uses an old pagan fable about the gods and by that indirection demythologizes Paul. As Mircea Eliade would undoubtedly point out, Emerson's prose reveals that he understands myth as only "fiction," as metaphor very distantly related to man's experience of reality. His own metaphor is revealing in this respect: there is for Emerson "One Man,—present to all particular men only partially, or through one faculty; and . . . you must take the whole society to find the whole man." Of this "body," the scholar is "Man Thinking." The Enlightenment deification of intramundane man permeates his address to the Harvard scholars.

But here we must make a distinction in our use of *myth* as applied to Emersonian thought. Eliade reminds us that, beginning with the Renaissance, *myth* came to mean *fiction*, as it did not to Homer or Plato or Dante. It clearly means fiction in such a mind as Emerson's, in which it becomes a strategy to arouse feelings in order to control the imagination of minds separate from his own and turn the power over imagination thus gained toward restructuring man himself. It is a rhetorical mode intending a "reprogramming" of human nature so that man wills himself to be his own god. That is the myth Emerson had proclaimed at Harvard in famous speeches.

That one addresses an "enlightened" audience at Harvard has been the assumption of any speaker there, at least since Charles W. Eliot's inaugural address as president in 1869. The new president appealed to the authority of John Locke, Francis Bacon, and Emerson in arguing that academic power is crucial to the effective operation of the state. In that address one discovers that the state is already becoming the substitute religion that Solzhenitsyn is to attack. "The community," says President Eliot, "does not owe superior education to all children, but only to the *elite*,—to those who, having the capacity, prove by hard work that they have also the necessary perseverance and endurance." Well enough, though Harvard has struggled mightily of late to accommodate itself to state-decreed definitions of *capacity, work, perseverance*. Such a struggle, which has spread throughout the American academy and surfaces locally in the promotion of college senior athletes failing sixth-grade grammar, is an inevitable extension of what President Eliot in his farewell doctrinal epistle in 1909 spoke of as "The Religion of the Future." In that document he is more explicit about the worship already latent in the inaugural address of 1869, for from the beginning he speaks on behalf of an intellectual priesthood dedicated to the state, rather than to any community in Saint Paul's sense of the term. He calls for Harvard to produce an "aristocracy which excels in manly sports, carries off the honors and prizes of the learned professions, and bears itself with distinction in all fields of intellectual labor and combat." Thus President Eliot's modifications of Emerson's scholar, a shift that moves the American intellectual further from Renaissance humanist toward pragmatist. And the first conspicuous model of Eliot's new man is to be that strong son of Harvard, Theodore Roosevelt.

President Eliot, on the authority of Emerson's assertion that history is but the lengthened shadow of a man (his cousin T. S. Eliot paid devastating respect to Emerson's aphorism in "Sweeney Erect"), sets about establishing a new program of specialization such as will provide the state a complex of long shadows that yet darken our days. Here is President Eliot's understanding of the educated man's proper role in the community: "As tools multiply, each is more ingeniously adapted to its own exclusive purpose. So with men that make the state. For the individual, concentration, and the highest development of his own peculiar faculty, is the only prudence. But for the state, it is variety, not uniformity, of intellectual produce, which is needful." How shallow a conception of the individual is here implied! The individual mind is raw material, to be turned into "produce" serviceable to the "state." The sweetener is that such a "product," turned out through the new elective system in higher education, will compose an aristocracy, specialized in its parts, though as members one of another constituting a whole machinery called the "state." Its central symbol, its "head" as one might say (borrowing from Saint Paul), may reflect the complex whole. That is, the president may have written books, stormed up San Juan Hill, explored the West, and so on. In a later day, he may be discovered writing a book on presidents, playing touch football on the White House lawn, and performing other athletic feats not proper to mention short of the daily press.

Thus President Eliot of Harvard College in 1869 called for a new intelligentsia whose principal virtue would be pragmatic variety, honed to an efficiency through the practice of intellectual abstractionism perfected in restricted specializations. And its principal devotion would find focus in the state. The new elite thus nurtured is to replace the older Puritan religious establishment that had governed intellect through Harvard, Yale, and Princeton before the war just over, or had controlled it at least till undermined by such progressive forces as Emerson's unitarianism. That old establishment had not made itself sufficiently powerful to control affairs of state in the days of Southern political ascendancy. It hardly promised to prove dependable to President Eliot's dream of what Solzhenitsyn was to castigate as the "enforced autonomy of man from any higher force above him."

Solzhenitsyn surely did not intend to include two hundred million Americans in his searing indictment of spiritual failures of the American intelligentsia, any more than President Eliot's inaugural address was intended to summon hordes of youth to Boston in an open admissions policy. Or any more than William F. Buckley was to mean Mississippi or Georgia or Oregon culpable for what went wrong between man and God at Yale. Yet a presumption of inclusiveness is reflected in the general response to Solzhenitsyn's speech in a spectrum ranging from righteous anger to mild regret, from Norman Cousins to William F. Buckley himself. Nor does Solzhenitsyn intend us to think, by his statement that

Russia has been purged by suffering, that all Russians have been "born again." "Is it true," asked the *National Review* on July 21, 1978, "that the Russian people have been purged by suffering, and are less materialistic and spiritually stronger than their Western counterparts?" And Buckley, in his syndicated column reprinted in the same issue, speaks of "Solzhenitsyn's confusion of his own greatness of spirit with that of most Russians." Not long since, Solzhenitsyn was being praised for that arresting portrait of endurance, Ivan Denisovich, in whom he shows a purging of one member of a community taken at its fundamental level. It is a more spiritual portrait by far than the one Hemingway gives us of his fisherman in *The Old Man and the Sea*, and it is so precisely because Ivan gains a complexity by being placed in community in such a way as to reveal him a remnant rescued out of the general decay. He is more complex than an allegorical figuring of Everyman such as that Emersonian self-reliant man with a Spanish accent which Hemingway gives us. But the greatness of spirit in Ivan does not encourage one to take him as the author's portrait of most Russians.

ii

On another occasion, Solzhenitsyn has remarked that a nation with a great writer has a separate government. That remark should help us set his Harvard address in better perspective—that remark, along with his extended analysis of the decline of the Russian intelligentsia called "The Smatterers," which appeared in his *From under the Rubble*. He must have supposed that his Harvard words would be heard against such as these. For he had experienced such an excessive and sudden veneration upon his exile that he might reasonably presume that pieces like his "Smatterers" had been digested with approval by his devouring hosts. Indeed, so generous had been the reception of this man who chose exile rather than abandon his words that he struggled almost helplessly for some privacy, finally settling in New England, a locale known for its close regard for the individual's privacy—so well known in this respect as to appear in comic portraits of the New Englander as inhospitable. He knew that *From under the Rubble* had enjoyed a brisk sale in its American edition, surely not through drugstore distribution. He *must* then have been read and pondered. And by whom if not by the American intelligentsia whose capital by popular consent is Harvard University?

Perhaps there was some confusion on Solzhenitsyn's part. Perhaps he assumed too easily that he spoke to a potentially viable community, one fallen on evil days no doubt, yet capable of recall to known but forgotten responsibilities by a prophet scorched in modern fires. The response to his address may well have been a further disappointment to him, exacerbating his sense of homesickness and deepening the disillusionment with Western civilization that was reflected in the speech itself. Perhaps he may even have forgotten for a moment his own portrait of the old Russian intelligentsia, or that it drank at the same waters the West had imbibed much longer than they. Or perhaps there are no longer many surprises possible to him in these matters of which man and his mind are a part. At any rate, he had already presented a portrait of the despiritualized intellectual of his own country, only now to discover that intellectual's doppelgänger in Western democracy.

In "The Smatterers" Solzhenitsyn analyzes the failures of the old Russian intelligentsia, failures in consequence of which the "smatterers" emerge as his principal antagonists. The "smatterers" constitute the new intellectual establishment now in control of thought and action in his homeland, but they turn out to be (and I suspect to his surprise) very like our own who have emerged from Charles W. Eliot's dream and exercise an analogous control in our own country. (A general control through unreflective "public opinion" is far more subtle than one through brute force, but not necessarily less vicious.) The Russian pilgrim thus discovered himself speaking, for the most part, to American "smatterers" in his address at Harvard. Indeed, his evaluation of that mind in *From under the Rubble* bears ironic echo of the evaluations President Eliot's dream began to receive at the turn of this century at the hands of such men as Irving Babbitt and George Santayana. For instance, we find him echoing Santayana's portrait of the intellectual of our "genteel tradition" who did not examine President Eliot's position or who would not oppose it. Santayana laments a general effect of Eliot's new Harvard elitism in words that would be at home in Solzhenitsyn's speech: "now analysis and psychology seem to stand alone: there is no spiritual interest, no spiritual need."

The old Russian intelligentsia (so runs the summary in "The Smatterers") became "clannish," with an "unnatural disengagement from the general life of the nation." It became possessed by "love of egalitarian justice, the social good and material well-being of the people, which paralyzed its love of and interest in the truth; [Dostoevsky's] 'temptation of the General Inquisitor': let the truth perish if people will be the happier for it." It was given to "day-dreaming, a naive idealism, an inadequate sense of reality." There is still present in the "smatterers" a central inheritance from the old intelligentsia: "dogmatic idolatry of man and mankind," a "replacement of religion by a faith in scientific progress" such as breeds the new elite, in whom there is a "lack of sympathetic interest in the history of our homeland, no feeling of blood relationships with its history. Insufficient sense of historical reality." Theirs is "the religion of self-deification—the intelligentsia sees its existence as providential for the country."

Thus it deified as if in its own image a "people whom it did not know and from whom it was hopelessly estranged." One recognizes here the Russian version of what Allen Tate called a "new provincialism": "that state of mind in which regional men lose their origin in the past and its continuity into the present, and begin every day as if there had been no yesterday." And did Solzhenitsyn or Tate say the following: "the provincial world of the present . . . sees in material welfare and legal justice the whole solution to the human problem. . . . [The provincials] do not live anywhere"? Or one might suppose that Solzhenitsyn has been reading Gerhart Niemeyer's *Between Nothingness and Paradise*, or perhaps Voegelin's own Harvard address (titled "Immortality: Reality and Symbol" and recorded in the *Harvard Theological Review* of July 1967), in which Voegelin gives us an analysis of the stages of the deformation of reality in the post-Renaissance world, from religious experience through dogma into ideology.

Given the direction taken by the old Russian intelligentsia, the elite "in Russia today is *the whole of the educated stratum*," says Solzhenitsyn, "every person who has been to school above the seventh grade." It is a group having "merely an outward polish," with little intellectual depth, and it includes bureaucrats, party agitators, political instructors. In short, it is made up of those in "the semieducated estate—the 'smatterers.'" Eric Voegelin, in the prefatory chapter he wrote in 1977 for Niemeyer's translation of *Anamnesis*, remarks our own smatterers. Our intellectual climate, he says, has been established as a result of the academy's absorbing "German intellectuals who emigrated to America" at the outset of World War II, bringing with them neo-Hegelian "ideologies, methodologies, . . . phenomenologies, hermeneutic profundities, and so on." This migration coincided with the "populist expansion of the universities, accompanied by the inevitable inrush of functional illiterates into academic positions in the 1950s and 60s." (When that evaluation gets around, Voegelin will become as popular among academics in the seventies as Arthur Jensen and William Shockley were among undergraduates in the sixties.) President Eliot in 1869 had promised that "it will be generations before the best of American institutions of education will get growth enough to bear pruning," and we set out on the road to the multiversities, each of them celebrating itself as "the best," usually by claiming kinship with Harvard or Yale or Princeton. The intellectual quality of academic debate as Voegelin witnesses it is still centered on those imported modernist ideas that Voegelin and others have shown to be bankrupt, but it is in considerable decline from the European versions of the same debates that went on at the turn of the century. (Imagine, for instance, the difficulty of showing such academics in a provincial university, bent on imitating Yale, the intellectual poverty of the "Bloomsbury" literary criticism centered at Yale and now widely imitated, the pale afterglow of Husserl's thought clothed in jargony terminology.) "Today," says Voegelin, "the academic world is plagued with figures who could not have gained public attention in the environment of the Weimar Republic," an intellectual milieu for which Voegelin holds scant brief.

In the wider, less provincial context that I have suggested, Solzhenitsyn's Harvard words carry more force of truth than perhaps even he might have supposed, or than it is comfortable for the Harvard establishment to admit, an establishment with long-lived branches in Washington and in universities across the country, principally the state-supported ones. The loss of courage and will in the new gnostic intellectual, whether he identify himself with the political left or right (and gnosticism has dominated American political thought in both camps since the War Between the States) is surely a conspicuous phenomenon in our time, reflected in the contending candidates in the last presidential elections. It reflects a condition of both spirit and will remarked by traditionalists—those "regionalists" Tate opposes to the "New Provincial"—within the classical-Christian world, "based [as Tate says] upon regional consciousness, which held that honor, truth, imagination, human dignity, and limited acquisitiveness, could alone justify a social order however rich and efficient it may be." That condition has also been increasingly under attack from the radical left, one political consequence being the election in the 1970s of a New Southist in populist clothing. The remedy for our national anemia seems fair to finish us off.

Solzhenitsyn said nothing at Harvard that had not been more violently said by word and deed in the 1960s, particularly in that traumatic period when the dominant symbol of our spiritual and intellectual vagaries became the Vietnam War. But our Russian friend is not speaking primarily of American millions in wandering mazes lost as compared to Russia's spiritual millions. Or at least he probably did not suppose himself speaking of so many. ("I had not thought death had undone so many," says Dante on a similar occasion.) But when he says that his country has now "achieved a spiritual development of such intensity that the Western system in its present state of spiritual exhaustion does not look attractive," he might have been Richard Weaver, or Flannery O'Connor, or Donald Davidson, or Allen Tate speaking twenty or thirty years earlier; in that possibility, the words would have been more internal to America: "Eastern system" to designate the modern gnostic state whose home territory seemed centered in New York City, with its business office charged with provincial affairs located in Washington, D.C., and its seminaries for the training of directors of the popular spirit at Harvard and similar institutions. Solzhenitsyn does say "Western *system*" in the translation we have, not "Western *people*," and he has already become aware of individuals here who have made their way up from liberal gnosticism through a "spiritual development." "I have received letters in America from highly intelligent persons, maybe a teacher in a far-away college who could do much for the renewal and salvation of his country, but his country cannot hear him because the media are not interested in him." (*Cannot*, not *will not.*)

iii

Solzhenitsyn means by "spiritual development" a return to what Tate speaks of as "regional consciousness" within the classical-Christian tradition. He explains the term in "The Smatterers" and he dramatizes it in Ivan Denisovich. We have recently been stirred by individuals such as he means: Alexander Ginzburg and Anatoly Shcharansky. There have been a number of particular instances called to our attention since the Stalin purge of 1937, fleeting dissidents who blossom in our attention for a moment before fading from our concern, as have literally millions in Cambodia recently, and before that in China, and before that the kulaks of central Russia and the Ukraine, the proud Estonians, and so on, and so forth. Solzhenitsyn is saying that out of such barbarism, fostered by the old intelligentsia and the new "smatterers," a new intelligentsia is being born. In "The Smatterers" he speaks of a "nucleus" that emerges from the smatterers, to be distinguished from them in being antipathetic to them.

Now there are such nuclei outside Russia as well. Recently there emerged in France, for instance, the *Nouveaux Philosophes*, accompanied by a general revival among young intellectuals disillusioned by the political left. This growing "nucleus" appears to be flourishing in opposition to the descendants of the Voltairean *philosophes*, as witnessed by the proliferation of periodicals and the appearance of a number of books that have excited debate, such as Bernard-Henri Lévy's recent *Barbarism with a Human Face* and (from across the channel) Arianna Stassinopoulos's *After Reason*. Thomas Molnar, in the *National Review* of November 24, 1978, pointed out that Solzhenitsyn is an important influence on the new spirit stirring in the West. If it has not embraced Solzhenitsyn's spiritual concern as yet, the signs of a movement in that direction are apparent.

Some Americans on the right, in speaking of that same spiritual phenomenon within our community, are likely to use *remnant* (as I do above) rather than *nucleus* to describe it, the difference in connotation being that between a gnawing despair in *remnant* and a generative hope in Solzhenitsyn's *nucleus*. The nucleus, he says, is to be recognized,

not by the academic qualifications of its members, nor the number of books that have been published, nor by the high level of those who "are accustomed to think and fond of thinking, but not of plowing the land," nor by the scientific cleverness of a methodology which so easily creates "professional subcultures," nor by a sense of alienation from state and people, nor by membership in a spiritual diaspora ("nowhere quite at home"). I would recognize this nucleus by the purity of its aspirations, by its spiritual selflessness in the name of truth, and above all for the sake of *this* country [Russia], in which it lives. This nucleus will have been brought up not so much in the libraries as on spiritual sufferings. . . . I have seen these modest and valiant young people with my own eyes, heard them with my own ears.

That is a statement the media ignores, though happy to report Lillian Hellman's full response: "When you're as close to God as Mr. Solzhenitsyn seems to be, then I suppose no world of any kind is good enough." And that Yale divine, William S. Coffin, Jr.: "Nixon used to talk the same language. . . . I suppose Solzhenitsyn would have cheered for the French fighting Ho Chi Minh." One needs little imagination, in the light of such responses as Hellman's and Coffin's and many others to Solzhenitsyn's Harvard commencement address, to anticipate the same respondents' probable outrage at such arguments as I am advancing, and especially to my assertion that Solzhenitsyn's "smatterers" largely control our own intellectual community.

Solzhenitsyn at Harvard assumed that he spoke to and of a more limited dimension of our complex country than it has been convenient to our intellectual left to admit. Some of the response has been almost at the level of suggesting that jets leave for the East every day, though expressed with more subtlety than our "Southern rabble" used to manage back in the 1950s: "If you don't like it down here, there're buses leaving for the North every hour." Dean Rusk, President Kennedy's secretary of state, assures us: "We should not roll over and play dead, because [Solzhenitsyn] does not have a strong personal commitment to constitutional democracy or to the notions of individual liberty which are fundamental to us here in the West. . . . we can't take our policy guidance from Mr. Solzhenitsyn." (Fundamental commitment to individual freedom ought to be stronger than a matter of *notions*.) But what is perhaps most shocking to our intellectual left is not Solzhenitsyn's policy guidance, or the absence of an evangelical "strong personal commitment" to an ambiguous abstraction, "constitutional democracy." (Dean Rusk sounds almost a strict constructionist here.) The intellectual left finds itself having too easily supposed its own members inhabitants of Solzhenitsyn's country of the mind, only to discover him dissolving those artificial boundaries prescribed by humanism as (in his words) "it makes itself increasingly accessible to speculation and manipulation." Thus does one see "the same stones in the foundations of a despiritualized humanism and of any type of socialism," including Marxism as practiced by Stalin or National Socialism of Hitler's variety. (Did either Stalin or Hitler commit any act except in the name of Humanity?) Solzhenitsyn's country of the spirit must inevitably modify the authority of abstract formality, the letter of the law divorced of spirit and exercised to the limit of pragmatic advantage through the letter itself—the state the highest symbolization in which *person* dissolves to *individual* and thence, by way of *integer*, into insignificance. By his emphasis on spiritual concerns, then, he declares the intellectual left's passport to reality out of order. That emphasis has been increasingly disturbing to the Western establishment since Walter Cronkite's puzzled encounter with Solzhenitsyn in Switzerland in the first days of his exile; in that interview, much more seemed afoot than political issues, but just what it was Cronkite could not find a handle to. For even then Solzhenitsyn was Russian and intended to remain Russian in ways that could not be reduced to ideological pattern, in ways that neither his nor our smatterers are likely ever to understand.

Little wonder then that in his Harvard sermon he exhibited a most "un-American" antipathy to President Eliot's dream of America. But the intellectual left had itself already prepared the stage for this most shocking episode. It had first made Solzhenitsyn, in a strange deformation of reality (as Eric Voegelin might put it), an expiatory figure, a living sacrifice for its own innocent evils of the 1930s. The Stalinist outrages of that decade, being reenacted with less physical but more intensely spiritual brutality on such men as Ginzburg and Shcharansky, remain still an embarrassment from which our older left has not yet recovered. (How nice of our secretary of state to find a few minutes for Shcharansky's "widow" before resuming business with Gromyko.) Because Solzhenitsyn was himself deceived in his youth and yet worked himself beyond deception to an immanence of articulated purgation—from *within* the system—he appeared a welcomed spectacle: mirror or doppelgänger. The Marxist system seemed in some degree vindicated. Perhaps the Western Stalinists (Lillian Hellman excluded) were not so simple in their errors. The god worshiped in the 1930s had not entirely failed, in spite of Arthur Koestler, if it could produce a Solzhenitsyn. But then, just as he is received with open arms, he turns insane; he begins an incessant burning spiritual theme.

Perhaps Solzhenitsyn was an answer to a psychological necessity to the waning left. He certainly found himself immediately elevated as a literary figure, a natural member in our decayed "genteel tradition," being offered naturalized citizenship in that floating country of mind in which one is "nowhere quite at home." He has not only refused that citizenship, but bears witness to a country quite antipathetic to the one offering him asylum, between which countries no detente will ever be established. We shall no doubt presently find reevaluations of Solzhenitsyn as literary man in the monthly and quarterly left—evaluations closer to the truth of his literary accomplishment than have been afforded him up to his uncouth violation of genteel manners at Harvard. (He at least, so far as I know, does not consider himself of that number that includes Tolstoy and Dostoevsky or—Henry James would wish us to say—Turgenev, though he is comfortable enough with Gorky and Gogol.) Such reconsiderations will have been undertaken, one fears, less to establish critical truth than to discount the prophet he is. Certainly, judging from the initial response of the dean of the literary left, Norman Cousins, we may expect as much. "He once described Roosevelt and Churchill as cowardly as a result of Yalta," Cousins says, to show what a wild man we have in Solzhenitsyn. "Yet if not for them, it's possible there would be no free world in which Solzhenitsyn could make such pronouncements about the evils of the West." (If not for them, so runs Solzhenitsyn's point, he might perhaps make such pronouncements from home rather than in exile.)

To reduce Solzhenitsyn as literary figure will seem to justify reducing him as prophet, in which office I find him at his greatest. He is a prophet addressing the intelligentsia's responsibility to matters moral and spiritual. As such he has proved as unsettling to the Western left as Jonathan Edwards must have been to Boston society in his surprising enthusiasm for the great awakening of the 1740s, with its loud emotional concern for the spirit lost in gnostic distortions of reality; as unsettling as the frontier evangelists of the great revival proved to Jefferson's dream of an egalitarianism engineered by an elite trained, if not by imported French deistic intellectuals, then at least by Boston unitarians.

The irony of the *place* at which Solzhenitsyn spoke, in the context of American intellectual history, is worthy of longer thought than has been so far afforded it. The ghosts of Emerson, Charles W. Eliot, FDR's Brain Trust, among many, sigh in the wings as he speaks. The late disciples of President Eliot's "Religion of the Future" will understandably be long in recovering from the shock of such violation of sacred ground as that given by this Jacksonian of the spirit, this Soviet misfit. His is a call for a return to the complexities of human existence in Plato's *metaxy*, in Eric Voegelin's In-Between. And by that call he seems to have desecrated the ground upon which the American intellectual left has built; an intellectual empire trembles. What is called in question is the doctrine (pronounced in President Eliot's farewell words in 1909) that the educated man must reject all "authority, either spiritual or temporal." There must be "no worship, express or implied, of dead ancestors, teachers, or rulers." Nor may the primary object of the new religion be "the personal welfare or safety of the individual in this world or the other . . . but . . . service to others [for which read the gnostic deity, 'Humanity'] and . . . contributions to the common good." This religion of the future "will not be propitiatory, sacrificial, or expiatory" or "perpetuate the Hebrew anthropomorphic representations of God." In such rejections as here prescribed we are nevertheless left with one authority not to be questioned lest one earn the epithet *reactionary* or *regressive*. That authority directs the rejections President Eliot finds necessary, thus purging the popular spirit of its roots in history and of its spiritual relation to the transcendent.

Little wonder that the angry, deracinated spirit of President Eliot stirs against Solzhenitsyn's rites of exorcism, or that it attempts to enlist the populace to remind Solzhenitsyn in a mannerly way that if he doesn't like "the American way" there are planes bound over the polar cap for Siberia (by way of Moscow) every day. This Misfit has attacked the religion our intellectual elite has substituted for our old concern for transcendence, a concern "progressively" lost to us on our way from the Renaissance. It is the loss of man given his own self-sufficiency, a loss engineered through the gnostic deification of man as created in the image of the post-Renaissance intelligentsia, "the proclaimed and enforced autonomy of man from any higher force." And that is precisely the doctrine most central to the thought of Ralph Waldo Emerson. This illusional reconstruction of reality has led us, in Solzhenitsyn's disturbing words, "to the calamity of a despiritualized and irreligious humanistic consciousness." We have become placid subjects to a new authoritarianism in which, as Santayana said long ago, "analysis and psychology seem to stand alone" as the ultimate measures of reality, in a world where "there is no spiritual interest, no spiritual need."

One can value Santayana's words in their poignancy, since he—like Henry Adams—recognized the intellectual and spiritual decay of the Western intelligentsia without himself being able to break from that decay that seemed to him so palpable at Harvard in his later days there, before he abandoned Boston for Italy. Stoicism of some coloring becomes the last decaying bastion given such a mind as his in this impasse, as is witnessed in the final days of both Adams and Santayana. (On his deathbed, Santayana is reported to have said to Sister Angela, who was tending him, that he continued to suffer, "not physically" at the end "but mentally." To her question "Why?" he uttered his last word: "Desperation!")

Certainly there is little evidence of an interest in or need for the spiritual dimension of man's being in the collapsing fabric of the intellectual community which Santayana fled and Solzhenitsyn affronted. Except in a negative sense. That is, for a moment at least in 1978 they seemed shocked by Solzhenitsyn and began sounding an emotional alarm. Fire in the night! And fire brought into this safe citadel by this wily Sinon from the East, no doubt with subversive collaboration of minds disaffected with the prevailing vision of Humanity as God that was locally dominant. But to admit calamity in the intellectual community might be to stir the popular spirit, a danger to that popular spirit's long and malleable consent to be directed. What if the popular spirit should indeed begin to stir, should break the bonds of its imprisonment to "humanistic man?" The question might well then become: what committee of Moseses has led us into this entrapping desert? A question to be asked, indeed, and one that has been increasingly asked in the past decade—by traditionalists and neoconservatives and fundamentalists and populists and libertarians—out of a growing if unified discomfort of mind and spirit with the reigning intellectual establishment.

What may follow from this partial awakening of collective integers into individuals, and at last perhaps even into *persons*, is the possible restoration of the family and community in the true ground of human nature—beyond the now stale and reflexive postulates of man as merely rationalist automaton, as an accident of nature now turned upon nature in the interest of its own survival—to an end hardly worth the struggle. For that end appears more and more to be, under the modernist vision of those intellectuals Solzhenitsyn called to account, the pathetic Alienated Self. It is a question to be asked: how came we into this spiritual desert in which intellect at its best seems bent on a surrender to the mechanical idol of intellect, Technology. And it is a question that may be answered by "nuclei" reared through the true virtues of intellect ordered to spiritual concerns. But these intellectuals must be reared not too far from the libraries. For certain ghosts out of history haunt our intellect, each man's, and must be called to account and thus exorcised from the popular spirit of our age so that the *person's* larger spirit may become generative in the desert. If with anger and terror those ghosts are cast out, without our understanding their nature and history, we shall but cast out some daemons to provide residence to others, though even so it taxes imagination to think them worse than the first.

VIII. Solzhenitsyn as Southerner

The dragon is by the side of the road, watching those who pass. Beware lest he devour you. We go to the Father of Souls, but it is necessary to pass by the dragon.

> —St. Cyril of Jerusalem, quoted as epigraph to
> *A Good Man Is Hard to Find* by Flannery O'Connor

I have been in the dragon's belly, in the red burning belly of the dragon. He wasn't able to digest me. He threw me up. I have come to you as a witness to what it's like there, in the dragon's belly.

> —Alexander Solzhenitsyn, to the AFL/CIO in
> New York City, July 9, 1975

i

When Alexander Solzhenitsyn was forced into exile in the West in February 1974, I was waiting the release of my new novel *Fugitive*, living (as I still do) in a small Georgia town in a sparsely populated county. Our citizens here, my neighbors, were largely unaware of either dramatic event, though I knew that my novel would be of passing interest since its setting was so local as to memorialize some community history and landmarks. What effect Solzhenitsyn's exile would have on local consciousness was doubtful. I don't know how many of my neighbors, even now, would recognize his name. Certainly a house-to-house poll made in the swift, efficient modernist mode would show him a stranger here, though were I to spend a morning at the barbershop or a few evenings on front porches talking about him, my neighbors would very soon recognize the sense in which Solzhenitsyn is our cousin. Such discovery of old relationships, though, requires the manners and pace of an older day. Aeneas, an unknown exile in Italy, discovered his old kinsman Evander and claimed Evander's aid because of blood ties and family honor: "We are bound together . . . by the old ancestral kinship and by your broad fame." And even under the pressure of defeat by the Turulians, Aeneas lingers with Evander to restore a relationship through ceremony stronger than the moment's crisis.

Such might be my own importuning words to the famous Solzhenitsyn, so that he might, as a strong exile himself, help me recall my neighbors to ancestral virtues now heavily besieged by the forces of modernism. Here in Oglethorpe County we are increasingly tempted to believe that some new Rome of a strange foreign devising might be built overnight, on principles of "need" determined by a house-to-house survey of our present appetites and then interpreted in Washington, D.C., or its branch offices, the social science departments of various universities. I fear tarpaper cities built on the rubble of older ways; I fear that uninhibited appetite is the end our natural hungers bring us to when unordered by ceremony. I notice, for instance, that the considerable advertising campaign in support of the 1980 census attempted to imbue a color-the-slot document with mystical powers: depending upon the citizen's faithful execution of the document and his faith in it as revealing his own essence, a general national revival is in the offing. That modern sibyl, the computer, will be giving us the necessary signals. If, as Solzhenitsyn said with shocking effect at Harvard, the West is increasingly given to operating "according to the letter of the law," at the "extreme limit of legal frames" in pursuit of "more things and a still better life" in the materialistic sense of those terms, it is also given to valuing the individual and his community as abstract facts, mystically interpreted by statistical priests. Our perfect response to the census will result, we are told, in a just and equitable distribution of goods and services by the Federal Father, and then we shall all be progressively happy.

I have watched Solzhenitsyn with fascination and with ironic pleasure, knowing that we both hold certain principles as central to the meaning of individual and community life, however much distorted and obscured those principles have been by the forces of modernism. I have listened to him with thanksgiving, pleased at the large and larger audience attracted to him in places where those principles seem more thoroughly clouded and obscured than they are here in Crawford, Georgia. So, whether or not particular of my neighbors at once recognize in Solzhenitsyn the kinships I see between them is not my concern. What is of concern is whether we here will continue to bear witness to those common principles. I have every confidence in Solzhenitsyn's steadfastness; but I am less certain about my community's, given the insidious and unspectacular invasions by that modernist spirit that I attempted to expose in my Fugitive-Agrarian novel. For in the South as in the nation there has been a subtle shifting of spiritual and political values to materialistic ends, as witnessed by the promotionalism surrounding our current census. Still, those kinships are strong enough at the moment to promise recovery. And I know that as Solzhenitsyn works his work in the larger arena of Western and American consciousness, we do the same here in Oglethorpe County—enough of us to keep the principles alive.

We Southerners in particular, then, welcome this displaced person from the East, whose enemies are our enemies—the man whom *Time Magazine* calls "Russia's greatest living writer." That description is *Time*'s apology to its readers for presenting an essay (February 18, 1980) it calls as "grim" as Solzhenitsyn's Harvard commencement address of 1978, an essay of "Advice to the West, in an 'Hour of Extremity.'" The apology is necessary, *Time* feels, since "many Americans will find Solzhenitsyn's views too harsh, his vision too chilling." Still, if popular comedians, actors, singers have been media-elevated to the rank of spiritual and political leaders, their random views certified by media exposure and validated by their "art," who is *Time* to deny Solzhenitsyn a hearing? For he, too, has become both popular artist and evening newsfare no less than were Jane Fonda or Joan Baez and a host of international statesmen née popular entertainers of the 1960s. Solzhenitsyn's reputation as fiction writer requires *Time* to give his views "wide attention," though the reader is warned to proceed at his own risk. (In its review of *From under the Rubble*, a Russian version of *I'll Take My Stand*, *Time* was even more cautionary on November 25, 1974: "In the West, the essays may buttress the conviction of Solzhenitsyn's critics that he is a mystical reactionary who places too much faith in the values of the Orthodox Church and Old Russia.")

My own *Fugitive* I shall set aside here after observing briefly that it grew out of a long devotion to Fugitive-Agrarian arguments, putting them to the test as they engage an accelerating modernism in this Southern ground, that insidious undermining that threatens the spirit I treasure here in Crawford. It explores the ground of a local experience out of which (in a phrase from *I'll Take My Stand*) a "genuine humanism" must grow, as opposed to that intellectually derived and largely academic and ultimately rootless "New Humanism" that the Agrarians found inadequate to rescue the life of man in community. The salient Agrarian passage is in their "Introduction: A Statement of Principles": "[Genuine humanism] was not an abstract moral 'check' derived from the classics—it was not soft material poured in from the top. It was deeply founded in the way of life itself—in its tables, chairs, portraits, festivals, laws, marriage customs." The drama I projected was of a would-be Agrarian's attempt to regain this genuine humanism. My protagonist, who comes by his principles through the academy (he is a Vanderbilt graduate), receives his comeuppance when he attempts to pour those valid principles "in from the top." I tried to dramatize the weakness of such misguided attempts and thereby imply the firmer ground necessary: the intimate experience of the world out of which intellectual principle emerges, our daily struggle in what Eric Voegelin calls the "In-Between."

For that is the ground where principle must take root and grow into one's life. Principle is seldom to be recovered or established by the forced spectacle that was so widespread in the 1960s, the daily confrontations between largely ignorant factions given to conflicting dreams of some instant Eden. It grows slowly in a struggle of spirit in oneself as it reaches outward to the world through the bonds of community. I might put that struggle in scholastic terms, to which such kindred spirits as Saint Thomas, T. S. Eliot and Donald Davidson, or Solzhenitsyn and my unlettered neighbors in Crawford would and do subscribe. For, though they may not share the terms, these diverse people share an understanding of the things the terms name out of experience. As Saint Thomas expresses the point: "Although the knowledge which is most characteristic of the human soul occurs in the mode of *ratio*, nevertheless there is in it a sort of participation in the simple knowledge which is proper to higher beings, of whom it is therefore said that they possess the faculty of spiritual being." One possessed of that distinction between *ratio* and *intellectus* may not command the terms, but he is already forearmed against the distortions of his soul which separate the two modes of knowledge in that soul. In our age the separation has occurred widely, elevating reason to an absolute in whose name "soft material is poured in from the top" through federal formulas. Accompanying such external imposition of abstract order is the elevation of feeling (the *understanding* divorced from *reason*) whereby occur radical denials and destructions of our sense of reality through vague collective social passions. In sum, we are being structured as a people through formulistically executed sentimentalities.

As a young man, T. S. Eliot was concerned with a "dissociation of sensibility" in English letters, a separation of thought and feeling which he declared to have occurred at about the time of Dryden and Milton. But that dissociation has been more general in our history than its literary symptoms reveal. It may be said to begin in the Renaissance, leading to the conspicuous antipathy of the nineteenth century to the eighteenth century—the struggle between an age of "reason" and an age of "romanticism." But the struggle is not one accounted for simply by reference to the dominance of one position at a particular time in the concourse of history. The antipathy of thought to feeling is fundamental in human nature, and the struggle occurs for each when he attempts to come to terms with creation. Excesses of thought or of feeling may give a particular color to a calendar segment of history, giving an age its name (ours seems to be the Age of Alienation). But the struggle against dissociation knows no date: it is the ambiguous sign in the individual soul of that fortunate curse called Original Sin, an inheritance from that "Fortunate Fall."

Whatever one's calendar reads for the particular person in time, his understanding calls him to an open surrender beyond himself. It is a call to see the self in a perspective of creation that acknowledges the Cause of creation, what Solzhenitsyn speaks of as "a Supreme Complete Entity." The Agrarians, characterizing the Southern address to this Cause, speak of "the God of nature," an openness toward whom helps distinguish the Southern mode of being, with its garrulous hospitality and celebrated manners. On the other hand, the individual's *ratio* is that consolidating inclination of the soul that attempts closure, that is tempted (when untempered by the understanding) to elevate the self by separation from the rest of creation through alienating Pride. Donald Davidson, seeing us "still Yankee, still Rebel," recognizes this difference in the more reserved manners and cautious hospitality of our New England cousin who is more given to *ratio* than we. But he knows a kinship, nevertheless, which rests on fundamental grounding of both Yankee and Rebel in our common human nature.

The Southerner's fascination with and fear of Pride and his sense of the relation of *intellectus* and *ratio* as faculties of the soul are still very much evident. As our literature shows, it affects our sense of drama to the degree that we are suspicious of deterministic ideas, seeing the dramatic center to be the individual will as it wrestles with dissociation of reason and understanding. Thus the Southerner tends to be suspicious of social programs that ignore the complexities of the real social world, in which for him Original Sin is an important complication; he is suspicious of abstract programs that would reform a community by pouring solutions to human problems "in from the top." In the 1960s such a Southerner watched with distress the rival attempts of a secularized Activist Left and a seemingly Establishment Right to gain dominion. If only, he might be heard to say, if only those mobs in the Chicago streets and those in conference at the 1968 Democratic National Convention would sit down and read *I'll Take My Stand*.

Another sign of the Southerner's attitude toward the complementary roles of reason and understanding is to be found in his strong sense of the family as the viable social structure, his sense that the family is bound together as individuals in a particular place and in a manner beyond the power of reason alone to comprehend. Accompanying this attitude is his address to nature as an existence in which one discovers the presence of the God of nature. The Nashville Agrarians took their stand upon historical ground heavy with these concerns. One might say that theirs was an "ecological" concern, but a concern built upon a spiritual base. But theirs is not simply "Southern" ground: it is more ancient than American history and more universal than the North American continent, to be recognized wherever man is in tune with his portion of the world. Here is that knowledge expressed by Heraclitus, who speaks of a vision of the creatures of nature through which one finds himself "listening to the essence of things"; by William Wordsworth, who through such a vision "sees into the life of things." It is in the biblical injunction to "be still, and know that I am God." It is in the plaintive lyric of a country singer, "Don't you hear that lonesome whippoorwill / So sad he cannot fly; / The moon has gone behind a cloud; / I'm so lonesome I could cry." (Such "lonesomeness" is not answered at last by another person, but only by another Being; the relation between country music and country religion has been almost destroyed by commercialism now, one of the insidious accomplishments of the enemy of spirit.)

Southern spokesmen have often failed to articulate this Southern position, which is pervasive of the "Southern life" they attempt to maintain. Or rather, they have not articulated it in a mode persuasive to its "Northern" opponents, particularly during the South's most spectacularly beleaguered history—the period from about 1850 to the publication of *I'll Take My Stand*. Some of the reasons they failed to do so are brilliantly presented by Richard Weaver in his *Southern Tradition at Bay* and in several of his essays. But the failure was a relative one. That is, the Southerner did not attempt his defense of principles in the strict mode of the *ratio*, and those in whose souls the *intellectus* had atrophied could hear little of what he had to say. Flannery O'Connor puts the difference succinctly when she says, "The Southerner knows he can do more justice to reality by telling a story than he can by discussing problems or proposing abstractions." It is "his way of reasoning and dealing with experience." The consequences of those differing modes she also remarks caustically: "I have found that anything that comes out of the South is going to be called grotesque by the Northern reader, unless it is grotesque, in which case it is going to be called realistic." The flowering of letters in the South in this century is directly out of the Southerner's concern to do justice to the complexity of reality, and that literature has in it a stand taken against the "Northern" inclination to value abstraction as reality, a species of gnosticism. For, again to quote that perceptive defender of the Southern vision, Flannery O'Connor, "a view taken in the light of the absolute will include a good deal more than one taken in the light provided by a house-to-house survey." And so she declares herself, as artist, to be "a realist of distances," through which vision she sees the transcendent in the immanent; as writer she dramatizes an active presence of the transcendent in the imminent action.

ii

Art, the Southerner believes (even when he does not call himself an artist), serves transcendent vision through its faithfulness to proximate nature. He is likely to see "science" as reducing nature to fact, which is then mystified by statistical exegesis. Thus storytelling becomes for the Southerner his homage to the largeness of reality, as well as a means of resisting deformations of reality by abstractionism. Indeed, storytelling becomes one of the modes of his worship of the God of reality through which he sustains a piety toward creation—and most particularly toward that special creature of God's creation, man. Through story he bears testimony on behalf of reality, whether in the courthouse or on its lawn in the shade of trees, or on his front porch, or in his multitudinous churches so given to dramatic revivals of the spirit. It is in the light of the absolute that he holds fill-in-the-blank questionnaires suspect. What he is and has been he finds better served through such documents as Ben Robertson's *Red Hills and Cotton*, Horace Kephart's *Our Southern Highlanders*, Andrew Lytle's *A Wake for the Living*. Faulkner's *Go Down, Moses* and *The Hamlet* and *Absalom, Absalom!* Tate's "Ode to the Confederate Dead" and Davidson's "Lee in the Mountains." Warren's *All the King's Men* and O'Connor's *Wise Blood* and "A Good Man Is Hard to Find."

I think it is safe to say that, although such works have sometimes received generous attention at the hands of critics, they have not often been wisely understood in their implications about man's spiritual place in the world. Miss O'Connor puts the matter more fiercely: "no matter how favorable all the critics in New York City may be, they are an unreliable lot, as incapable now as on the day they were born of interpreting Southern literature to the world." For they see Southern writers almost invariably as "unhappy combinations of Poe and Erskine Caldwell," especially when the grotesque is involved. Why has that vision Miss O'Connor defends failed to reach those critics and through them the popular American spirit? Because the Southern writer has been seen as separate from his vision? Seen as a reporter of social facts? Or separate because art is understood as trading in the grotesque to titillate the popular spirit rather than to celebrate reality? Miss O'Connor certainly felt those to be some of the reasons, insisting that in truth the grotesque character's "fanaticism is a reproach, not merely an eccentricity"—that "the freak can be sensed as a figure for our essential displacement" from reality in whom is revealed the drama of a struggle to regain his proper spiritual estate. Only in the disparity between his passion for reality which fuels his fanaticism and our age's general separation from complex reality does "he [attain] some depth in literature."

Miss O'Connor's "all the critics in New York City" is figurative, as a careful reading of her words in context shows. For though such critics as she means tend to congregate in certain places—New York City, for instance—she is speaking rather of a quality of mind than of all persons in a particular place. She is talking about a quality that one of the Fugitive poets characterizes as making one a "Yankee of the spirit." (Hence, my putting "North" or "Northern" in quotation marks is to suggest the distinction.) The "Southern" quality of mind tends to be most general in the South, though I know and value many "Southern" Yankees. The importance of this distinction will, I trust, emerge with increasing clarity as we proceed, through our focus upon Solzhenitsyn as "Southerner." Thus, in the light of this distinction, one surely sees Solzhenitsyn's Ivan Denisovich as a "Southern" grotesque character. But we must also observe in Ivan a depth not found in Erskine Caldwell's Jeeter Lester. All Southern writers are not Southern in the same sense, any more than all Soviet writers are Russian in the sense Solzhenitsyn distinguishes.

In Solzhenitsyn we have a Fugitive-Agrarian risen out of the most spectacularly suppressive regime of modern history, a regime that undertook a "Reconstruction" whose horrors the Southerner is better able to appreciate than most other Americans. For we endured the prelude to such modern reconstructions of reality as we see raised to an ultimate horror in the twentieth century. And though now exiled by the Soviet Reconstruction, Solzhenitsyn speaks as one deeply anchored in place. From "*what* soil should one fight the vices of one's country?" he asks in "The Smatterers." It is a plaintive cry of one whose native soil stains him in an unforgettable way. "I live," he says, "in constant awareness of my desire to return to Russia, and I know I will go back." We might recall Granny Millard's handful of Sartoris soil, which she carries with her as she flees the invader in Faulkner's *Unvanquished*. Or, less poignantly put than Granny's action or Solzhenitsyn's words though no less particularly tested by necessity, we remember Flannery O'Connor's remark that "the Southern writer apparently feels the need of expatriation less than other writers in this country. Moreover, when he does leave and stay gone, he does so at great peril to that balance between principle and fact, between judgment and observation, which is so necessary to maintain."

Of that "Northern" spirit (as we might label it) which denies Solzhenitsyn his roots, he says, "Spiritually all intellectuals nowadays belong to a diaspora. Nowhere are we complete strangers. And nowhere do we feel quite at home." He attacks that Sovietist spirit for its deliberate and systematic destruction of "men of the soil" so that they might be replaced by those "people of the air, who have lost all their roots in everyday existence." In distinguishing between "men of the soil" and "people of the air," he is making the separation that Allen Tate makes between men who are regional and those who are merely provincial. But we must recover our sight, says Solzhenitsyn, who speaks with a voice dedicated to and convinced of an ultimate emergence of the regional man over the provincial. That is the most healthful burden of his prophecy, without which his vision would be "grim," "harsh," and "chilling" indeed.

As I watched a provincial man, Walter Cronkite, interviewing this regional Russian soon after his exile, I had already been gathering myself for some time to explore the ground out of which Fugitive-Agrarian principles had grown, under the working title of "The Prophetic Poet and the Popular Spirit of the

Age." One might say that my study is an exploration of a remark Stark Young makes near the end of *I'll Take My Stand*: "Though the South . . . is our subject, we must remember that we are concerned first with a quality itself, not as our own but as found everywhere; and that we defend certain qualities not because they belong to the South, but because the South belongs to them." They are qualities, I contend, more easily discovered to us in a community at a particular time when that community is anchored in particular place. Life, we discover as regional men—as "men of the soil"—is enlarged by our participation in common humanity in the neighborhood of hills and valleys and by streams we know with the Psalmist's certainty. The enemy to this view is that provincial spirit which would gather all men up into an aimless drift, a journey whose only end is the journeying. The community of which I speak shows us to be members one of another in a mysterious and fundamental way that binds forebears and descendants within a life much larger than the provincialist can see. For when existence has been secularized by Hegelian thought in the provincialist mind, that mind sees only *with*, not *through*, the eye.

When history is secularized, whether by Hegel or Marx or the New Humanists, "humanity" becomes a shibboleth whereby all existence may be manipulated: the reality of human life is (to use Eric Voegelin's term) "deconstructed" by whatever self-proclaimed lords of existence have declared the world a mechanism in need of repair. Now the first deconstruction necessary to the manipulation of being is the reduction of regional man to provincial man, under a range of catchy slogans such as Progress or Humanity. Those manipulations do not necessarily reveal themselves as Leninist or Stalinist purges. But though less spectacular than mass purges, they may yet be more fatally destructive of one's life through gradual, almost imperceptible shifts. We react sharply to the suddenness of someone being shot by dictate or killed in a highway accident, but not to a gradual attrition of spirit in us. That is a truth extremely difficult to make heard in the popular spirit of our age precisely because spirit has been so gradually displaced from reality. Such is the point Flannery O'Connor makes through her grotesque characters, for as she says, "to the hard of hearing you shout, and for the almost blind you draw large and startling figures." Hers, then, is the same understanding of this hour of our spiritual extremity that Solzhenitsyn recognizes when he reminds us that the tsar executed about seventeen persons a year, while in Stalin's purge forty thousand persons were shot each month and "15 million peasants were sent off to extermination" by Lenin. But his impassioned call is itself more persuasive than his facts, for we have been so buffeted by facts, so immured of spirit by statistics, that his comparison registers less upon us than his burning personal, accusing presence. He is as uncomfortable to behold as Miss O'Connor's Haze Motes in *Wise Blood*.

Those twelve Southerners of *I'll Take My Stand* understood community to be much larger than its secular, geographical manifestation. The sense of place for them incorporated history in relation to the timeless, so that the local community of Harmony Grove, even when it changes its name to Commerce, carries in it a sense of the eternal. Through local particularity—*these* individuals of *these* families of *this* community—a sense of the spirit abiding in nature is acknowledged. Professor John Shelton Reed of the University of North Carolina pronounced at the annual meeting of the Southern Historical Society in Atlanta in 1979, "Industrialism is the Southern way of life. . . . The prototype of the New South may be the city we're in today." And C. Vann Woodward at that meeting, remarking the effect on the South of the Civil War, reminded his brethren, "The South did lose it, and one consequence was that the old planter influence was diminished, cut back, and the new group of industrialists and capitalists, typified by Henry Grady, took on a new role of leadership." I have pointed out elsewhere the interesting correspondence between Henry Grady's New York speech after the war, in which he warned the North that the South would bury it with its own industrial spirit, and Nikita Khrushchev's New York address to the West in which he asserted "we are going to bury you." (It is this same New South spirit that in fact led a town near Crawford to change its name from Harmony Grove to Commerce.) But though both historians pronounce the South now succumbing to a deracinating industrialism, Professor Reed goes on to point out the South's continuing attachment to local over world affairs and its continuing attachment to organized religion. Thus a Yankee, he says, may ask you what you do, but a Southerner still asks you where you are from. And Professor William C. Havard of Vanderbilt reports the response of a middle-aged black man to such a question: "I *stay* in Chicago, but I *live* in Alabama." I have heard Andrew Lytle argue that the most telling form of the Southerner's address to a new acquaintance is "Where do you bury?" In Lytle's inclusive sense of *you*, not only the individual and his immediate family are incorporated in a family body, but his "people" as well. In such language resides that Southern sense of place as a window upon the eternal.

The Agrarians understood and believed in these customs to which the South belonged, and still does. Finding them dangerously threatened by the industrial spirit, they celebrated such customs as essentially Southern, in the context of recent American history. They talked of "the South" as a "minority section" besieged by an "American industrial ideal." They saw such Southerners as Henry Grady as scalawags. Yet they were quite careful to make clear that an agrarian society such as they valued "is hardly one that has no use at all for industries, for professional vocations, for scholars and artists, and for the life of the cities." Their concern was that life be anchored in nature itself. Now this is not the same concern as Henry David Thoreau's. For Thoreau, an independent individual must be freed of community by his attachment to nature. Nevertheless, the Agrarian position was often attacked as if it were the same as Thoreau's, as if it were radically separatist. Since the 1960s Thoreau's influence has grown, but his is not an influence that will serve to strengthen community as the Agrarians sought to do.

The most immediate resistance to the Nashville Agrarians took the tack of distorting their position into a form of reactionary romanticism, whether of the Thoreauvian variety or of some vague throwback to an imaginary feudal dark age. These Agrarians, it was suggested, were merely a benighted remnant who attempted to advance long-since-discredited views of man and society. They wanted to "turn back the clock" largely because of their Bible Belt mentality. (This was a favorite phrase in Ralph McGill's annual attacks on their position in the *Atlanta Constitution*, McGill being the Henry Grady of the post–World War II South.) From our point of view in century's end, however, such arguments sound as shallow as Mrs. Lucynell Crater's provincial insistence to the drifter Mr. Shiftlet (in "The Life You Save May Be Your Own") that the "monks of old" just "wasn't as advanced as we are." The Agrarians said in 1930 that "modern man has lost his sense of vocation," that "the act of labor as one of the happy functions of human life has been in effect abandoned, and is practiced solely for its rewards." We know the observations as more intensely true than when spoken sixty years ago; we look back on the tumult of the 1960s with new eyes through *I'll Take My Stand* and better understand that recent painful decade.

The young in the 1960s were struggling, though most of them blindly, to escape those provincial reductions of life against which the Agrarian took a stand. But they found few of their elders who understood the causes of their discomfort any better than they did, few who could point them toward a sounder recovery than their confused actions promised. With no West to "light out to," they became deracinated Huck Finns, shrewd in their perception of society's failures but unwise in their pursuit of remedy. John F. Kennedy's "New Frontier" of space explorations hardly served their hunger. One could watch the first steps taken on the moon over and over, but not smell the dust stirred. Vicarious participation in such realities cannot satisfy the desire to participate in reality. It is an indictment of our intellectual community that many of those young people were cast wandering, becoming "people of the air." That phrase seems particularly suited to the so-called flower children, those frail orchids in the modernist jungle. Some of them turned, in desperation and with violent consequences, to such of their elders as Herbert Marcuse. For where could they learn of *I'll Take My Stand* or of Richard Weaver's *Ideas Have Consequences*, of Josef Pieper's *Leisure: The Basis of Culture* or his *In Tune with the World*?

Those young minds—many of them—would certainly have understood and responded to the Agrarian attack upon a rampant industrialism to which they gave a devil name, the Establishment; that was their attempt to name some Antichrist. They might have realized also that the Agrarian attack was upon both the secular left and the secular right and thus been rescued in some degree from recklessness. For it was the *secularist* aspect of industrialism that the Agrarian attacked, the reductions of both man and nature to efficient and material causes in the interest of product. The twelve Southerners saw such products as the dead end of applied scientism and said so. Hence they found little sympathy in either political camp. Nor did they find much support among those intellectuals increasingly encamped in the academy, those mediators of an optimism about the new god, Progress. By 1930 that new god had long since been established as worshipful in the American mind, and the God of nature as understood by regional man had been cast out by what the Agrarians called "the American or dominant" spirit. And here the academy's influence in this displacement needs brief consideration as a primary agent in our spiritual displacement.

iii

Near the turn of this century, Charles W. Eliot, having rescued Harvard University from its old role in American life as the formal support of mind in relation to spirit, bid farewell to that school which he had succeeded in tailoring to the service of the state through his long tenure. In his "Religion of the Future," as we have seen, he said that the new religion "will not be based on authority, either spiritual or temporal," since "the tendency towards liberty is progressive." There was to be "no worship, express or implied, of dead ancestors, teachers, or rulers." It would not be "propitiatory, sacrificial, or expiatory." Above all, it must not "perpetuate the Hebrew anthropomorphic representations of God." It would be dedicated to "service to others," and its contributions would be to "the common good." What, in such requirements, could Karl Marx object to? For either President Eliot or Marx, here was suitable ground upon which to build the future. The common good was now to be defined, whether in the name of Marx or Eliot, by a modernist spirit which understood man as a recent accident of an anciently accidental natural world, still genially referred to as "nature." Man by accident was somehow suited to elevate himself over nature as nature's god. President Eliot called for the reduction of regional man to provincial man; his sermon was a prophetic charge to educational institutions, a charge received and advanced since the 1909 address until it permeates the American academy. But the American academy, in modeling itself on Eliot's Harvard, has effected a displacement of man from reality. Thus, although Stalin's precipitous handling of the "kulak problem" registers upon us more spectacularly, the subtle displacement of regional man through "education" has been as destructive. Indeed, one suspects that it has been even more pervasively destructive of our nation than the Reconstruction of the South was to the South. The crises of the cities in the past two decades seem evidence to the point, about which problem a vast library now exists.

The Agrarian symposium ran headlong into that "American spirit" which Charles Eliot had conjured, a spirit as much at home on the political right as on the left. Solzhenitsyn encountered that spirit at Harvard in his commencement address. In the reaction to his address, as in the reaction to *I'll Take My Stand*, we discover that "Agrarian conservatism" is a creature apart. The Vanderbilt spokesman asserted that "the first principle of good labor is that it must be effective." But, they added, "the second principle is that it must be enjoyed." Labor must be enjoyed in and of itself, as one enjoys raising nature by art through an ordinate respect for the reality both of nature and of one's own gifts. The industrialism they saw as enemy to labor is "the economic organization of the collective American society," through which labor and pleasure have been effectively disjoined. Through that separation, harmony between community and nature became progressively dissonant. The good seen in labor, by either the laborer or his director, was translated into a final product, which in turn was translated by abstraction into dollar "value," in which figure *joy* was at best fractional. (The recent history of the American dollar on the world market is an ironic commentary on this point.) *Good* was lost to *goods*, and *goods* to abstract reckoning. Thus the spiritual struggle of answering one's "calling" in nature, of finding one's proper labor within the range of one's gifts, was shifted to an economic struggle, primarily a worldly and worldwide struggle. And that struggle came to center on the distribution of goods, in consequence of which (for the individual) labor became increasingly divorced from leisure, rather than being intimately related to leisure as it must be for one's spiritual health. Divided man is left in two worlds, the world of nine-to-five and the world of his ersatz leisure. But he can find satisfaction in neither.

Industrialism's "goods," from the Agrarian perspective, are seen as nature manipulated by abstraction for abstract ends. The holy texts of this new religion of nature, to be submitted to exegesis by both political left and right, are statistics. Thus an authorized text could be established upon which was founded an orthodoxy, President Eliot's "Religion of the Future." What followed was a Reformation, the breaking away of secularized labor from secularized capital. "But nature industrialized," the Agrarians had warned in their introduction, when "transformed into cities and artificial habitations, manufactured into commodities, is no longer nature but a highly simplified picture of nature."

Through such pictures "we receive the illusion of having power over nature, and lose our sense of nature as something mysterious and contingent." The God of nature under these conditions becomes "merely an amiable expression, a super- fluity, and the philosophical understanding ordinarily carried in the religious experience is not there for us to have." *God* as an amiable expression soon loses all meaning; profanity ceases to be profane. The order of language, whether in court or in conversation, begins a rapid decay; oaths speak less and less to the integrity of persons or community (though one is still well advised to choose words carefully in many Southern communities). As Miss O'Connor's Haze Motes discovers to his increasing frustration, blasphemy is impossible without belief, even as pornography is impossible where physical unions are reduced from a sacred sacrament to merely civil ceremony. Miss O'Connor's Shiftlet, in "The Life You Save May Be Your Own," remarks of his civil marriage to the idiot child Lucynell Crater, "That was just something a woman in an office did, nothing but paper work and blood tests."

To put our point from another perspective, the Agrarians were characteriz- ing industrialism as that aspect of the provincial mind which, since Eric Voe- gelin, has been spoken of increasingly as secular gnosticism. This modern gnostic attitude toward nature holds that man's mind is the first cause of crea- tion. Put in a Marxist form, as Voegelin shows by quoting Marx, "Nature as it develops in human history . . . as it develops through industry . . . is true *anthropological* nature." Now that conclusion is only a step down from the pre- Marxian position that God, rather than nature, is anthropological. Once God has been officially pronounced anthropological, as was done in the eighteenth century, one does with the term *God* whatever he will, using it amiably as Ralph Waldo Emerson tends to do or exiling it from the language altogether as the more rigidly deterministic positions require. But when the same conclusion as to the cause of nature is reached, whether by Emerson or by Marx, nature itself becomes merely prime matter for the exercise of one's will. There are no longer any strings attaching nature to a reality conceived as larger than man's con- sciousness; there are certainly no strings attaching nature to the God of nature.

Marx is observing, we note once more, an attitude toward nature that is compatible to gnostic capitalism no less than to gnostic communism. The structure he would build upon this view of nature differs from the capitalist structure, but it is not radically different because the first principle of man's relation to nature in each is the same. That is the point Solzhenitsyn made at Harvard in 1978. But in order for either Marxist or capitalistic structure to be erected on that first principle "reality must be destroyed" in the popular mind, as Voegelin says. "This is the great concern of gnosis," since gnosis "desires dominion over being" above all else. Such is the elevation of knowledge over nature by the *ratio*, and it leads to destructive separations within the individual soul. As Flannery O'Connor says, "Judgment will be separated from vision, nature from grace, reason from imagination." And the most significant aberration in this deconstructed nature is man himself. From a regional amplitude he is reduced to a provincial estate, to be exploited by the lords of gnostic power.

iv

In his Harvard commencement address, Solzhenitsyn took up the argument against the gnostic attitude toward creation. In that speech he quotes Marx as saying that "Communism is naturalized humanism," and adds: "One does see the same stones in the foundations of a despiritualized humanism and of any type of socialism: endless materialism; freedom from religion and religious responsibility . . .; concentration on social structures, with a seemingly scientific approach. . . . Such is the logic of materialistic development." The words were almost as direct an attack on President Eliot's Harvard as Solzhenitsyn might have made had he known in advance the prescription for "The Religion of the Future." Now the Agrarians included in their own indictment of the modern secularist world both the communist and the New Humanist. And they too saw the same stones in the foundations of capitalism. These several factions, supporting a common philosophy, were focused for them in the term *industrialism*. But in particular they characterized a species of socialist entrepreneur, the "Optimists," those advocates of gnosticism who "rely on the benevolence of capital, or the militancy of labor, to bring about a fairer division of the spoils. . . . And sometimes they expect to find super-engineers, in the shape of Boards of Control, who will adapt production to consumption and regulate prices and guarantee business against fluctuations: they are the Sovietists." They are also, we have pointed out, such "super-engineers" as President Eliot had geared Harvard to manufacture for the state, though the Agrarians in 1930 were looking primarily at the experiment underway in Russia and at the many "Sovietists" who were rising to activist roles in American society, particularly in industrial centers, rather than in the academy. (We remember that Warren had suggested calling the symposium "Tracts against Communism.") Nevertheless, their words were prophetic of the social and economic engineers who were even then entering the federal bureaucracy and would do so in swelling numbers after the election of that son of Harvard, FDR. Charles Eliot's inaugural address as president of Harvard in 1869 had laid out a program for the education of just such engineers. He restructured during his tenure not only the educational philosophy and its pragmatic program at Harvard but, through his influence, all higher education in this country. (His most generally remembered contribution is the elective system, through which mind is adjusted to pragmatic prospects by a tailored program of courses.) Thus he effectively undercut all that remained of the old ideal of a liberal education, though that ideal still has a struggling existence in many private and a few public schools.

Well aware of such destructions of higher learning, the Agrarians warned that the decay of human values, of "true humanism," would continue apace, whether under the auspices of the federal state through its boards of control or under those of corporations through their boards of directors. In either instance the first job of such engineers is to restructure the attitude toward nature held by the popular spirit. From that restructuring follows a redistribution of the spoils of nature, whether by the hands of Astors, Rockefellers, Goulds or by the hands of their counterparts, the managers of the socialist state. The point is worth emphasizing: whether the laws for the control of nature are advocated by the industrial right or the industrial left, those laws are derived from the same principle; the blueprints of laissez-faire capitalism, of state socialism, or of that totalitarian amalgam of the two, communism, are strikingly similar when the controlling vision has lost sight of the relation between nature and nature's God. But if man's final end is the consumption of goods, whatever the mechanism advocated, the "quality of life" thus championed must inevitably be determined at the level of a merely biological function. And however glowingly advertised in the name of the common good, the "good life" is still defined from a presumption that man is a self-refined animal and nothing more. Gone from one's labor is any sense of a calling, and gone from the laborer's "director" is any sense of stewardship under the grace of a Supreme Complete Entity.

Most tellingly, those losses are reflected in the reduction of mystery from ceremony, whether at the family supper or at the community feast. The bonding of community to a transcendent mystery dissolves along with its bonding to history. Thus we should observe with equal misgiving the Soviets' rewriting of history and our own rewriting. The pernicious docudramas of popular television and the manipulation of historical dates, initially to the convenience of federal labor schedules, are alike symptoms of a pervasive disease in the spirit. When Washington's or Lincoln's birthday is shifted to the proximity of Sunday, by acts of congress, those historical men begin to slip anchor in history and float as vague figures, more nearly disembodied gods than fathers, upon whom the rhetoric of a false worship may be the more easily focused. When manipulations of the reality of our history become an acceptable form of artificially induced ceremony, we end up with such radical deconstructions of community as I recently witnessed just across the county line. A historian of my acquaintance, whose field ironically is local history, engineered a Mardi Gras Ball in a dominantly Protestant neighborhood to raise funds for preserving the neighborhood. The "Fat Tuesday" dance was held on a Saturday night at the YWCO gym—a week and a half after Ash Wednesday. Such perversions of history, trading on nostalgia—that remnant of feeling out of a decaying spiritual hunger—make it evident that it were better for a people to tear down a neighborhood already lost and begin all over again. Genuine humanism emerges from our deportment in nature toward family and community history. It is revealed in our intimate relations to "tables, chairs, portraits, festivals, laws, marriage customs," as the Agrarian "Introduction" puts it. Which is to say that such a humanism requires that we value our history in nature with a piety that does not pervert community or its history for either sentimental or pragmatic ends.

Industrialism as we have been defining it—an attitude of the gnostic mind toward creation—leads men to lose that joy which is the effect of festival rightly taken. For, as Josef Pieper puts it, "Underlying all festival joy kindled by a specific circumstance [whether family supper, community gathering, or a legitimate Mardi Gras] there has to be an absolutely universal affirmation extending to the world as a whole, to the reality of things and the existence of man himself. . . . *To celebrate a festival means: to live out, for some special occasion and in an uncommon manner, the universal assent to the world as a whole.*" But a festival "without gods is a nonconcept, is inconceivable." However much Southern festival may have lacked the support of theological argument such as Pieper brings to his discussion in *In Tune with the World*, a festival joy is nevertheless the center of that Southern life the Agrarian defends. It is at the heart of Southern manners. It is in the ceremony of family reunions (see Eudora Welty's *Losing Battles*). It is in our regular church gatherings, but especially at those all-day gatherings to which people from California or New York return home, away from the place they stay to the place they live. It is in those more solemn gatherings with which we bury one of our own. It is in our storytelling on quiet summer evenings on the front porch, or when we draw about the kitchen or parlor fire on fall and winter evenings. For the Southerner knows, through an understanding beyond the reach of the *ratio*, that (in Pieper's words) "existence as we know it . . . does not just 'adjoin' the realm of Eternity; it is entirely permeated by it," whether we are at labor or at festive rest.

The gnostic address to existence, on the other hand, chooses as its absolute authority the *ratio*, denying the more fundamental truths about existence that the understanding must certify. By an act of will it chooses, through its gnosis as instrument, to disembody the self, to separate mind from nature in the interest of a dominance over nature, as it has already separated itself from the transcendent. And thus gnosticism comes to occupy a place which is no place, being neither in the natural nor in the spiritual world. But the gnostic must so deport himself, for otherwise he would be forced to abandon his insatiable hunger for power over being. John Milton cast the gnostic's motto in memorable, seductive verse. It is the battle cry of the New Prometheus who, since the Renaissance, would commandeer both theoretical and applied science: "The mind is its own place, and in itself / Can make a heaven of hell, a hell of heaven." But Milton puts those words in the mouth of that great angel fallen from brightness, who having denied reality must at last lament the hell within himself. He is doomed henceforth, as storytellers have it, to walk up and down, to and fro in the land, in an agony of placelessness, as the eternal tester, the canvasser of souls and salesman of emptiness.

V

The Southerner's suspicion of the traveling salesman is a commonplace in our folklore. It is a theme sufficiently present in our art to warrant a scholarly monograph. Thus Mrs. Lucynell Crater's suspicion of Shiftlet in O'Connor's "The Life You Save May Be Your Own" has initially to do with the question of what he has to peddle. "What you carry in that tin box?" she asks in response to Shiftlet's testing question "what is a man?" (There are certain touches in the story, incidentally, that suggest Miss O'Connor is mischievously reducing the story of Job to its modern ironic equivalent. Shiftlet is a wandering spirit presenting himself as carpenter, though he is of the company of Job's adversary rather than of Christ, and Mrs. Crater is hardly so just and upright as Job.) Salesmen are held suspect by the Agrarians as well, and they find advertising "along with its twin, personal salesmanship," a disturbing development out of industrialism. "Advertising means to persuade the consumers to want exactly what the applied sciences are able to furnish them. . . . It is the great effort of a false economy of life to approve itself."

The grounds of the Southerner's suspicions, however, are deeper than those exhibited by such writers as Sinclair Lewis in *Babbitt*, just as the Agrarian understanding of the nature of community differs from Lewis's version in *Main Street*. Lewis finds the difficulty of a Babbit or a Sauk Centre in their smallness and localness, the corrective perhaps lying in an enlargement, as is suggested by Lewis's own troubled journey eastward to New York and beyond. Advertising's effort to sell a false economy is not so simple as an attempt to sell a new soap or cereal to the unsuspecting. It is exhibited in its falseness in those attempts to move new federal programs; the advertising budgets of federal agencies have reached outrageous proportions since 1930. One finds the same procedures in the pages of *Pravda* as in the *New York Times*, the consumer providing the cost of wooing himself to a suspect cause in one way or another, whether through the open market, through his income tax, or through his labor in some Soviet factory or commune.

What profits it to lose one's soul in winning the world? Solzhenitsyn asks that question of a startled West, a question put in the arena of politics but at a level more radically disturbing than either economics or sociology or political science is usually willing to address. In 1980 he insists that the West is losing, if it has not already lost, another world war, "without a battle," through a "spiritual impotence that comes from living a life of ease." In 1974 he had come to us insisting that "the problems of the West are not political. They are psychological and moral. When dissatisfaction with government is expressed, it should be understood not in terms of political failure but in terms of weakened religious and ethical foundations of modern society." The only salvation for East or West, therefore, "lies in a moral and religious rebirth." That such a diagnosis touches a hunger in the popular spirit is at least suggested by the 1976 election in which, whatever the degree of naïveté in the candidate or the voters, an obscure rural candidate with a "born-again" message was elevated to the presidency. (Not without unfortunate consequences, however, for the *intellectus* [understanding] requires its complement, the *ratio*, without whose aid one stumbles toward recovery as if by instinct, guided only by "wise blood.") Those economists who approach the market in this present year of inflationary disaster through their applied science are more and more acknowledging the truth of Solzhenitsyn's judgment and increasingly warning that it is our "faith" which must overcome the panic reflected in the roller-coaster movements on Wall Street or the fluctuation of gold and silver on the world market.

Neither side of that division within the body of industry—labor or capital—is easily persuaded of the necessity of recovering spiritual being as the solution to social disorder, particularly since the residual faith of a whole people has been effectively shifted from the transcendent Cause of being to rest in an applied science that promises a multiplicity of temporary ends. Thus the Agrarians had to overcome difficulties larger than geographical divergences of "North and South." For when one's understanding does not support his reason in an encounter with the Agrarian position, whether he be of the secular right or left, one easily confuses the position with the hypothetical socialist position. Agrarianism must constantly extricate itself from that distortion. The confusion is understandable in part, given the celebrated "agrarian reforms" practiced in Russia, China, even in the Shah's Iran, and widely advocated as the solution of all problems in the Third World. Within the context of American history and closer to home, however, that confusion is worse confounded by the ambiguous presence of populism in the Southern mind. The Nashville position touches upon populism here as that phenomenon has emerged in the past hundred years from that increasingly beleaguered yeoman spirit which is deeply rooted in our Anglo-Saxon history. It would appear, however, that populism has been marginally effective in the national arena to the degree that it has been able to ride unmatched horses. For the populism that has grown out of an ancient English inheritance has increasingly revealed itself as *statist*, while advancing itself in the name of those regionalist ("conservative") principles which the Agrarians defended. Jimmy Carter would seem to have been successful largely through his pragmatic skill in riding these antithetical positions at a time of confused spiritual crisis in the national soul.

Since the Agrarian symposium, however, a host of Southern politicians not unlike Carter have maintained their base of local power largely through socialist programs, in spite of their national cartoon images as arch-conservatives. These politicians have argued in Congress for programs based on "conservative" principles—in the name of tradition, of the individual's birthright, of family and community. But beneath the surface of that posture has lain an egalitarianism through which local power has been maintained but which gnaws at our regionalist principles like cutworms among tomato plants. That specimen of our political bestiary, then, the Southern conservative congressman, has too often succeeded in his accumulation of power not simply through the conservative—"conservationist"—principle he embraces publicly once he has gotten to Washington while voting otherwise; that step is consequent upon egalitarian reductionism at the local level. Thus he has confused political issues to a degree that his conservative cousins outside the South, though allied with him on many issues, have felt uncomfortable in that alliance. One may appreciate the existential circumstances that tempt him to such strategy: it grows out of a forced unconditional surrender of the South in 1865 and the severe effects of Reconstruction. Yet we must recognize in such strategy the compromising of those abiding principles the Agrarians were recalling to us and the considerable damage done to those principles through such strategy.

The Agrarians were aware also of the confusing and often misleading emphasis in the dominant American mind upon that "Peculiar Institution," slavery. They resisted the growing insistence that slavery was *the* cause of their late unpleasantness with the North, memorialized under the dates 1861–1865. In consequence, they often found themselves unjustly labeled "racist." Slavery has been a highly visible issue in the political arena since the 1800s, as the whole nation is acutely aware in the current social concerns. But if we are to recover an equilibrium in a community of black and white, quiet minds must begin to consider whether racial problems are more symptomatic than pathological, a concern too easily raised by passion beyond the guides of understanding and reason. Consider how peculiar a circumstance is the "Southern system" in which the "little man," downtrodden by the rich and powerful (as an argument goes), maintains his "Jim Crow" institutions, whether under the leadership of Tom Watson or Gene Talmadge or Senator Bilbo. But equally, though less spectacularly, confusing are the obligations of Herman Talmadge to the remnants of the rural woolhatters, who have provided him the necessary popular vote, and to the industrialists, the corporations with seats of power in Atlanta. In such confusion, one must insist along with Solzhenitsyn that such political contradictions have cause in spiritual confusions about our relation to each other, to our place in nature, and to nature's God.

Beyond question the Southern Agrarian ground has in it the bacilli of a spiritual anthrax that breaks out in public as foot-in-mouth disease again and again. Money-lined raincoats are a recent symbol, causing Herman Talmadge the loss of his senate seat. Less recently, we remember the story of a folk politician who, when caught lining his pockets, insisted with vehement conviction, "Yes! I stole it! But I stole it for *you*!" We acknowledge the ground as contaminated, then, but it is contaminated as all lost Edens are—by a failure that is spiritual and not geographical or social or economic or political. Yet we necessarily return to that ground, which is a literal, geographical place: it is the ground upon which we must build, for there is no other. To exist at all, one must exist in some place at some time. But we may stand where we are in ways more knowing of dangers hidden in place so that our spiritual and moral failures will not allow us to abandon the valuable principles we have fallen from. There are still among us strong souls who insist that an always threatening failure requires that we regain those ceremonies through which alone lost innocence is ameliorated in community. Those ceremonies above all require that one resist a reduction of community, of family, to numbers in an egalitarian manipulation of souls to socialist or capitalist ends, especially when the manipulation is put in the name of Southern or states' rights. Such strong souls hold most firmly that community does not exist simply *now*, the point of time at which gnostic expedience is always attempting to obscure the reality of man's place in nature— always attempting to impose provincialism upon regional man. For this sense of community implies that the present moment bears in it the fruits of yesterday (not brought, or seldom brought, to full harvest) and the seed of tomorrow (flawed by the old loss we credit to Adam). Despite the imperfections, or rather more truly *because* of them, we hold to a truth inherited from our fathers and everywhere certified by present realities—a truth that reality itself refutes the reductionism in egalitarian shibboleths, those secular versions of lions and sheep and jackals in millennial Edens. Nature itself involves hierarchy, we observe; it is therefore a principle to be honored as the structure of reality, a structure particularly reflected in any viable community. That does not mean, of course, that such a truth does not carry with it the threat of spiritual destruction by prideful usurpation of authority in the structure of public office. Original sin is a principle Willie Stark insists upon most persuasively in *All the King's Men*.

vi

The hierarchic principle of reality which we see in nature and in community exists in an anagogic dimension for the Southerner; Saint Paul speaks of that dimension through a metaphor, and significantly to citizens of a corrupt Rome: "For as we have many members in one body, and all members have not the same office: So we, being many, are one body in Christ, and every one members one of another." The most immediate manifestation of Saint Paul's hierarchic principle, to the Southerner, is in his family. And because the family is the earthly structure through which the individual discovers his ordinate membership in a nature and state whose head is Christ, family structure is overridingly important. C. S. Lewis distinguishes the family from the collection of bodies to which modernism would reduce it, in words tellingly to my point:

> A row of identically dressed and identically trained soldiers set side by side, or a number of citizens listed as voters in a constituency, are not members of anything in the Pauline sense. . . . How true membership as a body differs from inclusion in a collective may be seen in the structure of a family. The grandfather, the parents, the grown-up son, the child, the dog, and the cat are true members (in the organic sense) precisely because they are not members or units of a homogeneous class. They are not interchangeable. . . . The mother is not simply a different person from the daughter, she is a different kind of person. The father and grandfather are almost as different as the cat and dog. If you subtract any one member you have not simply reduced the family in number, you have inflicted an injury on its structure.

Even so in the Southern understanding of family (as indeed in Lewis's own) a member is never subtracted, whether by death or by his own chosen expatriation. When he strikes out for the West, or even when he serves time at the county or state prison farm, his participation in the family body continues, though he may appear removed to the world's eye. Even death does not remove a member's presence, though that presence may be ignored. (The organic nature of the Southern family is spoken to beautifully by Ben Robertson in *Red Hills and Cotton*.)

This fundamental stone in community, the family, has to be torn down if the gnostic value of the individual as a unity of "homogeneous class" is to be established. The varied assaults of modernism on the family have been a conspicuous labor of the past two centuries, reaching disastrous proportions since World War II. For the organic structure of the family stands against those attempts to restructure human nature so that the individual may be displaced from his sustaining community membership and then artificially reassembled as a component of an abstract, rationalistic structure. The Southern family still contends with a perversion of family membership as affected by the natural-rights doctrine that rose ominously in the eighteenth century; in its most destructive guise this doctrine reduces man to the status of animal, as the term *animal* had already been reduced from its implications of naming the *creatura* of God. The holiness of existence, because it is God's creation, was thus exorcised from all nature; being was thus opened to the conquest of mind, and the strongest mind was justified in doing its own thing with nature. One might study at length, I believe, the destructive consequences of this displacement in the confused lives of estranged children, particularly the spectacular phenomenon of children's eruptions from the family in the 1960s. In "doing their own thing" so many of them were but imitating on a small scale the gnostic attitude of the powerful "Establishment" they took themselves to be opposing. Thus the family as we describe it here—the locus within which the individual discovers his bond with nature, with community, and with the God of nature and community—was eroded from within as it had been systematically deconstructed from without.

The Agrarian arguments, though blanketed and dampened by the advocates of the prevailing American way, smoldered but were not extinguished. They began to break into flame again in the popular fiction of Flannery O'Connor and the essays of Richard Weaver. Then came Alexander Solzhenitsyn, bearing his witness to a strikingly similar life, grown out of a common ground. His experiences were given magnitude by a political history larger than the personal, including the accelerated decline of the West and the ascendancy to power of the Soviet world; his prophecy could hardly be ignored. A Misfit rejecting the prevailing way of East and West, a disturbing displaced person pointing out to us the same stones in the foundations of East and West, he insisted that the fundamental crisis in modernism is spiritual. "Among enlightened people," he said with cutting irony in New York City (and how Miss O'Connor would have treasured the irony of place), "it is considered rather awkward to use seriously such words as 'good' and 'evil.' . . . But if we are to be deprived of the concepts of good and evil, what will be left? Nothing but the manipulation of one another." The protest he encourages is "a protest of our souls against those who tell us to forget the concepts of good and evil." For their evil counsel denies the nature of reality precisely so that the world may be made into an arena within which we manipulate each other, without the shadowing presence of conscience upon our manipulative acts.

Initially Solzhenitsyn was attempting to rally the West to an opposition to communism. Increasingly he has discovered a West so like his East in its spiritual decay, in its rejection of spiritual (as opposed to so-called social) conscience, that he engages us more and more as if a Southern evangelist at a summer revival. It was as embarrassing to some people, enlightened from a concern with good and evil, to have Solzhenitsyn deliver that Harvard commencement address as it might have been had Billy Graham delivered it, or Miss O'Connor's Haze Motes. For he raised fundamental questions about the quality of spiritual life in the materialistic West. And not a few of his listeners have come to agree with the woman in Haze Motes's audience: "He's nuts."

vii

So the Southerner may watch with concern the "Northern" reaction to the presence among us of that fearless, blunt man, but he will watch with some amusement as well. For Southern humor is one of the modes whereby the Southerner is enabled to endure the mystery of evil. Particularly he watches the drama of encounter between the "American or prevailing way" of life and the indomitable Solzhenitsyn. He will appreciate in particular Walter Cronkite, the Captain Kangaroo of the American way, in the presence of this strange prophet from the East. He will appreciate, as Solzhenitsyn's distress of the moment could not allow him to do, Cronkite's seeming bafflement over the Russian's outrage at being forced from his native ground. Why was this strange man not delighted by prospects of a new life in the enlightened West? Of course, one may also be moved to anger rather than amusement at a recent interview between Cronkite and a Sovietist, one Vitali Kobysh, a fellow journalist, an official of the Central Committee of the Communist party in Moscow, and quite possibly a KGB operator. This time Kobysh did the interviewing. According to Kobysh's version of the interview, to the question of why Cronkite would agree that "the Soviet Union menaces someone, that our people are preparing for war," Cronkite answered, "If you watched my program every evening for several years you must know that I never agreed with that and do not agree." (Lost in the response, of course, is the distinction between faith in a possible illusion and facts of reality, the lack of which distinction Reed Irvine's "Accuracy-in-Media" repeatedly shows to be a common failure of our media.) Furthermore,

Cronkite is said to have responded, "An honest person cannot believe that [the Soviets menace anyone or prepare for war], and I am positive that the overwhelming majority of Americans do not believe it. But they are thoroughly muddled. They are being scared on all sides." By whom? asked Kobysh. "By those who for various reasons consider it useful," Uncle Walter is reported as responding. Whether Kobysh's account of the interview is accurate I do not know, but Cronkite has not consented to correct the interview as printed in two Soviet magazines. Cronkite's administrative assistant reported to Reed Irvine that neither the tapes of the interview nor their transcription could be found, adding, "It's like Watergate." Perhaps, though, Uncle Walter has laid the groundwork necessary so that some year soon he may be commencement speaker at Harvard. If so, we Southerners will listen to the report of his address on our evening news with some amusement, but with some anger as well.

For a little while longer may we afford to be amused by the general circus displays of the spiritual displacement of our national spirit; we do not at the moment face the stark horrors of repression that Solzhenitsyn, Ginzburg, Sakharov, and the like have experienced. However, it is important that as we wait and watch we remember and keep alive the careful distinction Solzhenitsyn draws between the Russian spirit and the communist ideologist, a distinction with analogy in our separation of the regional man from the provincial man. "It pains us," says Solzhenitsyn, "that the West heedlessly confuses the words *Russian* and *Russia* with *Soviet* and *U.S.S.R.* To apply the former words to the latter concepts is tantamount to acknowledging a murderer's right to the clothes and identification papers of his victim." (It is the same pain I sometimes feel on hearing Jimmy Carter explained as a typical Southerner.) But leisure for amusement in such confusions is almost over; it is increasingly clear that Western gnosticism is more insidious and subtle but equally destructive, and its symptoms break out more violently at every hand in this new decade. Khrushchev's declaration to America was "We will bury you!" That bluff challenge, delivered as he pounded his shoe on the podium, has itself been buried under a new approach to the competition between Eastern and Western gnosticism. Solzhenitsyn observes, "Now they don't say 'we are going to bury you' anymore, now they say 'Detente.'" And it was a senator from Georgia, Sam Nunn, who saw in the Salt II negotiations the very Soviet strategy Solzhenitsyn warns against. But it was also a president from Georgia who only slowly began to suspect the possibility of Soviet subterfuge. That irony speaks a division in the South too troubling to be very amusing.

What a Southerner of my persuasion fears is that our national spirit more and more breathes within a world whose thermostat and filters are set by gnostic intellectuals; a climate in which there are more destructive contaminants than the Southern intelligence and will may detect, certainly more than the Midwest Research Institute can measure, given its emission standards in respect to "quality." Only after forty years have we become aware at last of the dangers to the human body of its breathing the air of asbestos plants. How long before we discover the effect upon spirit of those filaments of modernism taken in more gradually and revealed more slowly in the popular spirit? But these are the more fatal contaminants of being in the light of the transcendent vision upon which the Agrarian position is founded, ultimately more dangerous than the radiation level at Three Mile Island. If we watch a program of managed evening news night after night as if it were a bedtime story, accepting Uncle Walter's comfortable words that "that's the way it is," we may wake some morning to a strangely altered world.

And so we Southerners make welcome this outlandish Russian, who speaks so effectively against "the American or prevailing way" of life, recalling us to known but forgotten truths about man and his place in the world. We value his personal testimony, which our grandfathers would understand and which we trust our children may come to understand: "I have been in the dragon's belly, in the red burning belly of the dragon. He wasn't able to digest me. He threw me up. I have come to you as a witness to what it's like there, in the dragon's belly." He affirms and defends certain qualities of life not because they belong to the Russia he loves, but because the Russia he loves belongs to them. Without those qualities, life becomes meaningless. If we lose them, we shall wake to find only a dream world in which our bonds with illusion leave us in an ultimate horror of spiritual emptiness, the desperate moment Haze Motes experiences: "There are all kinds of truth, your truth, and somebody else's, but behind all of them, there's only one truth and that is that there's no truth. . . . Where you come from is gone, where you thought you were going to never was there, and where you are is no good unless you can get away from it." That is a dark morning of the regional man as he discovers himself transformed almost completely into the provincial man. He will live nowhere, only stay in random place. He will be citizen of a boundless state larger and more empty than can be described by *Southern* or *Northern* or *American* or *Russian* or *Soviet*—the state Milton's fallen spirit attempts to celebrate:

> The mind is its own place, and in itself
> Can make a heaven of hell, a hell of heaven.

In those words lies the death of family, community, country—the death of the whole person and of those workings of the spirit through such persons joined in a community, of which we should properly be members.

IX. Eric Voegelin and the End of Our Exploring

In our day, to raise the right questions is a deed already of a considerable magnitude, for only by doing so does it become possible to turn the mind toward some possibility of right answers.

Eric Voegelin has been increasingly recognized for his contributions to a recovery of the intellectual heritage of Western culture. His reconsiderations of our history and philosophy and political science as disciplines of intellect encourage us to ground those disciplines more firmly in the mystery of man's particular nature than has been usual in our century. That is because he discovers human nature to be more complex than the reductionism practiced by modernist readings of that nature for the past few centuries. His has been, above all, a searching encounter with mind and its response to the circumstances of its existence, from ancient times down to our own attempts to orient ourselves in the *metaxy*—the "In-Between" as he calls it, out of his own beloved Plato. The complex conditions of mind in existential reality, he comes to remind us, cannot be reconciled to the mystery of mind itself on any sound principle that does not turn at last toward transcendence. Nietzsche's "will to pure immanence," as a violent response to the universe declared mechanistic, must leave mind at last isolated from all being, in the last desperate fortress of mind, its own autonomy.

What one notices in the best response to Voegelin's work is that sort of tribute to it that he most desired: a searching consideration of what he has had to say about the Western intellectual voyage from the time of the ancient Egyptians to the traumatic storms and wreckage of our own century. The conspicuous spectacle for us of mind dislocated in this century has been devastating wars and radical rechartings of our world with political and sociological and philosophical lines that more often than not ignore the actualities of that world in the interest of gnostic mappings of being. In pursuing the causes of such spectacle forced upon reality, Voegelin summoned mind to the concern, always expecting an intense use of mind, so that we might recover and rediscover the proper order of our voyaging. I am thinking, as exemplum of the sort of response to his own thought that Voegelin valued, of a collection of essays edited by Stephen A. McKnight titled *Eric Voegelin's Search for Order in History* (1978), one of the early tributes to him, though not the last. Since this volume, several have been published. And many more are inevitable, such is the importance of the questions he raises.

But I do not intend a survey. I wish to consider this one volume as exemplary of the approach to his work that Voegelin himself would require of us. For there is in the volume a spirit of intellectual piety such as we need a more general recovery of. Now, in respect to things human in the proximate making—the intellectual labors of Eric Voegelin, for instance—the piety required is that balance of mind toward its object which truly values that object. When one's mind has as its object such a worthy one as *Order and History*, piety requires more than awe. One ought to be awed by such an arresting—astonishing—mind as Voegelin's, but that very mind expects of us, not adulation or an intimidated acceptance, but rather the labors of our own intellect toward rising to the level of an intellect such as his, directed in the common good. Voegelin's expectations of us, this is to say, are the surest sign that he is not himself entrapped by mind as its own cause and end. What he expects of us is not our embrace of or rejection of him, but a continuing engagement of those questions central to the mind's proper concern for being. That concern may keep us as a civilization from the general wreckage on the shores of being that seems the threatening circumstance of our journey in this century.

A principal virtue of this volume, then, is that in its colloquy with Voegelin, the minds gathered here look into contradictions, or seeming contradictions, into paradoxes and ambiguities in mind itself as a concept, but into particular minds, including Voegelin's own. It is an undertaking that requires a degree of faith in intellect. Voegelin might put it that we are required to make this act of faith if we are to become a viable community of the *spoudaioi*—if we are to become "mature human beings" worthy of our voyaging. It is especially required in such a dark age of intellect as ours if the light of intellect is to be preserved against an encroaching darkness. And so in this volume some hard questions are asked of Voegelin's thought, such questions as encourage a critical perspective upon the limits of philosophy and prophecy. It is a very old concern, this: for at what point does the lover of wisdom become the prophet? At what point does the philosopher require of us a consent to his wisdom in recovering a social order suited to community? Philosophers as prophets and poets as prophets have been insistent upon us for our intellectual consent, the more insistent as we become the more storm-tossed intellectually. And we seem to have reached a point where it is difficult to know whether the poet or philosopher is a cause of the storm or the storm the cause of him.

Which is by way of saying that, in reading our exemplary colloquy, we may be struck by the increasingly controversial effect of Voegelin's own thought, and most especially its effect upon academic philosophy and political science. But I want to call particular attention to delayed effects in the academy upon specifically literary concerns, since that is a particular interest of mine. Only gradually is it beginning to be recognized that such minds as Voegelin's are pertinent to literature, that compartment of the ship of intellect. And I introduce here a considerable literary figure to place beside Voegelin, a poet who seemed to many to have jumped ship. I mean Ezra Pound. The academy in its literary and philosophical concerns now begins to dwell upon both Pound's and Voegelin's work with similar intensity and with a growing respect. The delay is in part explained, perhaps, by Voegelin's and Pound's separate attacks upon the academy itself as principal cause of intellectual and literary failures. Each man is deeply concerned with an openness to reality, to be regained by revisiting our intellectual sources. Each finds the post-Renaissance mind increasingly removed from the experience of reality. For much of his life, Pound seems to find only Plato among the great Western philosophers as companionable to his own mind.

In consequence of their complex positions, each finds himself under attack from ideological left and right. Their own struggle for openness resists the imposition of order that would preclude such shifts of emphasis as Voegelin exhibits in *The Ecumenic Age*. How many *Cantos* make Pound's great poem, and is it complete or flawed in fundamental ways? How many volumes must there be in Voegelin's search for *Order and History*? At present there is an impressive (and sometimes oppressive) journal devoted to such questions in Pound, *Paideuma*; there is nothing comparable as yet for Voegelin, though one very likely will appear. Pound's signal cry to the poet to "Make It New" by returning to the roots of poetry, his own concern for the relation of order to beauty, speaks a kinship of the two. Indeed, the motto that is set to govern *Paideuma*, which Pound attempted to follow in his own quest for being, is descriptive of Voegelin's constancy of encounter with reality, though Pound (fundamentally an immanentist deeply suspicious of transcendency) found it in Confucius as enlightened by Mencius rather than in Plato as supplemented by Aristotle:

> the men of old wanting to clarify and diffuse throughout the empire that light which comes from looking straight into the heart then acting, first set up good government in their own states; wanting good government in their states, they first established order in their own families: wanting order in the home, they first disciplined themselves; desiring self-discipline, they rectified their own hearts: and wanting to rectify their own hearts they sought the precise verbal definitions of their inarticulate thoughts (the tones given off by the heart): wishing to attain precise verbal definitions, they set to extend their knowledge to the utmost. This completion of knowledge is rooted in sorting things into organic categories.

It is the movement from large to small to large, the constancy of growth, that finds parallel in each. Pound's concern for establishing order through action, through the law of the word as articulated by mind, of course separates him from Voegelin at last. Mencius says, "Having attained self-discipline, they set their own houses in order; having order in their homes, they brought good government to their own states, and when their states were well governed, the empire was brought into equilibrium." Self-discipline is "the root—i.e., the paideuma," says Pound. There is in Pound a confidence in man's power to order reality that Voegelin will have nought of, though he shares Pound's desire for order and beauty. Pound's belief in "the completion of knowledge" in the "men of old" brought him to grief, one could argue on the basis of the *Cantos*—it brought him to a realization that one must return to the roots of order in the experience of reality, but through the spirit of Voegelin's approach. There is dramatic irony in the two men's quests, Pound abandoning America for Europe as Voegelin is abandoning Europe for America as gnostic conflicts erupt into World War II.

As we engage such complex problems (as Voegelin would remind us) we must remember always that only false prophets promise to deliver us to the gates of that garden we remember vaguely having lost. Voegelin does not have that confidence in the poet as prophet that Pound exudes. Pound, such is his intense concern, will replace the philosopher-king with the poet-king. Voegelin, deeply respectful of the visionary poet, discovers T. S. Eliot the more companionable poet, Eliot's *Four Quartets* a sounder witness than Pound's *Cantos*. For the true prophet (Voegelin prefers the term *philosopher*) recalls to us *that* we are lost and reminds us that we must labor, each according to his gift, to recover the lost way. Being thus summoned to find ourselves, after recognizing ourselves lost in a dark world, it is little wonder that we struggle to apply terms like *prophet* or *philosopher* or *poet* to account for Voegelin's visionary work. We are fascinated as by an enchanter, and thus endangered to awe. The dangers of fascination, especially as an effect of taking words unexamined, trouble Voegelin. And so he would have us guard against fascination, infatuation, by words, our defense a severity of thought that requires a cautious reading of this very mind that summons us out of darkness toward the possibility of light. Voegelin is always aware that the prophet (or philosopher) who recalls us to known but forgotten or neglected truths does not have the power to answer all questions about our journey toward truth. Philosophical inquiry, he says, is what he is about; it is a way of diagnosing "modes of existence in untruth." His work invites us into a company engaged in discourse upon the supreme philosophical theme of being. He summons the *spoudaioi*—mature human beings—with whom he engages mind. Our responsibility, as the contributors to this symposium indicate, is to recognize the central questions. For Voegelin would protect us from too easy a transport through his words, lest we find ourselves isolated from the protean "complexity of reality" to which above all else our words are required to return us.

That is, words spoken *about* being must be brought to the test of experience, lest they disengage us from reality. Voegelin's suspicion of dogma as the first step away from participation in reality recognizes the human inclination to find comfortable resolution in the words of our poets and prophets and philosophers, a rest from the labor and hazard of our own long journey in history, our sojourn of the "In-Between." That is a reason for the constant theme in all his work, his attempt to explain to us (and to himself) what it means to be a philosopher. "Philosophy, the love of wisdom, becomes the tension of man's existence in search of truth." For "Philosophy springs from a love of being; it is man's loving endeavor to perceive the order of being and attune himself to it."[1]

Philosophy, in Voegelin's requirement of it, especially in consequence of his developing theory of consciousness, must return to the roots of consciousness. This requires a return within the philosopher himself to his own experience of reality and a return to the collective consciousness that is history. Still one finds relatively few personal events in Voegelin's work, relatively few attempts to anchor his quest in the literal world he inhabits. A consequence is, I think, a climate of abstractness in the very work which insists on the constant return to openness in the *metaxy* of reality. There is little direct suggestion of the world in which Voegelin has lived and breathed and had his being. Perhaps it is because, as John Hallowell says in his "Existence in Tension," "Voegelin has a tendency, which he shares with Plato, to disparage the body." He is we must notice intrigued by *symbol*, but less attentive to *image*, through which one attempts an anchor in the concrete world. This absence is particularly surprising, I think, when one considers that his conception of consciousness posits as a fundamental necessity a common experience of reality which provides at least analogy so that communication becomes possible—so that a community of "mature men" may rest in some faith that each man's experience of the *metaxy* bears correspondences to the experiences of others. To Voegelin, the philosopher's high duty is to recover to that community those truths of man's experiences of reality, known but forgotten through our deformations of reality in that limited rationalism which closes the consciousness to the complexities of the *metaxy*, the In-Between. It may be that Voegelin's interest in and use of imaginative testimonies of experience such as poetry and fiction seem to him to better serve the cause of experiential analogy; one is grateful nevertheless for the biographical account his longtime student William C. Havard gives us in this volume.

As for the philosopher (and here one experiences that tendency to abstrac-

---

1. *The Ecumenic Age*, vol. 4 of *Order and History* (Baton Rouge: Louisiana State University Press, 1974), 177.

tion), his nature "is distinguished by the virtues of justice, temperance, courage, love of wisdom, unrelenting zeal in the search for true being, great mindedness, ability to learn, and good memory."[2] Such properties of the philosopher are, as is appropriate to Voegelin's hard-won escape of modern ideologies, largely classical virtues applied to classical gifts. He is defining for us here the credentials for admission to that community biding in time of which he understands himself a member, the generation of the *spoudaios*, mature man, rather than that singularly perfect man who is Christ; and that is a point of distinction crucially important to him as to many of us who seek illumination through his work.

From the outset we expect too much of him if we require ambiguities dissolved, contradictions removed under the species of that discourse on mystery called paradox, and the way thus made easy. He insists that, though we move toward "mystery" and engage it on the cloudy border of consciousness as it touches the transcendent divine, we are at last unable to articulate that movement beyond tentative, provisional attempts which are most properly expositions of the modes of our existence in untruth. The fear of a violation of mystery haunts Voegelin throughout his post–World War II work, it seems to me, the fear that he (and through him, we ourselves) may elevate the tentative and provisional to an absolute and risk thereby elevating the articulator of the tentative to savior of mankind. Such, indeed, has been the history of ideologues such as Comte and Marx, as Voegelin's careful analysis of their consequential untruths has shown. For the Christian, as an act of faith, it is the savior and not the poet or prophet or philosopher in whom lies the promise of our return to the lost home.

Or to put the matter more accurately in respect to Christian orthodoxy: it is through a sacrifice once offered, and the will's emulation of that sacrifice by an openness of love for existence, that the soul at last arrives—not at a "lost home"— but to a state of perfection of its gift of being. But Voegelin is not prepared to make a surrender through faith to the mediator, though he values that surrender in others. It is as if he sees a danger that, at such a point in the quest, a surrender of faith is too near a surrender to dogma, a dogma descended to us from the medieval world. A dogma that, for Voegelin, seems to have prepared the ground in which modern gnostic ideologies have flourished. It is a lesson learned no doubt from his mentor Plato. Plato sees that same potential danger in the mimetic poet, who imitates not reality but the world of the senses, and so imitates the shadow of reality. Voegelin sees the ideologue in a similar light: since ideology is in reaction to dogma, and since dogma is a step away from that

---

2. *Plato and Aristotle*, vol. 3 of *Order and History* (Baton Rouge: Louisiana State University Press, 1957), 80–81.

participation in reality which moves us to dogma, the ideologue is at a second remove from reality in his "Secondary Constructions."[3]

To counter such a "progress" from participation into untruth, Voegelin proposes a trinitarian guide to the philosopher: Greek philosophy (principally Plato's), the gospel, and out of these his "Christianity," the spirit moving in the early Church fathers. In the *New Oxford Review* of June 1978, Russell Kirk tells us that Voegelin speaks of himself as a "pre-Reformation Christian." When we recall Voegelin's severe judgment on the medieval Church and the scholastics, we may suspect that for him the "Reformation" begins much earlier than the "Reformation" defined by academic historians. He points us to the dangerous rivalry between orthodox dogma and apocalyptic emotionalism in the middle ages which prepared the way for Renaissance ideologies, citing Norman Cohn's study of those preconditions of modernism, *The Pursuit of the Millennium*. One suspects, indeed, that for Voegelin the beginning of the Reformation is in Saint Augustine. (Professor Niemeyer has written me in response to this suggestion that Voegelin recently declared himself a "pre-Nicaean Christian.")

It seems pertinent here to recall an anecdote recorded by Julian Green about Camus, with whom Voegelin expresses a sympathetic recognition. At the end of World War II, Green attended a gathering at the Latour-Maubourg convent to hear Camus. After the talk an agitated "ex-revolutionary" startled the assemblage by saying, "I am in a state of grace and you, Monsieur Camus, I tell you very humbly that you are not." Camus's only answer, says Green, was a smile, "but he said a little later: 'I am your Augustine, before his conversion. I am struggling with the problem of evil and can't get to the end of it.'"[4] My point is that Voegelin, like Camus, is unwilling to relax from the struggle of individual consciousness as it engages those responsibilities of intellect's continuous encounter with existence. It is as if a "state of grace" presumed, as with Camus's accuser, may be in actuality a surrender to an illusion in the interest of premature rest.

Our own desire for a rest unearned by intellectual labors unquestionably tempts us to elevate poets, prophets, philosophers to the authority of saviors, the disastrous effects of which Voegelin surveys in the long history of man's struggle toward full being. Given our propensity to embrace messiahs unexamined, one understands Voegelin's suspicion of our innate desire for a rest in certainty. But his is an excessive suspicion perhaps. For the excesses to which one submits out of desire do not necessarily invalidate the desire. The desire for resolution that spurs intellect beyond question to answer, the desire for a rest for the will in certitude, need not lead us to the conclusion that rest is evil.

3. See "Immortality: Experience and Symbol," *Harvard Theological Review*, July 1967.
4. *Diary: 1928–1957* (New York: Harcourt, Brace & World, 1964).

There is a difference between coming to rest in false ground and in true. And even restlessness may itself be false, an agitation of spirit that seeks as its end of being only itself—the self irritated into being, as it were, under the presumption that such irritation precedes being. This is an abuse of restlessness which Voegelin himself castigates in Sartre and his followers.

Perhaps the most insistent questions raised in these essays on Eric Voegelin's "Search for Order," as we have anticipated, center on Voegelin's address to, or lack of a direct address to, Christianity. A number of the essays here (as well as in other places) begin to press the point. McKnight, the editor of the volume, laments in his own essay ("The Evolution of Voegelin's Theory of Politics and History: 1944–1975") the "lack of an extended study of Christianity" such as had been planned in the projected sequence of the volumes of *Order and History*, a study now abandoned in the departure from that sequence occasioned by Voegelin's emerging theory of consciousness. William C. Havard ("Voegelin's Changing Conception of History and Consciousness") comforts us somewhat by suggesting that "the underlying controls in the critical exegesis are clearly the experience of reality symbolized by philosophy as the love of wisdom which reaches out to its divine source and the pneumatic luminosity of Christianity." But Hans Aufricht ("A Restatement of Political Theory: A Note on Voegelin's *The New Science of Politics*") is not much comforted: "While under the gnostic view man has forsaken God, in Voegelin's system of metaphysics God, it seems, has forsaken man." That is, Voegelin "seems to deny man's capacity of experiencing God as 'way, truth and life,' since he designates all endeavors in this direction as 'fallacious immanentization' of God." (To the extent that Aufricht's charge bears a truth, we have, I think, a residual effect in Voegelin of his strong reaction not only to Nietzsche but also to the general attempt upon a theory of consciousness developing out of Husserl and Heidegger, an attempt he finds inadequate. He has not, one fears, escaped those influences entirely. It is in this battle with his old teachers that Voegelin came increasingly upon the necessity of some viable theory of consciousness.) Bruce Douglass, in the most severe of these essays, finds that Voegelin leaves us with "A Diminished Gospel." What is missing in Voegelin, he says, is "the sense of the Gospel as *salvation*."

Bernhard Anderson's "Politics and the Transcendent" considers the limits of Voegelin's philosophy of being in dealing with the fullness of biblical revelation, and he raises the question of Voegelin's address to the problem of evil, always a crucial burden in a visionary philosopher's world. It is a question tangential to the one Douglass raises about salvation, since one must ask what we are to be saved *from*, how we became endangered, and a congeries of like questions. One is disappointed, then, to find that neither Douglass nor Anderson presses the problem very far. In Anderson the conception of evil seems to border dangerously upon a Manichaean division such as I do not believe Voegelin himself to have entirely escaped in his appropriation of Anaximander; into which, indeed, his emerging theory of consciousness seems to draw him ever deeper, though he struggles brilliantly against that pull. Douglass's essay is more heavily given to a defense of the Reformation against Voegelin's devastating attack than to dealing with root questions about Voegelin's diminishment of the gospels. For Voegelin's avoiding the sense of the Gospel as salvation is not so much an avoidance as it is a radical transformation. It seems to Douglass that Voegelin "takes the Resurrection with the appropriate seriousness"; but it seems to me that he rather takes it and revises it to the purpose of his theory of emerging consciousness, diminishing the importance of what he has on other occasions called attention to: the particularity of the Incarnation. For that intrusion into history, as Saint Paul argues, is precisely and literally in time and for the purpose of man's salvation—salvation from *willful* evil. It seems strange that the examination of Voegelin's diminishment of the gospel message nowhere mentions the central condition in humanity which makes salvation possible through such an inordinate sacrifice as the Incarnation: the condition of man's sinful existence in the *metaxy*. Voegelin remarks ("History and Gnosis") that the Incarnation has not "affected the nature of man" since "the leap in being" of which the Incarnation is the event "is not a leap out of existence." But he does not, so far as I have discovered, indicate his understanding of the relation of evil and man's sinfulness to the nature of man.

Voegelin's adaptation of the resurrection to his own vision, then, is central in the questions raised about his friendliness toward Christianity. It is as if Christ is risen only symbolically for Voegelin, and (it would seem) specifically risen in man's imitations of Jesus' radical encounters of reality in the world. Thus Voegelin will say, in "Immortality: Experience and Symbol," that "History is Christ written large." When we consider that history has become for Voegelin the unfolding of humanity in the context of reality, we begin to suspect an aberrational construction of the meaning of the Incarnation, one which reduces the event of the Incarnation and replaces it with the "larger" event of the unfolding of humanity.

One is tempted to ask: if *any* experience in the *metaxy* may become an event in the constitution of history, are there any which are *not* events? What name do we give to the noneventful experience to set it aside from history? Those happenings that are not charged with the radiance of the theophanic fail as event, but why? Because not chosen by the divine for irradiation? Because not chosen by consciousness? Because not a "structure inherent to the experience of reality"? I leave these questions presently to shuck two bushels of corn on my back porch, an experience that I believe may be either filled by theophanic illumination through grace or not. But in either case I shall shuck the corn, as I pulled it this morning in the cornfield. Some hierarchy seems necessary in the structure inherent in our experience of reality, one that would embrace the radiant and the dark moments of experience by consciousness in the *metaxy*. But my very real desire tells me it is a hierarchy that reaches beyond my participation in collective consciousness as bounded by Anaximander's Unlimited (*apeiron*).

It is understandable that Voegelin would be more acutely interested in the event of Paul's encounter on the road to Damascus as a transformation of Paul's consciousness and through his, ours, than in the fundamental reality of the Incarnation as described by Christian dogma. Paul's experience is treated as of consequence to mature man. The gospel reveals a myth, says Voegelin, whose content is the story of the event—the entering of the divine *Logos* into a man (Jesus), and thence into society and history. Christ as "God with us," Immanuel, is a symbolization that undergoes such a deformation by the intrusion of a dogma of literalism (as it must appear to Voegelin) that the deformation stands in the way of one's dealing with the incarnation of symbolization in general. Thus Voegelin seems to take it that *to follow Christ* means to imitate Christ as an act of the mature man; for thus the act of matured consciousness makes possible a presence of the divine in history. Hence "History is Christ written large." But the Christian, who takes Christ to be what he says he is—the way and the truth and the life—questions such an aphoristic setting of incommensurates as Voegelin here presents. For if we take the words too carelessly, we may be tempted to the conclusion that history written large will necessarily overshadow Christ, as it has come to do in the modern mind. It is a quite different perspective to say that Christ is the *author* of all history, as Christian orthodoxy proclaims. That is the orthodox position that Ralph Waldo Emerson is intent on overthrowing through a "Self-Reliance" that declares "all history resolves itself very easily into the biography of a few stout and earnest persons." Thus history, Emerson concludes, is the "lengthened shadow" of man himself, so that it is little wonder the woods of the world are further darkened by that shadow as this doctrine is embraced and acted upon in the post-Renaissance world.

I have come to believe that Voegelin's deep suspicion of man's desire for rest colors his work with an intensity that requires exploring. If the shift in his central concern (witnessed by the position developed in *Anamnesis* and in *The Ecumenic Age*) is as Corrington suggests a shift from "a philosophy of history into a psychology of philosophy," that shift perhaps warrants my suggestive speculation, which a more thorough encounter with Voegelin's own development (as opposed to the historical content of his work) might undertake to verify or reject. One might begin by noting that there is continuously in him the vigorous activity of a mind agitated by questions. In respect to Voegelin's mood, revealed in his words, one is reminded of Homer's symbolization in Odysseus: in each of that old wanderer's encounters with "event," he too escapes a closing world, whether it be the destructive threat of the provincial Cyclops or the seductive "transcendent" rest promised by Calypso. And after each event Odysseus sails on, glad as one escaped, although in each encounter he has lost some of his dear companions. Displacement becomes a virtue posed against the threat of a closed placement (though Odysseus never loses his longing for Ithaca, we must remember). The fear of rest, I am suggesting, seems as much a motivating force in Voegelin's mind as the "question" upon which he comes to rest tentatively in the last but one of his volumes of *Order and History*.

We are reminded in Havard's account ("Voegelin's Changing Conception of History and Consciousness") of Voegelin's own narrow escape from the closing world of modern gnosticism. Havard quotes words the young Voegelin wrote before he won his way up from gnostic liberalism, advancing a neo-Kantian positivism in defense of his senior colleague Hans Kelsen in 1927: "By transforming the legal system into an ideal realm of meanings and reducing it to an instrument Kelsen destroys any undue respect for existing legal institutions. The content of the law is shown to be what it is: not an eternal sacred order, but a compromise of battling social forces—and this content may be changed every day by the chosen representatives of the people according to the wishes of their constituents without fear of endangering a divine law."

In retrospect there must be for Voegelin both the joy of escape and terror at the narrowness of his escape from that position. (One finds him particularly severe in examining his own near teachers like Husserl and Heidegger, an examination which finds entrapment in a closed consciousness to be the end toward which they tend.) But perhaps such experiences led Voegelin, the anti-dogmatist, into the most fundamental dogma of his own reconstruction of the experience of reality: any rest that seems to promise fulfillment of the desire in the human soul for rest is very probably a species of closure of the complexity of reality. In the terms developed in *The Ecumenic Age*, in his concern for man's relation to reality, any rest is a suspension of, a "death" of, consciousness, upon which the life of history is dependent. That position leads Hallowell to ask, "Is *every* attempt to express faith in doctrinal form necessarily doomed to become doctrinaire?"

Dante Germino (whose absence from this collection, along with Gerhart Niemeyer's, one regrets) raised a like question, before the publication of *The Ecumenic Age*, in his long exposition of *Anamnesis* in the *Southern Review* of winter 1971. He asks: "If Being is beyond experience, upon what basis can a philosophy of order assert anything at all about its constitution? If there are no 'absolute propositions' that can be put forward by a philosophy of the consciousness [as Voegelin contends], does this not undermine the remarkable confidence with which Voegelin dismisses so great a part of western speculation?"

Voegelin's answer, judging from both his *Anamnesis* and his *Ecumenic Age*, would rest in his faith in mature man (*spoudaios*), a faith placed in each by the other and in the sheltering comfort of the intellectual dialogue which houses that community within the *metaxy*. But the criteria for recognizing the members of that community would seem to rest most heavily upon the one dogma: the refusal of conclusion, the refusal of rest in conclusion, so that dialogue becomes a movable place to be. Thus we encounter the principal dogma at the heart of Voegelin's own work and can recognize the one sin against the holiness of consciousness: Thou shalt not rest in conclusion lest thou fall into certitude, the unforgivable sin against openness. It is the principle that leads him to assert that gnostic man is possessed by "a drive for certitude." The mature man, to the contrary, is motivated by the question, to which there is no answer, but only tentative answers. There is a reluctance to admit to the dialogue, as an act of openness, the possibility of an answer. But one misses a significant point thereby: when gnostic "modes of existence in untruth" are elevated to the rank of absolute answer, to the general deconstruction of reality, that action does not therefore preclude an absolute answer nor the possibility of the wise man's drawing nearer to that answer with a certitude reduced from arrogant pride.

The question, he says in *The Ecumenic Age*, "appears as the motivating force in the act of symbolizing the origin of things" in the "setting of the primary experience." Thus the "motion" of consciousness is explained. The question represents "a structure inherent to the experience of reality." But what calls up the question so that it appears in us as an instrument or engine of structure? Is it inherent, or an accident of the collision of consciousness with that which is not consciousness but somehow contains consciousness? (Consciousness as *included* in complex reality is Voegelin's bid to escape the dangers of solipsism.) Is the question's origin somehow spoken to more effectively by the schoolman's Prevenient Grace? Why does consciousness ask the metaphysical question if there is no answer, as Voegelin maintains, but only provisional answers? For Voegelin the discovery that unanswerability is the answer to the question is the mystical revelation through which experience becomes luminous, an excitement of consciousness which appears to be its fulfillment. Thus Voegelin's eschatological vision appears to rest on the theophanic event as a present experience in consciousness, lest the apocalyptic temptation in us (out of eschatological desire) restrict or even annihilate the tension of existence in the *metaxy* and lead us to deconstructions by conquest or exodus. There is in his thought a certain cheerful "stoic" mood which endures the present event as an end: questions of the ultimate appear deferred; he refrains from presumption upon mystery toward which process tends. The luminosity of consciousness in the present thus seems the substance of things hoped for.

There appears then a scar on the general body of Voegelin's work whose cause, one hazards, was a deeply personal wound sustained in a devastating encounter. His narrow escape of the neo-Kantian world of continental thought in the 1920s and 1930s, followed by his very literal narrow escape from Austria into Switzerland from that spectacular manifestation of gnostic thought, Hitler, may well symbolize a fundamental problem in his work. And this returns us to the relation of the Incarnation to Voegelin's pursuit. His arguments come increasingly to rest upon what is in effect a second dogma which he discovers in Anaximander, as we have once more anticipated, and explored as differentiated by Plato and Aristotle: "The origin (*arche*) of things is the *Apeiron* [the Boundless or Unlimited]. . . . It is necessary for things to perish into that from which they were born; for they pay one another penalty for their injustice." Thus in *The Ecumenic Age* Voegelin insists, "The experience of the cosmos existing in precarious balance on the edge of emergence from nothing and return to nothing must be acknowledged . . . as lying at the center of the primary experience of the cosmos." Only within the conception of a whole bounded by the boundless nothing does it seem possible to Voegelin to maintain that openness to existence without which spirit atrophies.

It would appear then that for the Unknown God (the boundless or unlimited) to become the revealed God in history, in whose name we pray for rescue from our willful failures (the Christ of Christian doctrine), would destroy the one mystery Voegelin thinks his vision to rest upon. Consciousness requires for its life, for its rescue from death, an ultimate unknowable. One wonders whether such a position, which may be a reaction to arrogant and prideful certainty such as one finds in the generality of mankind (whose symbolization is the Christian doctrine of original sin) does not in fact distort the complexity of reality. One finds such imperfect certitude in all sorts and conditions of man, whether mature, growing, or arrested. And the opposition that Voegelin raises to the apocalyptic dimension of Christianity lies also in part perhaps in its threat of a conclusion to that finite openness represented in the mature man's encounter with the teasing presence of being within the In-Between. For the hunger for resolution is the driving force within the apocalyptic. A consequence of this Voegelinian fear is, as Douglass says, that in place of the "biblical image of God whose presence and purposes in history are made manifest we are given a divine flux whose direction is a mystery."

Douglass's "image" suggests why Voegelin's pursuit of symbol leaves his work, the texture of it, imaginistically weak in general. Voegelin recognizes that our awareness of the experience of reality has as one of its dangers our separation from the complex reality that engenders the experience; awareness of experience through reflection upon it may falsify experience into an idea which bears an illusion of being an object. Symbolization is the nearest one comes, it would seem, to the enlivening of the "object-idea" toward a recovery of primary experience, toward a participation in Being, a surrender through "myth" to a complexity in which openness is maintained. One might anticipate, then, that Voegelin would (as Heidegger does) turn to the poet to accomplish the final return to reality, and in a sense he does, as his constant attention to and exegesis of poetry suggests. Nevertheless, he has reservations about "myth" that do not seem quite worked out to resolution. Thus he says, in his "Postscript: On Paradise and Revolution,"[5] that "mytho-speculation is not a philosopher's or Christian's meditative *via negativa* toward the one divine ground of the world and man. The divinity of the myth is not world-transcendent but intra-cosmic." The Platonic myth, a creation of the philosopher by his imagination to solve the impasse his reason reaches in pursuit of the question, is a device only, it would appear, rather than a residual form from an encounter with the ineffable, a symbolization (as seen from the outside) of primary participation. (Plato "dressed" his eschatological interpretations "in the mantle of myth," Voegelin says.)

For Voegelin, the uncaused cause is the *apeiron*, the unlimited, which he concludes divine. The *apeiron* appears rather a Greek version of Yahweh in this approach to the absolute. It is, nevertheless, an approach through an intellectual ground that is governed by a most rare and admirable piety. But it is a piety in which on occasion the fear of transgression seems to prevent that necessary openness that Eliot is forced to acknowledge in *The Waste Land*: "The awful daring of a moment's surrender." The cost of that surrender? "Little Gidding" puts it as "A condition of complete simplicity / (Costing not less than everything)."

We come now to summary observations on that theory of consciousness which Voegelin is in the process of advancing, to which the writers in this symposium are often drawn. We do so starkly, leaving aside the theory's refinements so that the problem of its central burden may be suggested. (Voegelin himself has suggested that a phenomenon may "be studied in its radical expressions where it is not obscured by compromises with the exigencies of political [or polemical] success.") His brilliant recovery of classical philosophy, especially his reading of Plato, points to an important affinity between Plato and Voegelin that we have already touched upon: for each of them man's fall is not into sin, but into doctrine, so that evil is error made by the thinker in his unfolding of history, to be righted by right thinking.

Philosophy, says Voegelin in *Plato and Aristotle*, is not "a doctrine of right order" or "a piece of information about truth, but the arduous effort to locate the forces of evil and identify their nature. For half of the battle is won when the soul can recognize the shape of the enemy and, consequently, know that the way it must follow leads in the opposite direction." But here once more the mystery of evil seems to yield to philosophy—to right reason. Little wonder that Voegelin is sometimes puzzled, as Anderson remarks in his essay, as to why

5. *Southern Review*, Winter 1971.

men reject the vision delivered by prophets, philosophers, and saints. Again we are reminded of that inclination in Plato which holds toward the good as achieved by right thinking about the right questions, an inclination easily raised toward dogma by the less than thorough, the pseudo, Platonist. Only where one admits the freedom of a willed rejection of right thinking, an aspect of human existence to which the doctrine of original sin speaks, may one understand how a mature man does not invariably experience a happy sense of community with the generations of the *spoudaioi*. One might conclude, contra Voegelin, that history is Christ written small, the Christ-likeness of the *spoudaioi* falling considerably short of the goodness of the Son except as sacrificial grave may rescue them to a higher brotherhood.

For Plato, and seemingly for Voegelin, evil is a mistake, a failure of intellectual process in dealing with the shadowy flux within which one struggles toward encounter with the divine. This is to say that evil is not a willful perversion of reality. The "process" of right thinking becomes then the ultimate good, the movement of consciousness in the recovery of reality. Consciousness is actively sustained within reality by mutual exchanges revealed by our reflection as the flux of history—the unfolding of humanity in which the unlimited participates as first and final cause. There seems to hover about this conception of the drama of humanity, just offstage, a suggestion of circularity which bends the transcendent upon the immanent. I am reminded of Virgil's uses of Plato in this problem of origins and ends—of Anchises' explanation to Aeneas in the underworld of how things come into existence and go out of existence. One does not, of course, establish political empire through Voegelin's construction so directly as does Aeneas in Virgil's vatic poem. As philosopher, one rather participates through openness, becoming a medium of Divinity into the world through that community of mature men, the *spoudaioi*. This is the body of which we may find ourselves member in Voegelin, though the body has no head such as Saint Paul declares Christ to be. The openness of the philosopher as conceived by Voegelin is quite different from the openness of the saint as revealed through Saint Paul, when Paul is read from an orthodox Christian rather than from a classical Greek perspective.

A complaint increasingly common in Voegelin's respectful audience is that, while he asserts that philosophy, myth, revelation, mysticism are ways of man's recovery from his fall from being, he does not distinguish clearly among these ways nor show the relation among them. The way of the philosopher is clearly the way he sees for himself, the action of consciousness in relation to the tension of existence. But that appears to be the highest calling Voegelin will acknowledge, in which respect he is once more closely akin to Plato, his mentor who also honors myth and even at times through myth approaches mysticism. It is thus that we have a Platonic rendering of Paul in *The Ecumenic Age*. In *meta-*

lepsis, Plato's mutual participation of the self with the ineffable, the self is dissolved in the motion of encounter. But in the action of grace that so concerns Paul it appears rather that the self is fulfilled—filled full of its own potential being. The "new" man is born, but he is not the Platonic new man, the philosopher, the mature man, though he partakes of some of the qualities of the *spoudaios* as defined by Voegelin and is thus bound in a community, larger than they: particularly he shares a piety toward and humility before the mystery of existence, those virtues binding him to those not of the *spoudaioi*.

Voegelin's vision of consciousness in reality as it emerges out of his Platonism bears interesting parallel, it seems to me, to the vision of a recent child of the Church with whom the Church struggles to reach an accommodation, Pierre Teilhard de Chardin. Not the least likeness is the very limited (I am tempted to say "naturalistic") sense each has of evil. "History" as "Christ written large" has its analogue in Teilhard in his wider span of the history of the cosmos which discovers the enlargement of process toward mystery reaching a conclusion at point omega. Voegelin's researches into prehistory also extend his arena toward Teilhardian inclusiveness. And already in *The Ecumenic Age* his view of history as the growth of consciousness from compactness to differentiation suggests Teilhard's vision of the evolution of consciousness through "vertical energy." Unlike Teilhard, however, Voegelin seems to allow a participation in his own version of point omega at the present moment of our own consciousness as it perceives itself bounded by the *apeiron*; hence it is not quite a participation in the fullness of being as envisaged by Teilhard. For Voegelin "the new center of consciousness itself is not that of a disembodied mind . . . , but the consciousness of a greater number of human beings, widely dispersed in space and time over a socially and culturally diversified mankind, in whom the epochal event becomes reality in a wide spectrum of degrees of differentiation, of degrees of disengagement from the primary experience of the cosmos and specifically from the mytho-speculative, historiogenetic experiences."

Such a dispersion is rather surely threatened by a considerable disembodiment, lacking as *community* the organic nature of a community anchored in place and there nurtured in part by history as well as by nature. Where Teilhard's poetic vision of creation posits the ultimate rescue of *all* creation (and not just man) through perfection of consciousness, Voegelin at this point in his visionary attempt does not include even all of mankind. Nevertheless in respect to Teilhardian parallels, in *The Ecumenic Age* the drama of humanity which is pursued in the first volumes of *Order and History* becomes subordinate to the drama of the cosmos. Thus one may be wise to return often to the embodiment of reality in trees and grass, in the house and street and town where he exists at this point of time and place. For reality as an encounter by consciousness of a flux in time carries in it the old dangers of abstractionism though made mystically attractive.

What also seems troublesome in Voegelin's new emphasis is an apparent shift from a history as discovered or recovered through particular concrete minds in particular social and political epochs, to a history discovered in a somewhat ambiguous consciousness, the pursuit of which seems to lose textual concreteness and to diminish the sense of the particularity of the quarry as well. No one is more acutely aware of the dangers of abstractionism than Voegelin; in that most difficult of his works, *Anamnesis*, he is insistent upon the necessity of concreteness as the pursuit leads us into the rarefied interior of psychological reality, where we struggle to grasp the ungraspable that we begin to fear. The encounter between the moving consciousness and the divine ground, provided by the unlimited, is of consequence to men (it seems to be suggested) only insofar as they participate in the process of mankind whose only dependable locus is the separate concrete consciousness of the man. But the unfolding of humanity in "the flux of presence" would seem to depend crucially upon shared experience, a participation in the community of mature men. One's humanity, as well as one's specific engagement of the eternal ground, appears limited by the adequacy of one's participation in the *metaxy* at the level of *spoudaioi*. Additionally, the prospect of order in society or state seems increasingly dependent on a consensus of the *spoudaioi* radiated to the whole of mankind, rather than advanced by articulation or by some formal action within the flux. In this mystical unfolding of mankind which would bypass dogma and thereby avoid an eventual derailment into ideology, there stirs faintly an ascetic desert wind, tempting indeed, but seductive with a temptation to sentimentality about the ends of being in time, the "unfolding mankind." *Mankind* proved, as Voegelin has already decisively shown us in works such as *From Enlightenment to Revolution*, the catch term to power as that term is manipulated by ideologues through a sentimentality cultivated and nurtured as a pervasive mood in the popular spirit. Through that manipulation of sentiment, actions of decomposition—a restructuring of reality—have been precipitated by the secular gnostic.

For Voegelin, as he says in "The Concrete Consciousness" in *Anamnesis*, "Human consciousness is not a free-floating something but always the concrete consciousness of concrete persons." And again:

> The concrete consciousness of concrete man is the only consciousness given in our experience. Such constructions as a collective consciousness—either the consciousness of a society or the consciousness of mankind in history [the ideological construct or the Jungian immanence]—are hypostases that have no standing in theory. For instance, when we said that each society produces the symbols through which it expresses its experience of order, we did not mean that the society is a subject having

a consciousness that could interpret itself through symbols. Such statements are, rather, an abbreviated way of talking about the process by which concrete persons create a social field, i.e., a field in which their experiences of order are understood by other concrete men who accept them as their own and make them into the motive of their habitual actions.[6]

Thus Voegelin rejects utopian gnosticism, the apocalyptic destruction by particular manipulators of society's individuals as they experience separately a participation in the ground: "When a theorist [such as a Marx or Nietzsche] is inclined to liberate consciousness from man's corporeality [and so make of it a 'free-floating something'], there arise symbols of order like the realm of the spirits, or the perfect realm of reason to which mankind is approaching, or the withering away of the state and the coming of the *Third Reich* of the Spirit." But neither is concrete consciousness a Jungian immanence in the concrete man, a consciousness marked with "the symbols found by man for expressing his experiences in the *metaxy* into apeirontic archetypes" through transformation in "a collective unconscious," in which theory of consciousness a relation to symbol is an implicit evolutionary process.

In his theory of consciousness, Voegelin presents consciousness as an active, present participation in the ground of being. Through that action the necessary symbols are generated, so that symbols do not abide the generations of man in a dependable way. To adapt Ezra Pound's famous imperative command to the poet concerning the making of poetry, concrete man is compelled to "make it [the symbol] new." Such an action *recovers*, rather than the consciousness finding itself an inheritor of, a past participation in being which is designated "history." History is "the interpretive field of consciousness that experiences its essential humanity," and essential humanity is the action of participation in the ground of being in the present concrete *metaxy*. History is a "field of interpretation" available to the *spoudaios*. The succeeding generations of the *spoudaioi* enjoy, it would appear, at least the possibility of an increasing purchase upon that field by leaps of being, though the "total structure of the universal field, which conventionally is called 'the meaning of history,' is no possible object of knowledge." Such advances upon the field are to be seen as "acts of the self-interpretation of ideological social fields rather than noetic interpretation of history and its order," this latter being Voegelin's own central pursuit as philosopher. The derailment of consciousness from its proper movement in history continues since "the middle of the eighteenth century under the title 'philosophy of history,'" taking us away from the consciousness's proper deportment toward its proper goal, namely, "the optimum luminosity of consciousness" in

6. *Anamnesis* (Notre Dame: University of Notre Dame Press, 1978), 201–2.

which man "experiences himself both as existing in time and as participating in the eternity of the ground." In a proper deportment toward its own existence, consciousness experiences the tension toward the eternity of the ground which belongs to the universal field, expressed in a symbolism "usually called eschatologies," though not necessarily Christian eschatologies, he adds. For Plato provides the same class of symbolization: "Plato was a philosopher who knew how to philosophize. His eschatological interpretations never raise the claim to be noetic analysis or empirical propositions: he always dressed them in the mantle of the myth."

Consciousness as advanced by Voegelin, then, appears to be not a collective which, in a Jungian sense, determines the experience of the *metaxy* by a symbolism immanent in the particular concrete consciousness; neither is it a collective which has been constructed by the symbol's release from corporeality, the willful deformation by gnostic dreams of power that end in apocalyptic deformations. But he does seem to warrant, if not imply, a oneness to consciousness (*unfolding mankind*) beyond the limited participation of consciousness in particular concrete man, a oneness continuously fed by the generations of mature man, though it remains ambiguous also whether mature man is such because he is elected by accidents of nature or by transcendent grace. Such a vision seems to me to risk sacrificing the individual soul—unless it belong to the *spoudios*—to a closed "system" within flux, a system that allows too little account of the "I" whose memory and desire lead it to reject the explanation of its being as out of the unlimited, which term Voegelin glosses as "nothing" in *The Ecumenic Age*. (Teilhard's evolutionary vision, more overtly than Voegelin's, sacrifices particularity.)

I am aware that Voegelin brings a heavy emphasis to bear upon the concrete consciousness as anchored in the concrete man in his *Anamnesis*. The difficulty, then, is doubtless my own. But it is a difficulty exacerbated by the implication that concrete consciousness is the creator of symbol in its action with the *metaxy*, therefore the creator of forms of order, and therefore both origin and agent of form in the ground. Symbolizing is the activity whereby consciousness constructs itself, sees itself as existing in time and as participating in the eternity of the ground. The theory seems to suggest that consciousness is drawn toward luminosity by focusing upon its goal, the luminous self, by its own power. The danger appears to be that consciousness becomes revealed to itself as its own creator out of the mysterious presence of the "question" which gives it a first impulse toward itself. Consciousness thus appears endangered in that it becomes its own most dependable object, but within the little world of concrete man: a present creation which—if not "something free-floating" within that little world—bears semblance of such an object. Not a collective in the social or historical or cosmic field of mankind, and yet a collective within the limited field of concrete man inasmuch as he is individually *unfolding mankind*. I do not understand the position I am left with to be a considerable advance upon Heidegger's valiant attempt to recover the ground, though I am confident that Voegelin's labor attempts to be such. Nor can I solve the additional difficulty of reconciling (1) that which is actively aware of creating itself toward luminosity to (2) the created consciousness itself. It is as if consciousness lifts itself by its own bootstraps. At the same time I realize that Voegelin, as philosopher in the present chaos of modernism, sees it necessary to achieve a solution through thought. In addition, it must prove a more persuasive journey to the remnant to move toward a resolution, or some promise of resolution, than to "philosophize" from a conclusion grounded in a faith so largely abandoned. The popular spirit of our age does not allow the philosopher that comfort as he seemed to enjoy it in the medieval world.

Voegelin's theory of consciousness, I conclude, appears to be established on the border of philosophy with poetry, as Teilhard's theory of creation is established on the border of science with poetry. Both thinkers exhilarate us as they call us back to the hard questions which require help beyond that which philosopher or scientist, prophet or poet, can afford us at the last. And even if we become uneasy about the conclusions implied by some of Voegelin's argument, we know that he has nevertheless brought us to the precincts of vision again. As we turn those hard questions upon his own arguments, as he expects us to do, with knowledge of our own ignorance in the matter but confident of the firm generosity of spirit and high intelligence which his work reveals, we must remember also that he attempts always to set us right as to the limits of our dependence upon him. He insists on our own intellectual responsibility in these high matters.

"A vision," he says in *The Ecumenic Age*, "is not a dogma but an event in metoleptic reality which the philosopher can do no more than try to understand to the best of his ability." He is speaking of Paul and has just remarked, "The present concern is not with points of Christological dogma but with a vision of Paul and its exegesis by its recipient. Hence, there can arise no question of 'accepting' or 'rejecting' a theological doctrine." At this point of his concern, and at this level, no question need arise; for here he is testing the question that stirs life in his mind. It is the theologian who must address the complexities opened by Voegelin's theory, his attempt to save the appearances in the manner of Plato, as it is the problem of the individual person as he reads to test the grounds of his own faith and his experience of complex reality.

Reality is, for Voegelin, a process, the experience of which "has the character of a perspective." But the "knowledge of reality conveyed by the symbols of experience of that reality can never become a final truth for the luminous perspective that we call experiences, as well as the symbols engendered by them, are part of reality in process."[7] This aspect of Voegelin's pursuit of consciousness is anticipated perhaps by Owen Barfield in *Saving the Appearances: A Study in Idolatry*.[8] The titles of opening chapters are suggestive of the kinship: "Collective Representations"; "Figuration and Thinking"; "Participation"; "Prehistory"; "Original Participation." The "saving of appearances" through "hypotheses," in the Greek and (Barfield insists) medieval understanding of the manner in which consciousness participates in reality, protects one against turning phenomena into idol. A "representation, which is collectively mistaken for an ultimate," ought to be called an "idol": thus Barfield's address to ideological deconstructions of reality. The arresting of phenomena into objects is for Barfield the process whereby existence is reduced to secondary structures from its transcendent involvements. Barfield speaks as well to the modern confusion whereby a present reading of history presumes that history at the moment of "event" in the past was "literally" as it appears from our present perspective: his concern here is with Voegelin's own concern for the effect of participation in reality by consciousness which misunderstands the reality as an "object" unaffected by participation. Barfield says, in "The Incarnation of the Word": "I believe that the blind-spot which posterity will find most startling in the last hundred years or so of Western civilization, is, that it had, on the one hand, a picture in its mind of the history of the earth and man as an evolutionary process; and that it neither saw nor supposed any connection whatever between the two."

Clearly Voegelin is attempting to discover the connection. But Barfield finds the connection precisely in the meaning of the Incarnation, in Christ's declarations that "I am the way, the truth, and the life," "I am the light of the world," "I and the Father are one." Voegelin's contention that "the knowledge of reality conveyed by the symbols can never become a final truth" in our luminous experience of reality, it seems to me, denies immortality of the soul in the Christian understanding of that immortality. As philosopher at least, he is reluctant to conclude the fullness of knowledge of God promised in Christ. If Voegelin added the limit "in time," one would have little argument with his general position, for his argument for the limits of knowledge because of limited knowers' participation in the process of history is not so far removed from Saint Augustine or Saint Thomas—or Owen Barfield—as he would seem to believe. Perhaps Barfield's little book rescues his theory of consciousness from many of the objections it is otherwise open to. The final chapter, "The Mystery of the Kingdom," is particularly illuminating in this perspective.

7. "Equivalenses of Experience and Symbolization in History," *Eternità e Storia* (Florence: Valecchi, 1970). Quoted by Wiser in his essay.
8. New York: Harcourt, Brace & World, 1965.

It is the theologian, we said, who must address the complexities of consciousness in history as opened by Voegelin's theory. That at any rate appears to be his own position in the matter, a position he has advanced perhaps as far as he can before he must appeal more openly to the theologian, whom he has many times invited to his dialogue, or (in my own anticipation) before he must move beyond faith in mature man to a faith anchored more precisely than in the unlimited. There are signs of that coming necessity here and there in his work. There may even be his own anticipation of the coming necessity in his rather severe remark on Toynbee's willingness to rest halfway the journey rather than force a way on to the encounter with mystery which might reconcile the philosopher to a certainty beyond absolute uncertainty, beyond the *Apeiron*. Toynbee, Voegelin says, should not have been surprised that he must eventually arrive at a "spiritual crossroads" and "sooner or later, when engaged in a study of this kind . . . have to confess himself either an existentialist of the nihilistic variety, or a philosopher and Christian." The key word here is *and*. At present he insists that he is only a philosopher and "a philosopher can do no more than work himself free from the rubble of idols which under the name of 'Age' threatens to cripple and bury him; and he can hope that the example of his efforts will be of help to others who find themselves in the same situation and experience the same desire to gain their humanity under God." He has not, I have said, escaped the struggle unscathed. (One does not gain his humanity except as aided by grace, or so Christian dogma tells us.) But his very scars make him a welcomed example to those multitudes of us trapped and struggling to win free from under the rubble of our "age's" deconstructions of reality.

X. Eric Voegelin as Prophetic Philosopher

Existence has the structure of the In-Between, of the Platonic metaxy, and if anything is constant in the history of mankind it is the language of tension between life and death, immortality and mortality, perfection and imperfection, time and timelessness, between order and disorder, truth and untruth, sense and senselessness; between amor Dei *and* amor sui, *l'âme ouverte and* l'âme close; *between the virtues of openness toward the ground of being such as faith, hope and love and the vices of infolding closure such as hybris and revolt.*

—Eric Voegelin

i

Among the many arguments to be made in pointing the poet toward Eric Voegelin as a steadying presence in an unsteady time, one of the most helpful may be implicit in the last of his gifts to us, "Quod Deus dicitur," especially in that portion in which he examines the role of fool in that dialectic whereby we attempt to arrive at a name of God. For through that struggle with the *insipiens*, the intellectual problem of name may be at last calmed. The text upon which Voegelin meditates is from David's lament upon the depravity of the natural man, Psalm 53, the first half of verse 1: "The fool hath said in his heart, There is no God." I should like to include here the last of that verse as well: "Corrupt are they, and have done abominable iniquity: there is none that doeth good." What we will know already, from even a casual acquaintance with Voegelin's work, is an appropriateness of the text to his own devotion to existence. He has chosen in his last hours not only an Old Testament text, but words from a poet as well. In his lifelong examination of the relation of the signs we use to the reality we attempt to touch by signs, he is always quick to turn, as philosopher, to the poets, and the poet engaged in the same quest may well turn to him. Indeed, one might contend, with considerable justice, that his lifelong devotion to Plato is as much to Plato the poet as to Plato the philosopher. I have contended already that Voegelin attempts to rescue us from a

194

Renaissance and post-Renaissance corruption of our understanding of Plato's own address to the poet, a point of considerable importance, whether one be poet or philosopher.

I have specifically in mind what he has to say on the matter in *Plato and Aristotle*, concerning the hierarchy of souls one discovers in Plato's *Phaedrus*. He says: "We find the poets relegated to the sixth place. . . . We find also, however, that not all poets are relegated to this low rank, for in the first group there appears, side by side with the *philosophos*, a new figure, the *philokalos*, the Lover of Beauty; and we find this new figure characterized, together with the *philosophos*, as a soul which is inspired by the Muses and by Eros. This *philokalos* is the new poet, truly possessed by the *mania*."

What we may notice here, then, is a relegation of the poet as mimetic artist to the sixth position in this hierarchy, a relegation generally understood in Western thought, I suspect, and certainly in most of our addresses to Plato's view of the poet, as Plato's denigration of the poet. We know what Socrates has to say on the matter in the *Ion*: the poet, through no virtues of thought, becomes a reflective medium as it were, an instrument of the gods. But if there is a country beyond the gods in which one is to discover the final truth about poets and philosophers and gods and creation, this species of the mimetic poet is undependable in the concern. So the poet is reduced—as it has proved convenient to do, especially in the academy as it has accelerated the processing of Western thought for a general consumption. Such reduction of the poet's office means that he, as mimetic artist, imitates at best an imitation of a reality. His signs are shadows of the sign we are tempted to designate creation, since he takes the shadow world to be reality. Plato, says this reading of the philosopher, sees all creation as but shadow. But Voegelin urges upon us the question of whether this is a reductive reading of Plato, of whether we may not thus be taking Plato the poet as Plato the idealist philosopher.

I think this a fair summary of the general understanding of Plato's view of the poet to which we have been conditioned and against whose reductionism Voegelin cautions us. It has been, one might say, an intellectual custom since Sir Philip Sidney's struggle in his "Defense of Poesie" (1583) with the implications to the poet of Plato's argument. At that point in our history, the Republic seemed most promising of fulfillment. Nations were rising in a glory of self-discovery whose celebration was to be, perhaps, the poet's contribution. The poets themselves were bringing to the community of mind a recognition of Plato's arguments about the *polis*, and indeed they were active agents in the establishment of the Republic, some of them losing their heads in consequence. It is disconcerting at least, then, to find Plato rejecting the poet as even suitable citizen of that emerging Republic, let alone spokesman for it. A part of the dilemma for Sidney and others, however, is precisely that Plato's works in general are so richly suggestive to poetry. Surely, then, Plato could not intend to dismiss the poet out of hand. Put another way, Plato is too much a poet himself to consent, even as philosopher, to cast the poet out of the Republic. Indeed, one will find Plato a principal father of allegory in the English poetic tradition. From *Piers Plowman* to *The Faerie Queene* to *Pilgrim's Progress*, the shadow of Plato's mind falls upon our poets' understanding of metaphor. When I say "upon *our* poets' understanding," I mean something rather limited in the general context of Western culture and thought: I mean rather specifically (though not exclusively) the poets of the English tradition. In this respect I would mark a difference in, say, Dante's interest in allegory. For Dante's Platonism is rather crucially modified, I believe, by Dante's awareness of Aristotle, and especially of Aristotle as himself modified—as baptized—by Saint Thomas Aquinas. One might explore the distinction by comparing *The Faerie Queen* to the *Divine Comedy*. I intend here no concern for relative merit of the two works as works of art. I mean only to call attention to the quite different sense of reality that rises out of those works. And those realities both point us toward Plato, but from very different aspects of a seemingly common interest: again I must use shorthand or (I'd prefer to say) metaphor to distinguish the interests. I mean that there is a difference in the address to myth as one finds it in Dante and as one finds it in English Renaissance poetry from Sidney and Spenser down to a recovery of myth in a poet like T. S. Eliot.

Mircea Eliade very shrewdly points the matter when he remarks that with the Renaissance the concept of myth becomes translated into a concept of fiction. Voegelin might say, and probably does somewhere, that myth thus loses its anchor in reality. That is rather certainly a cause of that effect upon our signs that Voegelin speaks of, in relation to a general disorientation in the nineteenth century: the loss of order that results when our signs become "opaque." In this context we ought to remember how disturbingly haunted the nineteenth-century poet becomes. And the haunting presence is that of Plato. His presence is in Keats and Shelley most conspicuously. But he hovers about Coleridge and Wordsworth as well, though those two older poets I believe attempt to anchor their inherited Platonism in creation in such a way as to come to terms with creation as more than shadow. Again, metaphorically, it is as if they, and especially Coleridge, attempt to bring Aristotle to bear upon their Platonism. The point is borne out by Wordsworth's concern for the body as a desirable medium to visionary thought, as in his "Tintern Abbey" and in portions of the *Prelude*. It is in Coleridge's concern for the imagination, a faculty which seemed to him to have so lost its anchor in the interval from Chaucer to his own day as to require reminding us of its being anchored in the poet, in the created nature of man as understood by Aristotle and Saint Thomas. Man, created in the image of God, possesses a position mediate, a position to be understood if we understand the relation of what Coleridge calls the Primary and the Secondary Imagination. Coleridge sees Primary Imagination as anchored in that transcendent being which, in the Old Testament naming he uses, is the "I AM THAT I AM."

In that recognition by Coleridge lies an orientation lost to Keats and Shelley, those younger "Romantics." Keats, through an anguished desire, supposes the imagination somehow a faculty that promises rescue from the shadow world of nature, within which we are doomed. In that shadow world "but to think is to be filled with sorrow and leaden-eyed despair" he says. In this view the poet, by his imaginative actions, would lift himself out of shadow-strewn decay, that region which is for Keats the realm of nature. His great odes are ripe with the point. As for Shelley, so modern in this respect, the imagination is to be used by a fierce action of the will to take the country of the transcendent by violence through imagination's conquering nature. One thereby transforms creation itself into a shadow of the violent imagination. His "Hymn to Intellectual Beauty" is a text to my point, a poem that reveals Shelley as one of those modern gnostics about whom Voegelin so often talks. His "Ode to the West Wind" is another. Our twentieth-century romantics, and I have in mind here poets like A. E. Robinson and Wallace Stevens and Ezra Pound, are very much children of these younger nineteenth-century Romantics, Keats and Shelley. One finds the same anguished desire for a rescue of consciousness by the imagination in Robinson, and in him also the same melancholy failure. In Stevens, the arrogant gnosticism that is conspicuous in Shelley is tempered. Where Shelley is not content to rescue himself alone by the fierceness of his imagination but would force everyone else's rescue as well, Stevens is content to make a modern poem that suffices to his private moment of rescue; he is, in fact, rather indifferent to the rescue of any soul else.

Now Ezra Pound is a somewhat different case and one that will lead us back to Plato and to the *Phaedrus* and to Voegelin's attention to the importance of that Platonic work in our accommodation of Plato as poet. One encountering Ezra Pound as a presence in his poetry, a poetry he does not attempt to separate from the rest of Pound as Wallace Stevens so carefully does separate himself from his masque, may be even more struck by Pound's kinship to Shelley. In both one finds that fierce will to rescue all creation by the power of the imagination. In both is an insistence on the validity of the poet as philosopher and as theologian, the latter a term I use quite deliberately here in anticipation of a point Voegelin makes about the term's origin in Plato, as we shall see. In assuming and combining the several offices of the intellect in relation to the community of man, Pound and Shelley focus the offices through an assumed authority of the poet. It is the poet who is to be purveyor of order both social and political. There is a sufficient spectacle accompanying Pound's life that we may not at first see how closely parallel he is to Shelley. For one thing, we are closer to Pound in the long haul of history, with more traumatic disturbances to civilization apparent as the immediate context to Pound's own hour of our Western journey. We remember Shelley setting tracts adrift in bottles in the Irish Sea, an act that from our distance appears comic because inconsequential to subsequent events. His floating arguments came to no considerable effect in spectacle, as Pound's radio addresses from Mussolini's Rome appeared to do. And there were certainly consequences more dramatic to Pound. In addition to the broadcasts, Pound also wrote a treatise provocatively called *Jefferson and/or Mussolini*.

The large events of Western history between 1918 and 1945 are such that his arguments appear more shocking to us, though it is doubtful that his influence through his words proves any greater upon our history than Shelley's drifting treatises. It pleased us in our day to raise the Pound question to a high level of attention, ever since debated in the academy with a fierceness of partisanship that led, in one instance at least, to a distinguished American poet's challenging a distinguished editor to a duel over the awarding of the Bollingen Prize in Poetry to Pound for his *Pisan Cantos*. I introduce Pound's address to the poet and the poet's place in the Republic not because I think it decisive in events but in order to return to Plato's address. We may remember that Pound finds Plato alone of all Western philosophers worthy of his admiration. Aristotle for him, in *Guide to Culture* for instance, is a name to be spat out. I myself take Pound to be a gifted lyric poet, given to intuitive moments of brilliance, but not to any sustained moments such as would or might make him that necessary poet to serve the republic as he believed the times required. Sadly, he even more firmly believed himself suited to that special calling.

What I am suggesting—again metaphorically—is that, more intuitively than rationally, Pound senses a difference between Aristotle and Plato that makes Aristotle troubling to him. We all remember Plato's elevation of the philosopher-king—at least that is the coloring of his concern that impresses us. What Pound sees in Plato is a concern for the sign, for the true word, which is such that *philosopher* and *poet* are terms barely to be distinguished for Pound. Thus, the savior of the world for Pound must be the poet-king, and in Confucius he finds a suitable figure wedding a Platonic sense of the sign with a pragmatic, activist use of sign in ordering nature, particularly human nature in its social context. Of course Aristotle will not at last secure either poet or philosopher at the apex of active social order. But neither, as I shall argue, will Plato. Still, this is an argument we are not quite ready to make.

ii

Now it is somewhat reductive of me to make the suggestion that follows. But if we remember that I myself speak all along more as struggling poet than as mature philosopher, we may take the suggestion as only that of a poet. To do so allows us as philosophers to entertain the suggestion with a willing suspension of disbelief such as we could not allow if a philosopher were to put the suggestion as a proposition. What I wish to suggest is that Pound never sufficiently distinguishes the mimetic poet from what Plato calls, in the *Phaedrus*, the *philokalos*. The mimetic poet for Pound, let us say, is an activist presence in the social order, imitating in himself an order which in turn should be imitated in part by the several social integers of mankind in social community, "each in his own nature" as he says in Canto XIII. Insofar as he, Pound, has intimations of the poet as *philokalos*, I would find this glimmering recognition in him valid. But it is as if he cannot escape the vision of himself as poet, as seen through the post-Renaissance distortion of Plato's vision of the poet as *philokalos*. If we explore the point a bit further, through Voegelin's observations, we may see perhaps the causes of violence in a Shelley or a Pound whereby each would raise the poet from his seemingly lowly rank in Plato's hierarchy to the central position of man's social order.

Voegelin points us to the distinction we must make. In the *Phaedrus*, the soul at the apex of the order of souls is called "The philosopher, the *philokalos* [not the same as the *philosophos*], the music and erotic soul." Second in the hierarchy is "the law-observing king, the soul of the war leader and ruler." Beneath these, in order, are (3) the statesmen, economic administrators, traders; (4) the trainers of the body and physicians; (5) the seer and priest; and at last (6) the poets and other mimetic artists. We need pursue the hierarchy no further down the chain of souls for our purposes. Indeed, our point has most to do with the top two: the *philokalos* and *philosophos* in relation to the law-observing king. And our point is that, in the structure of souls in Plato's paradigm, there is a separateness implicit between the highest soul, the "philosopher-poet," and the second highest, the king. The separateness has precisely to do with the special calling of the philosopher-poet to a service toward that whole structure of souls which one understands as constituting social order, the community of souls in the Platonic paradigm of souls. I leave aside the inviting consideration that these Platonic souls in their several callings also lend themselves to a vision of the particular discrete soul as being itself constituted of the several callings. For, in the actions of the discrete soul in creation, in some points that soul is, for instance, "king," in some others "statesman," in some even "philosopher." Indeed a purpose of formal education ought to be to help the discrete soul discover its special calling or callings, its dominant gifts of being whereby it at once recognizes a kinship to other discrete souls and understands prudentially in itself the limits of its authority in respect to particular gifts. It is a failing of prudence in Pound, in the scholastic sense of the term *prudence*, that makes him a tragic figure in the context of political history.

The point, then, is that in Plato's hierarchy of souls we should notice the special relation of the philosopher-poet to the other members of the social structure. In the ranking, as Voegelin says, the *philosophos* and the *philokalos* are joined together. That is, the lover of wisdom and the lover of beauty are proconsul to the *polis* as it were. But not, let us add, in the activist manner demanded by Shelley or Pound, who would be proconsul. This is a point Socrates makes in many places in respect to his holding a private station, in the *Apology* and *Phaedo* for instance. Yet these souls are necessary presences to that body of the *polis* (as also to the unity of the discrete soul in my own suggestion that the soul is moved by several callings). Voegelin remarks, "We find this new figure the *philokalos* characterized, together with the *philosophos*, as a soul which is inspired by the Muses and by Eros. This *philokalos* is the new poet, truly possessed by the *mania*." Remember my own argument that these highest reaches of soul, seemingly placed at the apex of social structure by Plato's argument, are indeed in a sense separate from that structure, or tangent to it, in respect to any social activist dimension within that structure. We may then turn at last to a figure with whom I have been often concerned—a melding of the *philosophos* and the *philokalos*. This figure I speak of as the prophetic poet. And this soul's aspect of being possessed by the *mania* I would wish to speak of in relation to what Voegelin has to say about the fool in the last of his writings. For what he has to say of the fool's contribution to philosophy is rich indeed. As we turn to this exploration, we may carry with us as well the long history of the poet as fool, especially insofar as he too is seen as fool by his fellows, who tend incidentally to attach the same epithet to the philosopher.

iii

Let me here remark Voegelin's long devotion to Plato in relation to his own lifelong concern to come to terms with Christianity, a concern that comes toward a focus in his "Quod Deus dicitur." And I summon as aide a prophetic poet with whom I have dealt at some length, Flannery O'Connor. Miss O'Connor was much taken with Voegelin, reviewing the first three volumes of his

Order and History for her diocesan paper, calling attention to his importance to the Catholic mind. In a letter to a friend, she corrects a statement apparently made by the friend: "Voegelin, incidentally, is not a Catholic. He calls himself a 'Pre-Reformation Christian.'" She adds, "I don't know what that would be." I think from our reading of "Quod Deus dicitur" we may see something of what he means, and insofar as I understand the two of them—Eric Voegelin and Flannery O'Connor—they are rather closer than she may have thought at that moment. Actually, I think she does recognize a closeness more than she admits. In reviewing *Plato and Aristotle*, being allowed a very brief space, she singles out Voegelin's remark that for Plato (and these are Voegelin's words) "the philosopher is man in the anxiety of his fall from being; and philosophy is the ascent toward salvation for Everyman. . . . Plato's philosophy, therefore, is not a philosophy but the symbolic form in which a Dionysiac soul expresses its ascent to God." Having quoted this, she remarks that thus Voegelin "makes it clear that the leap in being toward the transcendent source of order is real in Plato but that it stems from the depth of the Dionysiac soul; the prefiguration of the Christian solution is prefiguration only." She adds, "Plato's enemies were the Sophists and Socrates' arguments against them are still today the classical arguments against the sophistic philosophy of existence which characterizes positivism and the age of enlightenment."

One familiar with Miss O'Connor knows that these Platonic arguments are implicit in her fiction and often explicit in her letters and talks, though they are arguments she finds more firmly anchored in Saint Thomas Aquinas than in Plato. That makes it doubly interesting to us that in his last work Voegelin himself chooses Saint Thomas as a point of departure as he attempts to focus his long quest into a view of the transcendent. The title of his final words to us is from Thomas. From Thomas's "Quod Deus dicitur," out of the *Summa*, we begin a meditation that leads us once more back to Voegelin's beloved Plato. Let us note, then, a relation between this last drama of mind and the passage from *Plato and Aristotle* that Miss O'Connor chooses to quote in her review out of the vast richness she might have quoted. The few words she chooses are a key to a piety required of both the *philosophos* and the *philokalos*, required of both the prophetic philosopher such as Voegelin and the prophetic poet such as Miss O'Connor. Both must, in such an age as ours, act out a recovery of being; both must submit to the perils of that activity of becoming an "Everyman" in an ascent toward salvation, in order to bear witness—each in a separate mode—to the necessity of that journey. If the modes differ (for that of fiction is not that of essaying upon being), in a real and common way separate from modal surfaces, both philosopher and poet attempt to recover that movement of soul toward God whose point of departure lies in an awakening of consciousness at the "depth of the Dionysiac soul." It is thus that each dramatizes a "prefiguring of the Christian solution." But in philosophy as in art, for Voegelin as for Miss O'Connor, that foreshadowing of the necessary journey must be a "prefiguration only."

Now the point at issue here is a delicate one, to be most carefully made. Otherwise we shall fail to appreciate the magnitude of either poet or philosopher. Let us go about it in this way: a question that haunts our reading of Voegelin is this—*Was* he a Christian? The analogous question, in relation to Miss O'Connor, is this—Is she the dedicated Christian she declares herself to be, given the strange fiction she writes? What poet and philosopher would say in response, I should think, is that a fundamental misunderstanding gives rise to both these questions—a misunderstanding on our part about the piety properly required of these discrete souls in relation to their particular gifts, those of the philosopher and those of the poet. One soul here is by its calling dominantly philosopher; the other dominantly poet. The inappropriate question was often asked Miss O'Connor, one of the recorded forms of it by an interviewer who wanted to know whether she was trying to prove the truth of Christianity through her stories. Was her concern the Christian message? Miss O'Connor responded instantly: "You never 'prove' anything with a story." In "Quod Deus dicitur," Voegelin makes the same point on behalf of the philosopher such as himself. Concerning the argument he has been pursuing he says: "The argument, of course, is not a 'proof' in the sense of logical demonstration, of an *apodeixis*, but only in sense of an *epideixis*, of a pointing to an area of reality which the constructor of the negative propositions has chosen to overlook or to ignore, or refuse to perceive."

Now as both he and Miss O'Connor are acutely aware, the "negative propositions" are dominant in the modernist mind, and both are very much about the enormous task of pointing to realities denied by that mind. Miss O'Connor, for instance, calls herself a "realist of distances." Voegelin, concerned with the same distances, increasingly concentrates on the point of departure for such visionary perspective in the consciousness itself as that consciousness engages symbols toward that larger visionary perspective. We know from long experience that a pragmatic, empiricist climate of thought narrows the vision to a concern for what lies under the microscope of the moment, but a pragmatic address is careless of fundamental beginnings and ultimate ends. The relation of the beginning point of consciousness to an ultimate perspective upon complex reality has no admissible reality in this limited vision. The address is to ideological uses through sophistic rhetoric, in the interest of converting minds to a faith in the narrow moment's focus. For such a faith is necessary to the siphoning of power to ideological uses. That is the end intended, however much confused by millenarian poetry of five-year plans. In short, the address is that of what Voegelin calls modern gnosticism, its end a dominance over being itself.

It is in the mode of their pointing that Flannery O'Connor and Eric Voegelin are at once discovered to share a common end and discovered as well to be unlike each other in consequence of the nature of their differing modes. By exploring these likenesses and unlikenesses, I think we shall make clear an important contribution Voegelin makes to any poet with ears to hear, as we may make clear as well a gift to any philosopher by a poet such as Flannery O'Connor. Fundamentally they share a recognition of the necessity, given our disoriented world, of acting out through their work a recovery of openness toward being. Thereby the soul may rediscover the possibility of an ascent from its Dionysiac depths. Put compactly, each undertakes a prophetic mission. But each as prophet is concerned with that limit of the prophetic office described by Saint Thomas: their mission is to recall us to known but forgotten things.

In their exercise of this prophetic service through the modes of poet on the one hand and philosopher on the other, we discover in each an appropriateness of Plato's terms *philosophos* and *philokalos*. What is at issue is a deepened love of being, arrived at through our understanding why existence is beautiful. And we begin to see in what sense Plato's characterizing of these two species of soul makes them separate from and in important ways transcendent of the other callings within the hierarchy of souls propounded in the *Phaedrus*. By such exploration, we better understand that part of our intellectual inheritance which I speak of as the post-Renaissance struggle with Platonism, a struggle that so largely affects not only our philosophy since Descartes and Bacon, but our literature since the Elizabethans as well. That struggle, Voegelin suggests, is from our mis-taking of Plato. The influence of this mis-taking on our poetry is perhaps not the highest concern at stake, though it is an important one to the academy's address to the humanities. That is, the concern is important to that peculiar office of mind we characterize as academic insofar as that mind is charged to recover its own openness to existence through letters.

Let us, then, turn to what Voegelin says of the fool, the academic mind itself a suitable enough transition perhaps. Specifically, let us begin with the "negative propositions" of the fool, a concern that orients Voegelin's final essay in a quest for the actions of mind in naming God. We emphasize in doing so Miss O'Connor's fictional treatment of the fool, which bears striking parallels, for she is very much aware of that modern sophistry which is but our version of the pre-Socratic position on those propositions. With a mischief appropriate to her fiction she locates the sophistry not in sophisticated minds for the most part but in semiliterate country characters, as if to remind us that one need not hold graduate degrees in Existentialism from the Sorbonne to arrive at negative propositions. Voegelin cites a statement of the propositions by Gorgias in the treatise *On Being*:

(1) Nothing exists;

(2) If anything exists, it is incomprehensible;

(3) If it is comprehensible, it is incommunicable.

I think I am required to make no long proof that these propositions are indeed the ground increasingly assumed in modernist thought since the Renaissance, a great deal of the poetic activity in that interval of Western history spent in attempting a recovery out of these assumptions. We need only recall Voegelin's impressive explorations of the struggle or to read Miss O'Connor's letters and talks to see how acutely aware each is of those propositions as predicating modern man's address to creation. What we are concerned with, in the light of these recognitions, is this question: How may the prophetic poet or prophetic philosopher best address himself to what is a seemingly overwhelming opposition to his attempt to recall us to an openness to being; how may he point toward aspects of reality overlooked or ignored or refused by modern sophistry?

One problem they face, and the first that must be dealt with, is that the very signs necessary to poet or philosopher are denied any but arbitrary signification, given the initial acceptance of Gorgias's negative propositions. Of course, there is an inescapable contradiction here: in order to accept the negative propositions one must first accept a positive value to the signs that formulate the negative propositions. Some of you will recognize an immediate pertinence to a current critical fad thus built shakily on these propositions, the movement called Deconstruction, whose point of departure is the proposition that not only God is dead, but also the author of any text and consequently any text itself—the only life an exercise of wit upon the dead text by the Deconstructionist.

For the Voegelinian philosopher it may appear that what is required is a reliving of the history of the mind in such a manner that mind may be recovered beyond history. This requires an entering into mind at an ancient level, as it were, a growing with it, a failing with it, always coming closer and closer perhaps to this present moment of the philosopher's own mind. And for Voegelin this is a fundamental concern in *Order and History*. The danger of the attempt is that the particular recovering mind may lose itself in the act of reliving, the act of recapitulating the history of mind toward transcending history. In that reliving, the fullness of the philosopher's experience of the reality of mind itself is at risk. That means that the recovering mind—the mind acting out an ascent toward God out of its ancient Dionysiac depths in Voegelin's characterization of it—has not the luxury of standing aside from any danger to itself. It may not rest in an acceptance through faith of a particular end for its actions as an inevitable end. That would be to presume its own rescue as already determined. That would be to presume conclusion before setting out, mind's private version of a "five-year plan." Certainly, insofar as that mind wishes to become fully an Everyman to bear full witness, as opposed to merely posing as a symbolic figure for Mind as Everyman, and thereby do its pointing toward an openness to being through an inadequate sort of allegory, it cannot at the same time represent itself as having arrived at visionary certainty. Its authority must be that of the quest, not of the conclusion. This, indeed, is the crux out of which rises our inappropriate question, "Was Eric Voegelin a Christian?" In an analogous way, this is also the crux of our problem with that prophetic poet Flannery O'Connor. The poet is the maker of a thing (the story) that reflects the Dionysiac depths which may open us more largely upon being, given sufficient art and gift in the poet. Thus the question inappropriate to such a poet: What is Miss O'Connor proving by her story?

In Voegelin's own long acting out of man's fall from openness, his struggle to recover the soul's being, he comes at the end to point us to the complexity of the discrete soul, wherein the tensional pulls toward a fullness of being are given symbolic representation by the negative and the positive propositions. Here, too, is the center vital to the poet in his separate mode of making. For both, let me suggest, are engaging what Saint Thomas describes as the fundamental nature of art, equally applicable to philosophy and to poetry. Each is imitating not simply the nature of his own discrete soul in its act of becoming, since that would yield only narcissistic art, witnessing in a limited way the artist's lonely soul in its realization of its gifts of discrete potentiality. As prophetic poet, each is rather imitating actions possible or probable to souls struggling within the In-Between toward a fullness of discrete being. The soul beholding such art, responding to its own nature from its encounter with such an art, must itself come to a conclusion of its activated quest by its own volition.

For both poet and philosopher—if they are O'Connor and Voegelin—there is the necessity of recognizing not only the fundamental reality to the soul of positive propositions, which taken alone may tempt one to "prove" something with story or argument, but the negative propositions as well. In the tensional suspensions of soul between and among the pulls upon it, the soul becomes more fully responsive not only to the complexity of the In-Between beyond itself but to the complexity of its own reality. Voegelin suggests that to ignore the negative propositions by addressing only the positive as if they were logically demonstrable (thereby implying the negative as nonexistent) is to ignore a part of reality no less than do those modernist minds who deny or ignore the positive. Concomitantly, for the poet to refuse the negative propositions—even by simply satirizing the negative—would mean that he inclines to embrace an attempt fatal to art, trying to "prove" something by his poem or story. That would be a violation of art comparable to the philosopher's attempt to prove positive propositions apodictically.

iv

We know that both Flannery O'Connor and Eric Voegelin recognize that ours is a "pre-Socratic" world in respect to its general embrace of the negative proposition. As Voegelin turns to Plato through his action of mind, Miss O'Connor turns to Saint Thomas Aquinas. Let us observe that the very form of the *Summa Theologia* sets the tensions of positive and negative propositions. When we observe as well that Thomas nevertheless emphatically asserts the positive over the negative, that does not negate the point of similarity. But Thomas is not acting out the philosophical mind in the same way that Voegelin or Plato does. However, should we gain a more distant perspective upon Saint Thomas, I think we might well say that the *Summa* is itself such an acting out. What I mean is this: in reading Thomas we tend to overlook the mystical dimension in him, particularly insofar as we concentrate closely upon the text of the *Summa*, a text as authoritative as he can make it in respect to logical proofs. But I would contend that Thomas, no less than Saint Augustine, is mystically inclined, is a visionary. He is moved by a tensional relation between the *ratio* and the *intellectus*, the head and the heart. The task he is set upon in the *Summa* is as pure a pursuit through the *ratio* as mind can manage. But it is a task undertaken to justify the heart, the *intellectus*. In this respect, he stands to Saint Augustine as Aristotle to Plato, a point, incidentally, which I am not sure was sufficiently appreciated by Voegelin until his final assay.

But this aside on Thomas does not bear directly upon our present concern. Rather, our concern is with the active imitation by the soul of the philosopher-poet of its possible or probable journey. What Voegelin reveals to us on the point, to the benefit of the poet, is a necessary openness to the complexity of the soul itself insofar as the poet or philosopher makes an attempt, as both *philosophos* and *philokalos*, to recover to us an openness to being. If the poet were to express our concern, in respect to his office as poet, he might well borrow a term from John Keats, a term notorious to the literary scholar but one pursued often in very shallow ways by those who celebrate the poet. Keats's term is *negative capability*. He remarks, in this connection, that when he reads the *Iliad* (a work Miss O'Connor finds Voegelin engaging with "masterful analysis"), he is with Achilles shouting in the trenches. He would similarly enter into the sparrow and peck about the gravel. If one were to approach the concern from another perspective, he might summon T. S. Eliot's own concern for a failure in our poetry since the Renaissance; Eliot speaks of the "dissociation of sensibility," a separation of thought and feeling, the grounds of which separation were more profound than he recognized when he made the phrase a popular critical cliché. That dissociation one might explore in Eliot himself, seeing his discoveries of the depths of the problem in the *Four Quartets*. And one might thus discover something about Voegelin's partiality to those poems, in which he recognizes kindred concerns. Or one might turn to Coleridge's remark that a reader, experiencing such an imitation of the actions of the soul as a poem, should assume a "willing suspension of disbelief." The concern in all these approaches is for openness of the soul to being, through which alone it may respond toward its own fulfillment through the larger complexities of being.

It is only after this necessary preparation that we may come at last directly to the text announced at the outset, the question of the fool's role for that prophetic poet in whom we find a mutuality of *philokalos* and *philosophos*. The term *fool*, Voegelin remarks, is a translation of the Hebrew *nabal*, in its Latin form *insipiens*—the English word an unfortunate translation since the origin of *fool* is *follis*, a bellows or wind-bag, connotations of which still cling to the concept in the English text. Thus *Dixit insipiens in corde suo: Non est Deus* becomes "The fool hath said in his heart, There is no God." As we saw from the full text, King David, whose line of descent will intersect the transcendent at Bethlehem, finds that there is "none that doeth good" in consequence of this rank seed sprouting in the heart.

In order that we might somewhat modify the unfortunate connotations of *fool*, and come closer to the intentions of the biblical text and to Voegelin's arguments from it, may I suggest that we say it this way: the *reckless*, the *unreckoning*, says in his heart there is no God. What is at issue is the sin of presumption whereby one overlooks or ignores or denies a dimension of reality spoken to through positive propositions, a sin in that it is the step taken in an alienation not only from God but from all being. In that movement, the reckless (the fool) would become the center from which any being is denied other than itself.[1] Unrestrained, in its full recklessness, it is that satanic denial of being that John Milton dramatizes in *Paradise Lost* in words prophetic of the modern gnostic mind which Voegelin explores in so much of his work:

> The mind is its own place, and in itself
> Can make a heaven of hell, a hell of heaven.

This is the nadir in that fall from being that gives rise to anxiety, to *angst*. Voegelin remarks that this is the beginning point for the philosopher Plato. I

---

1. On this discussion of the *fool* in its philosophical context, one should bring Josef Pieper's theological discussion of *acedia* to bear. See his *On Hope* (San Francisco: Ignatius Press, 1986), 54ff and 65ff.

mention Milton here as well to remind us of the somewhat innocent, younger Eliot, who finds the beginning of our dissociation of sensibility occurring at about the time of Milton. The truth is that Milton recognizes and dramatizes the condition of the dissociation in his great poem and is not the cause of it, as readers of Eliot have sometimes taken Eliot's remark to mean.

Voegelin calls attention to the locus of this dissertation. It is the soul, but not the soul at the time of Plato or of Milton or of T. S. Eliot. It is a point of a consciousness in history. And the crucial effect of dissociation upon any soul at any time is the inadequacy of its signs, its words through which it attempts to move in relation to being. Thus of the word in the reckless heart, Voegelin says, "The deformative confusion in the 'heart' of the insipiens . . . is the experiential source which brings the problem of the non-thingly structure of divine symbols to attention. It is *cor suum* in man which is the experiential place of a hypostatising position or negation of divinity." But it would be reckless of one supposing himself not the fool to deny the reality of this doubt as possible in and through the heart. That is, it would be reckless to dismiss the fool, lest a new fool at last attempt to lead the old fool from his foolishness by such dismissal. That makes poet or philosopher obsessively committed to proving the unprovable. The battle on between Creationists and Evolutionists is a parable of the point.

Voegelin reminds us, then, that "the existence of God can become doubtful because, without a doubt, the fool exists." And he adds, "As a potentiality [denial] is present in every man, including the believer; and in certain historical situations its actualization can become a massive social force." This is to say that it became so at Athens, before and after the death of Socrates; it is so in our day, following the triumph of nominalism whereby divine symbols have lost for us their complex resonance in our attempt, out of our finitude, to approach the non-thingly nature of the divine. Since the fool, even as the poor, is not only with us always but is in the very ground of our soul's being, he may not be lightly dismissed. To emphasize the importance of this point, let me quote once more from "Quod Deus dicitur":

> The fool of the Psalm is certainly not a man wanting in intellectual acumen or worldly judgment. . . . In Psalm 13 (14), the *nabel* signifies the mass phenomenon of men who do evil rather than good because they do not 'seek after God' and his justice. . . . In these Israelite contexts [the psalms, in Jeremiah and Isaiah] the contempt, the *nebala*, does not necessarily denote so differentiated a phenomenon as dogmatic atheism, but rather a state of spiritual dullness that will permit the indulgence of greed, sex, and power without fear of divine judgment. . . . The fool stands against the revealed God, he does not stand against a *fides quaerens intellectum* [such as Anselm]. This further component . . . must be sought rather in the philosophers' tradition that has entered Christian theology. It is Plato who describes the phenom-

enon of existential foolishness, as well as the challenge it presents to the noetic quest, for the case of Sophistic folly.

Voegelin turns to Plato's *Laws* and *Republic*, in which are advanced the argument that the reckless, the fool, suffers a disease of the soul. For the "negative propositions are the syndrome of a disease that affects man's humanity and destroys the order of society." But what we may not ignore is that, though such propositions reflect a deformation of the heart, they nevertheless as such bear a truth. It is a truth beyond even the nominalist distortions of the very signs used, and the deformed signs themselves point to a truth; they bear witness to a truth, though false in themselves. A distinction is therefore necessary between falsehood in words and falsehood in the soul. In Plato's words, "the ignorance within the soul" is "truly the falsehood" that is borne in the words; the words themselves are "the after-rising image" of that falsehood. And so the words are not an unmixed falsehood; they bear true witness in respect to that diseased soul; the diseased soul utters false words that truly reflect its disease. We underline the point by saying that those utterances bear true witness: that is, they testify to the falseness of the soul that gives utterance to them. And so, says Voegelin out of this argument by Plato, that old philosopher "created a neologism of world-historic consequences," namely *theology*. For as he says in the *Republic*, negative propositions are "types of theology." The positive propositions are also types of theology, but they are true in that the words both reflect true souls and are present to us as words true in themselves. This enticing country for our exploration has its geography laid out in Étienne Gilson's *Philosophy and Linguistics*, we note in passing.

We have come to the profound articulation by Voegelin of that state of the soul which it is the prophetic poet's obligation to point us toward, and as we move ourselves toward a conclusion, I would ask that we keep in mind (since we may not suitably introduce and explicate at length the relevant evidence from our prophetic poet) a dramatic revelation of the soul caught up in this struggle. I have in mind Flannery O'Connor's protagonist in *Wise Blood*, Haze Motes. One might remember as well Miss O'Connor's marvelous humor that rises out of her use of clichés, within which lie marvelous complexities of words in relation to reality, in relation to the truth of things visible and invisible. To notice those words in relation to the agents of those words will be to see true words revealing to us false souls. What she must do, as prophetic poet, as an artist committed to the good of the thing she makes, if she is to render justice to the complexity of being, is to recover through the presence of fictional tensions both theologies within the one soul—within her protagonist, Haze Motes. That marks her highest tribute to the complexity of being, in celebration of which through art there is no necessity of "proving" anything.

In the following remarks by Voegelin, he is concerned to make clear the necessity of openness within the philosopher such as he was. But in those words we should recognize the close kinship of the two, our philosopher and our poet. In her letters, having already reviewed the *World of the Polis*, she remarks to her correspondent that in the volume Voegelin "has some masterful analysis of the Iliad & of Aeschylus but other huge hunks are dull or over my head." Again to the same correspondent: "Parts of [*World of the Polis*] were very exciting but for the most part you need to be a Greek scholar to read it." Could we pursue her here, we would undoubtedly find that she absorbs more of the argument than she says. Perhaps her demurral is in part a strategy in relation to the correspondent, in whose spiritual estate she is deeply interested, so that she may guide that correspondent in directions that may be more fruitful to an agitated soul than the philosopher's mode. What I am emphasizing is that kinship between the philosopher Voegelin and the poet Flannery O'Connor which makes of them both prophetic poets, though differing in mode. Both are concerned with the timeless contention of the two theologies within each soul, the struggle within the soul between being the fool and being wise.

Here, then, the passage from Voegelin, at the latest, and perhaps highest, moment of his long journeying:

> Both types [negative and positive] are theologies, because they both express a human response to the divine appeal; they both are, in Plato's language, the verbal mimesis respectively of man's existence in truth or falsehood. Not the existence of God is at stake, but the true order of existence in man; . . . the propositions, positive and negative, have no autonomous truth. . . . Hence the verbal mimesis of the positive type, as it has no truth of its own, can be no more than a first line of defense or persuasion in a social confrontation with the verbal mimesis of the negative type. Even more, the positive propositions derive an essential part of their meaning from their character as a defense against the negative propositions. As a consequence, the two types of theology together represent the verbal mimesis of the human tension between the potentialities of response or non-response to divine presence in personal, social, and historical existence. If the fool's part in the positive propositions is forgotten, there is always the danger of derailing into the foolishness of believing the truth of these propositions to be ultimate. But the presumption of ultimacy would make them indeed as empty of the experiential truth in the background as the fools pretend to be.

On the conclusion, Miss O'Connor might well point to the argument she would find in Saint Thomas, which says that our words, necessary to our pursuit of being, nevertheless are inadequate to the comprehension of truth in a literal sense of comprehension. To understand any proposition as ultimate, rather than as directing attention toward the ultimate, is the distortion of the reckless mind.

It remains to me only to pay my deepest respect to Voegelin for the labor toward a fullness of being he undertook for me and for all of us in the mode of the lover of the truth of reality. Most of us, once we discover ourselves possessed of the gift of mind, incline to lament that we were not born ancient in that gift, at the same time wishing to be possessed as well of eternal youth. George Bernard Shaw remarks the one inclination when he says how unfortunate it is that youth is wasted on the young. Descartes laments the other in his *Discourse*: "Since we have all been children before being men, and since it has for long fallen to us to be governed by our appetites and our teachers . . . it is almost impossible that our judgments should be so excellent or solid as they should have been had we had complete use of our reason since birth, and had been guided by its means alone." Meanwhile, a mind like Voegelin's undertakes the labor of recovering a mode of philosophy, quite consciously and deliberately on our behalf no less than on his own, increasingly recognizing his calling to be that of that soul at the apex of Plato's hierarchy of souls whom I have called the prophetic poet. In that labor he recognized the necessity of removing the rubble of thought that we so blithely speak of as history, thus to point to a similar necessity for each of us if we are to recover our potential soul toward a fullness of being.

In this labor he is concerned to discover to us the initial movement of consciousness at a point in the being of our soul that is therefore an initial movement of the soul. It is the concern to bear witness to an action whose articulation would begin, "in the beginning was," the point from which the discrete soul moves toward God or away from God. It is the genesis of soul discovered within our consciousness itself, in which respect as philosopher he is closer in mode to Plato, but also to Saint Augustine. In this final commentary concerning our struggle to say the name of God, he takes recourse to Saint Anselm and Saint Augustine, two "pre-Reformation Christians" for whom he has an affinity, attempting to reveal a movement of soul toward God without using theological terms. What he says concerning Saint Anselm, for instance, in exploring the movement of soul witnessed in Saint Anselm's prayer, might be acceptably glossed under the rubric of illuminating grace, though that might be too easy a bypassing of the action of entering into and reliving Anselm's movement of soul. He recognizes, in reading Anselm,

the living desire of the soul to move toward the divine light. The divine light lets the light of its perfection fall into the soul; the illumination of the soul arouses the awareness of man's existence as a state of imperfection, and this awareness provokes the human movement in response to the divine appeal. . . . Anselm's Prayer is a *meditatio de ratione fidei* as he formulates the nature of the quest in the first title of the

Monologion. The praying quest responds to the appeal of reason in the *fides*; the *Proslogion* is the *fides* in action, in pursuit of its own reason. St. Anselm . . . clearly understood the cognitive structure as internal to the Metaxy, the in-between of the soul in the Platonic sense.

It is the "living desire of the soul to move toward the divine light" that is celebrated in Anselm. And that is what Voegelin celebrates as well.

To discover, or rediscover, the reality—the actual existence of this non-thingly thing: this desire prompts Voegelin's quest, and his pursuit is saintly, though its mode may appear historical or philosophical as those terms are decayed from high meaning for us. I think Voegelin would approve of my saying that T. S. Eliot has summarized his own message to us in words that support us in the quest Voegelin, too, invites us upon. In the final lines of what is in reality his final poem, "Little Gidding," Eliot says:

> We shall not cease from exploration
> And the end of all our exploring
> Will be to arrive where we started
> And know the place for the first time.

Nor do I think Eric Voegelin would set aside my epithet for him as prophetic poet, understanding the meaning I intend as derived from Saint Thomas Aquinas and as embraced by Flannery O'Connor. For the prophetic poet does not predict. As we have emphasized, he recalls us to known but forgotten things. He returns us to the complex ground within which the soul struggles joyfully in its suspension among tensional poles, restoring us from negative deconstructions of the soul and positive presumptions by the soul through our recognitions of that mystery of existence which Voegelin speaks of as the In-Between.

Eric Voegelin as Prophetic Philosopher
Afterthoughts

I. On the Poet's Openness to Being

The poet, committed to the uses of prudence in his address to art, most properly discovers the wisdom of Aristotle's distinction between history and art, recognizing the importance of the *possible* or *probable* as distinct from the *actual*. He will as well, I believe, add to this recognition that definition of his responsibility as artist which Saint Thomas Aquinas makes: the artist's responsibility is to the good of the thing he makes. This does not mean that he necessarily comes to this recognition *through* Saint Thomas; he will do so as Thomas himself did: through a lively recognition of art's diversity from nature and of his peculiar responsibility to art in distinction from his responsibility to nature. He does so, nevertheless, through a further recognition that he is not the primary cause of the thing he makes, though tempted to a contrary conclusion. His prudence reveals to him a reality upon which he must depend as artist in projecting the possible or probable dimensions of an imagined history, conspicuously illustrated in the imagined history of fictional minds in a drama of signs. He must come, then, to the recognition that art is an imitation, not of nature in the large inclusiveness of the term *nature*, but rather that his actions as artist are an imitation of the actions of nature, a distinction rationalized by Saint Thomas out of the truth of the matter—with which truth the artist must contend, whether or not guided by Saint Thomas or Aristotle.

We are concerned here with a "mimesis" considerably more complex than that sense of mimetic art usually encountered in literary or art criticism. That criticism has lately foregone the discipline of formal philosophy in the interest of a limited defense of the particular critical position, and so it has increasingly failed to serve the artist well. That limited defense may of course take a point of departure in an established philosopher, whose words support the critical position, but most usually it is but an initiating support rather than a conviction of the truth of things discovered through the philosopher upon whom the critic purports to depend. That is why, conspicuously in the academy, we have such a multitude of *experts in* rather than *disciples of*. Such an approach may find itself comfortable enough with Hegel or Kant or Wittgenstein, at different times but in an occasional relation to the particular philosopher.

What Voegelin offers the critic, no less than the poet, is an address to primary concerns in the interest of truth, not as an occasion for verbalizing only. One might take as a rubric describing his concern words from Saint Thomas: "The purpose of the study of philosophy is not to learn what others have thought, but to learn how the truth of things stands." Thus critic or poet or philosopher labors to become a disciple of truth, not an expert in what has been said or what might be said of truth. Now the truth of things in relation to the mind and to the nature of the mind was surely Voegelin's devotion through a long career of asking fundamental questions of philosophers and poets and critics, measuring their answers against his very acute sense of his own experience of the reality of his experience of things. What he practiced with diligence was an openness to being; what he discovered in that diligent practice was the complexity of our experience of being, within the tensional suspensions of mind between its recognitions of its own being and its pull toward that complex being which is neither itself (the mind) nor caused by itself. In exploring this country of the soul suspended in history, he more and more discovers not only the metaxy of which the soul is part but what one must call an inner metaxy of the soul itself, the complexity of the soul's discrete being. To that concern he devoted the last days of his life, in evidence of which he leaves us "Quod Deus dicitur."

In respect to the necessary openness to being in pursuit of the complexity of the world, through which the complexity of the soul itself is more and more revealed, the poet would bear dramatic witness. But there are complications, perhaps initially more crucial to the philosopher or theologian than to the poet since theirs is from the outset a concern for the perfection of the soul. Only initially, I say, meaning thereby to suggest that the poet is more likely to be captivated by an innocent awe he would celebrate with art. Perhaps that is why art seems so hazardous to the poet. It does seem usual, at least, that the poet tends to develop from lyrical outburst toward larger drama, the middle-aged lyric poet rather an unusual presence in the history of letters. (In an analogous way, Greek tragedy grows out of hymns to Dionysus.) What I am saying is that, for philosopher or theologian, there can be no perpetual neutrality within the tensional poles as there is initially for the poet, whose delight is an imitation of the possible or probable drama of the soul, that being the proper action of his art. If there is a truth about how things stand, there is also a falsehood, which the poet must dramatically imitate, as opposed to the philosopher's or theologian's reckoning with those opposites to truth. The philosopher must at last conclude that the false is false, feeding upon the true. In this respect, the commitment of the philosopher to truth differs from that of the poet. The poet, concerned for the good of the thing he *makes*, is in a sense committed to a certain good even in the false or evil. Thus there is a recognizable good in such a figure as Iago or Mephistopheles, properly celebrated as a good in the realm of art, insofar as such made creatures echo a facet of the complexity of being through the art of the possible or probable. In this point lies no doubt a particular temptation to the poet, who may easily mistake his authority in making a good of a bad as a godlike power, from which position he may in the end mistake himself for God. James Joyce has made effective imitation of such a possible consequence in his *Portrait of the Artist as a Young Man*.

It is nevertheless true that the poet, no less than the philosopher, is a part of the arena of the In-Between, a circumstance complicating the problem of his prudential balance within the arena of being. He does not escape at last truth or good, or the false or evil, by art, though many poets have supposed it possible to do so through their art. Especially since the nineteenth century, a mystique of the imagination as a substitute for the Holy Ghost has come into prominence, a mystique out of which Joyce derives his possible portrait, Stephen Dedalus. The imagination, through an assumption of absolute power with sign, builds a world—or attempts to build a world—constituted of sign divorced from reality. Now this is very near the center of Voegelin's concern in his pursuit of what may be said of God, and his last essay most particularly calls our attention to the problem of the sign, the word, and its relation both to the question of how the truth of things stands and to the health of the soul in its quest for that truth through the sign. His center of concern and the poet's must at last be the same.

II. On the Limits of Logic to the Visionary

Voegelin, in advancing the two theologies as explored by Plato in the *Republic* and *Laws*, arrives at a position very like that necessary to the poet in his address to being through words. The dangers Voegelin cautions against are precisely those that threaten the poet, who is ever tempted to the exhilarating conclusion that through words he has somehow managed to capture being, to comprehend being in a literal sense of comprehend. In the circumstances of its reality, its being within a complex that stretches to the edge of mystery, the soul finds its most crucial circumstance the In-Between-ness that is also within itself, about which we talk when we pose the "fool" who says in his heart there is no God against the wise man who affirms God. Voegelin's position, which he derives from Plato primarily—though he brings Saint Augustine and Saint Anselm and Saint Thomas Aquinas to the support of the position in his final essay—describes the state of the soul this side beatitude, this side its transcendence. The reality of its being is its tensional existence, whose poles are established within the soul itself.

Flannery O'Connor remarks that one never proves anything with a story, objecting to those who would see her fiction as either a philosophical or a theological argument attempting to prove the existence of God. But she nevertheless shares the position Voegelin holds as philosopher, in that both engage a concern beyond the limits of logic. The positive argument one poses against the negative argument, as Voegelin says, is of course no proof "in the sense of a logical demonstration . . . , but only in the sense . . . of a pointing to an area of reality." To miss this distinction is to miss the truth about words and their relation to reality by the presumption that words comprehend reality. It is a position most tempting to the soul in its first unfolding toward its cause, as in the position developed by the old testament fool or the Sophists preceding Plato with whom Plato contends or—much closer home—the young artist Stephen Dedalus, who presumes the world he makes of words obviates reality, in effect casts creation into an outer darkness in relation to his own made world of words.

What Voegelin offers the poet, at last, is a reminder of the intellectual and spiritual deportment toward reality which, were he to put it directly in Christian terms, would be characterized by prudence, a condition of heart and mind through which one is heartily mindful of man's finitude, of his incompleteness. It is the position of our first awakening, as it were, which Voegelin finds Saint Anselm declaring in his prayer. Through this awakening the soul experiences itself in relation to an illumination of itself whose light is not essentially of itself but a gift; Voegelin speaks of the consequence as a "living desire of the soul to move toward the divine light." The "illumination of the soul arouses the awareness of man's existence," he says, "as a state of imperfection, and this awareness provokes the human movement in response to the divine appeal." If I were to speak of this moment of the soul's awakening to itself in my own way, I would take recourse to such a term as *grace* and speak of that free gift to the soul which Saint Thomas would call "illuminating grace."

III. On Myth and Countermyth

Voegelin remarks, "If there were no symbol of faith already in historical existence there would be no question. The article of faith is part of the procedure of noetic questioning regarding its meaning. The 'question of God' cannot be made intelligible unless the question of God is part of the reality to be explored." This is to say two things: first, that the question is a precondition of historical consciousness, bequeathed to consciousness necessarily by history; and second, that at the level of understanding, independent of history, a conclusion such as "God does not exist" is one following from a conclusion that "God does exist." The negation depends from affirmation, as evil from good. The latter point is of importance in relation to Voegelin's analysis of Plato's response to the pre-Socratic position. Negative propositions dominate as Plato comes to oppose the Sophists. But that pre-Socratic position is a consequence of intellectual deconstructions of precedent positive propositions, propositions imaginatively propounded in the myths and celebrated by the poets. Without this recognition, one might mistake the pre-Socratic negative position as the point of departure. A suitable locus for explication of this point is Aeschylus, in whom both poet and philosopher contend, as in the trilogy dealing with the house of Atreus. When Voegelin remarks this concern in "Quod Deus dicitur," he says that the Sophist's position "had to be couched in the form of a counter-myth to the symbolization of divine order in reality by the cosmogonic myth of the Hesiodian type. The form actually assumed by the argument apparently was a cosmogony in which the gods of myth are replaced by the elements in the material sense as the 'oldest' creative reality." My point is that the gods of myth are precedent, upon them depending both the countermyth of elemental reality of the Hesiodian type and the counter-countermyth of the Sophists. These vestigial remainders of a myth engaging an older myth have been very much with us these past two or three centuries, of course—since the Enlightenment. Voegelin reminds us that in our engagement of them through history we are well advised not to become entrapped at the level of history, since that entraps us in the illusional address typical of a Toynbee or a Spengler. History as ferris wheel rises with the Renaissance to an insistent presence, out of Vico, affecting even the poet (*vide* James Joyce). But Voegelin warns us: we deal with questions neither ancient nor modern. "The argument sounds quite modern in its recourse to the reality of the psyche, and of its experiences, against constructions which express the loss of reality and the contraction of the self—though the modern constructors do not have to deform a Hesiodian myth for their purpose but must replace the divine ground of Being by an item from the world-immanent hierarchy of being as the ultimate 'ground' of reality." He says in a preceding sentence: "In a genetic construction of Being, the elements cannot function as the 'oldest' reality; only the divine Psyche, as experienced by the human psyche, can be 'oldest' in the sense of self-movement in which all ordered movement in the world originates." (This is the rock genetic Darwinism currently founders on.) As we consider patterns in history, then, we must be cautious in recognizing that such argument is "neither modern nor ancient; it rather is the argument that will recur whenever the quest of divine reality has to be resumed in a situation in which the 'rationalization' of contracted existence, the existence of the fool, has become a mass phenomenon." Much earlier, Flannery O'Connor, in reviewing *Israel and Revelation*, calls attention to the importance of this message of Voegelin's as central to his exploration of order in history; summarizing the point she says, "In the Hellenic world man was seeking God, in the Hebrew world God was seeking man. Real history begins when man accepts the God Who is, Who seeks him." She notes that for Voegelin history is "a journey away from civilizations by a people which has taken the 'leap in being', and has accepted existence under God." It is in this respect that Voegelin's work is for her an "advance over Toynbee."

IV. On the Sign's Anchor in Mind and in Reality

On the problem of the sign's anchor of mind in reality, Voegelin reminds us that "the world of symbols compactly symbolizing reality at any given historical point has to submit to the pressure of noetic analysis." But further, "The hypostatisation of the reflective symbols leads to the deformative construction of the process of thought into the finished thought of a System of conceptual science." Not only are we constantly testing inherited signs analytically, but any reformation of symbols in consequence of analysis erodes, in some degree, the intimate relation of thought to its new sign. This is the crucial region of thought's attempt to touch reality, but our characteristic mode of the *ratio* in this attempt nevertheless requires the always-decaying symbol. Such is the process that moves Plato, Aristotle, Thomas, Descartes, Kant, Hegel, and so on. This is the country shared by any willing mind. The problem for the philosopher (and for any active mind for that matter) is to express a reality with signs that are doomed to be tainted by a seeming *thingness* in the sign itself. The sign, thus, has a seeming reality which on the one hand is not thought and on the other is not a reality of thingness per se. (Concerning this rugged country, Gilson's *Philosophy and Linguistics* is cogent, especially in his analysis of the distinction between thought and word.) The problem is especially exacerbated when the signified, toward which thought would point by symbol, is a being beyond thingness. To attempt to say a true "thing" about God or about beatitude is to become at once engaged by the "pressure of neotic analysis" upon the symbol—

beatitude, for instance—and by an insufficiency in the reconstituted reflective symbol. Consider the following attempts to provide reflective symbol toward a satisfactory finite conception of the "state of the blessed": Saint Thomas would argue it "the ultimate goal of human life," adding, "We move toward this goal, beatitude, and come nigh to it by actions springing from the virtues and particularly from the gifts of the Holy Ghost." Compare these lines from a current country gospel song: "Today we call it Heaven, / But tomorrow we'll call it home." Which, one might ask, moves us nearer the ineffable estate of reality we call beatitude by its language and through its language? Which bears a presence of the *intellectus* more conspicuously?

V. On the Philosophers' Common Ground

On Leibniz's solution to a pursuit of a grounding in reality, Voegelin says, "The quest of the sufficient reason culminates in the two questions: (a) Why is there something rather than nothing, and, (b) Why are the things as they are? On this level of symbolization Leibniz arrives at the formulations closely resembling those of Thomas. The experience of contingent reality implies a non-contingent reason for what is experienced as contingent." Thus reason is a "place" as it were which is "non-contingent" to reality. But so stated, without recourse to the gift of grace in our being, reason is necessarily contingent to reality. That is why we encounter such complex problems as that of saying (in Voegelin's words) that the "noetic search for the structure of reality that includes divinity is itself an event within the reality we are questioning." The logical difficulty of a divinity *included* in reality is seen quite differently under the aspect of grace, as when we say that the quest for the structure of reality, necessarily within the reality including us (*within* the discrete person, *this* soul), must inevitably encounter a presence not included by reality, as reality is available to the finite soul; it is indeed a presence of Reality which is larger than, and in some mystery beyond, finite knowing, is itself inclusive of reality. The encounter spoken of as an event made possible through grace is open to less difficulty than if spoken of as made possible through finite recognition of the event alone. Voegelin's intellectual antagonist, not accepting the reality of grace beyond demonstration, will not allow the point as valid. And it is in anticipation of this reluctance, I believe, that he develops this line out of Leibniz, nevertheless pointing out affinities in the "symbolization" in Leibniz and in Saint

Thomas. His acknowledgment of the dependence of a noncontingent reason upon a "being" separate from the reason's contingency upon reality appears in the remark following: "The ego doubts and desires," a movement out of Cartesian thought. Thus "an ego that doubts and desires to go beyond itself is not the creator and maintainer of its doubting existence, and that cause is the 'God' who appears in the analyses of [Descartes's] *Third Meditation* and the *Principles*. There is no doubting contingency without the tension toward the necessity which makes the doubt evident as such." And that necessity must be, therefore, noncontingent to the ego or reason or whatever symbolization one gives the noetic quester. It is in this very ground of similarity between Descartes and Leibniz and Thomas that one might wish the more careful distinguishing of modes and grounds of the neotic quest. For it is in respect to the *initiating* "doubts and desires" that these separate philosophers most resemble each other and not in their characterizations of the causes and ends of those doubts and desires.

VI. On Deconstruction

Since the invention of movable type, the precision of voice in the printed sign—the suggestions of gesture and tone accompanying voice—has been increasingly a challenge to the poet. The critic has enlarged his office largely in this ambiguous ground, appropriating to himself increasingly an authority whose culmination has been the establishment of ambiguity in the sign as the dominant mystery of sign, separate from the ambiguity of being itself. Within the ambiguity the critic may hope to establish a supreme reign. The consequence has been, most recently, an absolute decree of the infinity of the text itself, that first article of faith held by the Deconstructionist, the critic as poet. The necessary premise of this latest gnostic act of faith is the dissociation of the text from any mind that is not the present mind of the new artist, the critic as poet. In addition, the text is dissociated from any signified reality. In that double operation, the text may then be declared infinite.

Now the critic as poet has as his especial act, in consequence of the double dissociation, a spontaneous performance of acrobatics upon the now infinitely pliable trampoline, the text. That is the declared arena from which all other aspects of being are not simply exiled but denied, in a severely Heideggerian voiding of being. But the end is no encounter of being, but an existential gesture in which the isolated mind encounters the void. Thus this arena allows no grandstand for spectators, or at least the performer must admit no grandstand, since the logical consequence of such an admission opens the established vacuum to being—to an intrusion of separate mind and an implication of a relation of sign to the signified. Thus the premise of the infinite text and the authoritarian play by the critic as poet explodes.

What one has is a strange principle of mind in relation to sign. A general anarchy of mind is the assumed prerequisite to the principle of an absolutism of the particular mind as the nearest that the particular mind may come to the pure vacuum of its arena. That assumption may not be given explicit assertion—though in fact it repeatedly is so given—since an assertion of the principle and a defense of it through signs is a contradiction of and so destructive to the initial article of faith: namely, the infinity of text, an infinity of the sign and any complex of signs including the defense. That article of faith must include the assertion of the principle itself, since the assertion is a text.

At this point of a radical absurdity of mind's indifference to sign—except as sign is assumed a prime matter for the performance of a world by the dancing, isolated mind—we discover the collapse of what in retrospect must be called at best a critical fad, Deconstruction. The evidence of that collapse is increasingly apparent, though the academy—always a decade or a century behind in its recognitions of untenable positions of mind—struggles to establish Deconstruction as part of an ordered curriculum. One need but read current catalogs from larger universities to discover the evidence. What is happening, beyond these belated official encounters, is a very ancient and inescapable principle of signs: a relation of an originating mind to the text itself. One need not deny ambiguity in signs to recognize as well the necessary consent of mind to sign. That consent is an action of finite mind in its attempt to establish a relation between its finitude and an infinitude which is not in the sign per se but subscedent to, and transcendent of, the sign. The effective demonstrations of the point one may explore in Eric Voegelin's *Anamnesis*, as his exploration there is complemented by Étienne Gilson's *Philosophy and Linguistics*.

Between the finite and infinite, sign becomes mediator, its engagement mediating and alleviating incommensurates in the mystery of the encounter of thought with being. The scholastic point (as in Saint Augustine and Saint Thomas) that sign cannot comprehend being, while it may lead to a despair of mind in its attempt to escape its own finitude or to an arrogance of presumption in declaring mind's infinitude as borrowed from the "text" of being, nevertheless reminds one that the implication of infinitude is not a property of sign itself but of that being toward which thought reaches through sign. Thus one must at last recognize the absurdity in the proposition that the sign—the text—has as its own property infinitude. What one recognizes in such games with signs is an intellectual alchemy, whereby mind would dance its own being as its own first and final cause.

What one has, then, is a gnosticism such as that which Eric Voegelin spent his life studying and exposing in its multiple manifestations in the sweep of recorded intellectual history. He comes to a recapitulation of his long quest in that compact, if finally incomplete, statement whose articulation he struggled with up to the very point of his death. "Quod Deus dicitur" is a reflection on what may be said about the mind's experience of the infinite through sign. It is a recalling to fundamental questions, a hopeful voice reaching us through signs. Even the academy, the center of intellectual confusions at this juncture of history, may well respond in a recovery from a Dadaist address to the problem of finitude's relation to infinitude, one species of the academy's Dadaist creations being the Deconstructionists. (It is not the *only* species, of course, another instanced by the confused salient of biotechnology, in which it is not easy to separate science from alchemy any more than in the confused battlefield of linguistics.) We shall, I believe, become increasingly aware—in and out of the academy—of the necessity of recovering that property common to mind, the sign itself. Thus we may recover some community of mind with the truth of things, a necessity more fundamental and complex than the shallow cries of alarm about education's getting *back to the basics*, a subscribed shibboleth which at the moment has no intellectual substance, only an impetus of confused alarm.

It is such an anticipation of a return to a sanity of mind that I find in the work of Eric Voegelin, in his concern for consciousness in relation to the complexity of existence, for instance. In this respect, he leaves us a considerable legacy. It is a prophetic gift that the poet, philosopher, theologian, scientist may both profit from and celebrate. For he has succeeded in recalling us to the known but forgotten gifts of voice in signs, that voice of thought deeper than merely the ear's response. He recalls the possibility of a community of mind whose geography is the border between finitude and infinitude. In this place of mind, between extremes, we may recover both the music and the gestures that mind makes in the immediacy of existence. He saw that we have allowed ourselves to be gradually wooed from that immediacy through mechanisms of mind taken as if movable type itself, developed through a series of questionable intricacies to new alchemistic formulas of the relation of thought to being. As we have done so, we have developed a new idol of mind, at the moment making us breathless with its spectacle. We have given it a mechanistic body refined almost to spirit, save for the continuing tribute of living mind sacrificed to it. The new homunculus, the computer, waits the collapse of mind, when it too must crumble as the mummy touched by the reality of air. Meanwhile, there is that quieter, slower, surer and more patient voice to guide us in this arena of our confusions so that we may at last put all man's makings—those of scientist or philosopher—in ordinate relation to being. If we happen to be poets, we might find the voice of Eric Voegelin to be our Virgil, leading us out of a collapse of mind toward mystery larger than mind, toward a recovered encounter with being.

VII. On *Fides*, *Intellectus*, *Ratio*

In my celebration of Voegelin, I nevertheless recognize certain difficulties with his position, inevitable to any struggle to control sign in an ordinate relation to the signified. It is certain that he expects of us that we test his signs in our common pursuit of the truth of things which those signs point toward. Consider as an instance the following sentences from "Quod Deus dicitus":

> We are not facing God as a thing but as a partner in a questing search that moves within a reality formed by participatory language. . . . The noetic search for the structure of reality that includes divinity is itself an event within the reality we are questioning. Hence, at every point in the process, we are faced with the problem of an inquiry into something experienced as real before the inquiry into the structure of reality has begun. The process of our *intellectus* in quest of our *fides*, a process that also can be formulated as our *fides* in quest of our *intellectus*, is a primary event.

The passage leads me to a speculative consideration of the appropriateness of or clarity of some of the several signs composing the passage, though I am carried by the general movement of those signs in such a way that I do not suppose myself misled. I recognize as well, of course, the possibility of my own mistaking of the signs here given. Nevertheless, the speculative commentary:

(a) Concerning *the structure of reality that includes divinity*: The assertion that "the noetic search" is "an event within the reality" being questioned by the act of the search itself addresses an inescapable problem: the searching mind may occupy no position that is not itself a part of the complex that mind would or might wish to be disengaged from in order to search reality "purely." The existence of mind makes that impossible, given the Thomistic "principle of proper proportionality": creatures (in this instance the discrete questing mind) *have* esse but *are not* esse; God alone *is* esse. This distinction points to the obstacle the philosopher encounters always in his attempt to *say* Being, as opposed to *pointing toward* Being, an obstacle Voegelin progressively engages. Nevertheless, in this last attempt upon the problem it leads to the complication of his saying that the structure of reality "includes divinity." The person of God is beyond thingness, in my way of pointing. But *person* as attached to the concept of mind is ours by our discrete existence, by our *having esse*. It is this incommensurate difference that handicaps us as we attempt to distinguish God from thingness. Hence there is a vagueness in speaking of the "structure of a reality" that "includes divinity." The same vagueness attaches to words if we speak of "facing God . . . as the partner in a questing search." I recognize the burden of difficulty that leads Voegelin here to speak more as poet than philosopher.

(b) Concerning the relation of *intellectus* and *fides*: If one moves (as I attempt to do) from a scholastic understanding of these terms as a means of intersecting the meaning Voegelin intends, *intellectus* and *fides* seem to me to lack the counterpoint (in one respect) and the complementary confluence (in another respect) that are clearer to me through the terms *intellectus* and *ratio*, terms the scholastic poses as modes of the soul's knowing. In these modes, that of the *intellectus* is of the "heart," that of the *ratio* of the "head." That is the viable distinction I think Saint Thomas makes when he says (in the *Questiones disputate de veritate*): "Although the knowledge which is most characteristic of the human soul occurs in the mode of *ratio*, nevertheless there is in it a sort of participation in the simple knowledge which is proper to higher beings, of whom it is therefore said that they possess the faculty of spiritual vision." This distinction I believe useful in the discussion of the text from the psalm, "The fool hath said in his heart, There is no God," a text upon which "Quod Deus dicitur" turns. The fool has not governed a negative act of faith, out of the "heart," by his rational faculty, and hence his "reckless" proposition. Rather the ground of this perversion of knowledge is in the angelic mode of knowing, the *intellectus*, in which ground lies that potential of denial which subverts the *ratio* in support of a rejection of being, first the soul's potential being, after which the *ratio* gains an apparent dominance. This is, I believe, the region Voegelin speaks of (in *Plato and Aristotle*) as the fall from being from whence the Dionysiac soul "must struggle in its ascent to God." In this view, the faith that God exists or the faith that God does not exist springs from the *intellectus* or is forced into the purview of the *ratio* from the *intellectus*. That is, the *intellectus* is, as it were, an initiating ground within the discrete soul, which the *ratio* as man's (the soul's) characteristic mode of knowing responds to. I believe that Voegelin's attempt is a recovery of this initiating experience of reality by the soul, to which the next point speaks.

(c) The *quest of our fides* as *a primary event*: Voegelin is concerned to recover a pristine encounter of the soul with reality—a Husserlian attempt as it were to get back to the encounter itself. The difficulty he engages is the circumstance of one's being born into history and therefore forced, as philosopher, to recover a prehistorical experience through intellectual act. That act attempts to exorcise the marks on the *intellectus* consequent upon being born into history. For Voegelin, this is a most Platonic concern, as if the primary event were a coming into the existential world out of a prior angelic mode of existence. The "fall" is thus a coming into history, which (were one a poet) might be described as William Wordsworth indeed does in his famous "Ode: Intimations of Immortality from Recollections of Early Childhood." The end desired by Voegelin is a recovery of a pure *fides* against the handicap upon the actions of the *intellectus* imposed by that characteristic mode of knowing, the *ratio*. It is an attempt through a philosophy in the Platonic mode to overcome what the Thomistic mode would name original sin, history itself in this respect an evidence of original sin. Or one might say that philosophy for Voegelin is the price historical innocence pays in consequence of its prehistorical, prephilosophical fall. If one is to make this attempt as philosopher, from Voegelin's point of view Plato is the point of departure. We note, then, Voegelin's remark in describing Plato (in *Plato and Aristotle*): "The philosopher is man in the anxiety of his fall from being: and philosophy is the ascent toward salvation for Everyman." In these words, seen in relation to "Quod Deus dicitur," we see how resolutely conscious Voegelin is, not only of the necessity of philosophy as the way to overcome the soul's entrapment by history, but of his version of Platonic philosophy as his own particular calling within history. To see this is to better understand that disinclination in him to be lured into the calling of the theologian. It is also to see why such a question as whether Voegelin is himself Christian is an inevitable one—unless we understand the pious response he makes to the particular gift he believes to be his: his calling to be Platonic philosopher. It is also perhaps to understand what he means, when pressed, by declaring himself a "Pre-Reformation Christian," though I believe he would wish us at last to appreciate his affinity to those Pre-Reformation Christians from Saint Paul to the early Middle Ages. One senses a greater comfort for him, for instance, to be found with Saint Augustine and Saint Anselm than with Saint Thomas in his last pursuit of an answer to Thomas's question: what may be said of God. It is as if he finds in them that necessary (to him) *epideixis*, a "pointing to" the complexities of reality, but finds in Thomas (I believe in a degree mistaken) an *apodeixis*, an attempt too severely given to logical demonstration.

VIII. On the Blessing of the Antecedent as Antidote to Negative Theology

One may reach a level of thought through the *ratio* which allows the mind to profess a strict empiricism or rationalism or nominalism or pragmatism—a pure system of symbolic pronouncements. But one does not arrive at such a purity of symbolic action having set out from the position itself. That is, the purist cannot start out from the position itself. He cannot start out as Socrates or Saint Paul ends, cannot be born mature, though the legitimate desire in us for perfection may too easily tempt us to distort the limits inherent in our finitude. Our willfulness may at once demand an angelic perfection of mind and protest that it is not ours at birth. One reaches an intensity of desire to *have fulfilled* potential, and that desire may lead us to distortions of the present we cannot avoid in relation to the past we would escape. Such is the existential ground of thought out of which utopian projections of the future are generated in a denial of the very reality of those grounds upon which present, past, and future are established. When such denials become programmatic in the public mind, there follows a general loss of reality—such as I contend to have occurred in Western civilization beginning with the Renaissance.

One reaches such a conditioning or wayward thought in relation to the symbols of thought through the desire's simplification of reality. That desire, though thus distorted, is not in itself the difficulty, since the desire, when ordinate, is a legitimate hunger for a perfection of the potential that is the very gift of our discrete being. This distorted thought may thus seem to us, not the constricted simplification of the complexity of thought itself in relation to the complexity of reality (which is mediated by the complexity of symbol), but a clear vision of reality, a visionary entry by thought into an absolute. A Descartes or a Bacon or a Locke may come increasingly to a simplified "vision" of the growth of his particular mind, only to discover at last that his visionary position cannot fully explain the mind that holds the visions. That is because the visionary mind can never be pure in itself. It cannot deny at last having risen to its supposedly pure position through a denial of the antecedent, a denial of the ground of the very rising itself.

Our experience of our own mind and of that world which is not mind is mediated, then, not simply by symbol structured in a visionary pattern out of desire insufficiently affected by the antecedent. The mediation begins at the most elementary ground of our being and of our coming to be, as when we are in our mother's arms (or *not* in our mother's arms)—to put the point in synecdoche in respect to the discrete soul's relation to the complexity of being. One's consciousness discovers one's self already possessed of a considerable inheritance of being when one first encounters the self in self-consciousness. But that is a reality which makes it difficult for the purist to forgive being itself, since it means the self is necessarily beholden to being. On occasion such an unforgiving purist self will respond to being as the transformed princess might to her peasant origins, by willful denial of reality. A Hobbes, nevertheless, in reacting to the metaphysical tradition that attempts to account for the conditions of being out of which such ungratefulness rises, cannot escape reality antecedent to his posited denial, though he may ignore altogether or symbolically restructure the antecedent. But the reality that an antecedent metaphysical tradition exists which has largely made the complex intellectual world out of which rises his own mind: that may be ignored only for an illusional moment. It is the prophetic poet-philosopher who must remind a Descartes or Bacon or Hobbes or Locke of this reality and so return him to the realities of being.

The point is that realities antecedent to, say, either empirical or rational attempts to limit being have already begun to enter thought out of the realities of being. They are realities requiring a sense of mystery as governing the rational or empirical pursuit of the truth of things because of the finitude of thought itself. Lacking that piety of mind required for such realization, one's thought can but become fanatic in its exclusions of complex reality, thus establishing the condition of the gnostic mind. Hobbes on the nature of the imagination is advancing a finite vision of the imagination, juxtaposed to antecedent finite visions of the imagination by the very symbolic projection he makes. He is not obliterating the antecedent, though the desire to do so is not wanting perhaps. Einsteinian physics does not obliterate Newtonian physics, though such is the nature of the mind's desire that it may too easily believe so. The Hobbsian or Einsteinian mind, such is mind's hunger for absolute vision, would obliterate antecedent representations of complex reality by asserting *The* reality of its imaginative vision. Progressively, the pressure from a legitimate desire, become inordinate in its desire for perfection, requires of the increasingly fanatic mind an obliteration of the antecedent.

That is surely one of the reasons John Locke's epistemology proved so captivating with the rise of our sense that power in the mind could command and transform being. The mind as *tabula rasa*, however, is posited when Locke's own mind is long since overwritten. And not the least scribbling upon it has been made by his Puritan family, within a pervasive climate of Puritan thought. (I have argued elsewhere that it is this climate of thought which largely introduced gnostic obfuscations of being, feeding a rationalist-empiricist-pragmatic programming of the popular mind, thereby establishing faith in a new beginning for mind in nature against all precedent history of mind in nature. Thus it becomes possible to build "a city on a hill" very far removed from Plato's or Paul's.) Lockean epistemology seems to make possible a self-generation of mind through an empirical command of the thing through the sign, whether that thing be the mind and its self-purified signs or corporeal creation itself. But there begins to grow a desperation out of this elementary attempt to restructure being itself to please mind's desire for self-generation, since the attempt requires denial of the antecedent. The desperation is exacerbated by the very necessity of either denying or ignoring the antecedent. Thus the anxious note struck by

Descartes, out of this desperation. It is "almost impossible that our judgments should be so excellent or solid as they should have been had we had complete use of reason since our birth, and had been guided by its means alone." A reminiscent note is struck in the lament, acknowledging the antecedent, but there is also a forlorn note in his "almost," suggesting that reason may yet expunge the antecedent.

As the reason attempts to establish absolute hegemony, an absolute measure of the truth of things that excludes the antecedent, it sees an unavoidable preliminary: it must first declare itself into existence *ex nihilo*, its Lockean mind as a *tabula rasa* the most niggardly admission of the antecedent possible—mind as blank being. The *ratio* is to make it what it is to be—a mind—through symbols structured. The symbolic structure then is declared the thing itself, created by the *ratio* out of the act of faith in reason's transcendence of being. There is finally, however, an inescapable contradiction in the structure which the actual mind, as opposed to the prescribed mind, cannot hide from itself; the *tabula rasa* is after all precedent. And so the continuing frustration to the fanatic gnostic *ratio*.

Perhaps it is the frustration resulting from the pressure of the antecedent upon the reckless *ratio* that explains a historical progression in the distortion of mind, a deconstruction of the antecedent in an illusional pursuit of the future. Eric Voegelin cites a repeated pattern of argument rising in the postmedieval world, in which the antecedent is declared benighted. His point of departure is Joachim of Floris at the end of the twelfth century. Gerhart Niemeyer, in *Between Nothingness and Paradise*, traces the line of descent to Hegel and Comte and others. Though there is variety of mind in this progression, they share a basic paradigm: the past is primitive; the present is an awakening from the primitive and thereby an anticipation of a quantum leap to a fulfillment in the future. But as the paradigm wavers and collapses in future failures—our present—the vision of reality narrows further toward abstraction in a frantic attempt by the *ratio* to escape not only the antecedent but the collapsing present; the *ratio's* visions of Beulah Land are downplayed. The narrowing, let me suggest, attempts to escape not only the antecedent but the immediate present, though there continues paradoxically a nostalgia about the future. To make the generalization somewhat clearer, the following:

We appear increasingly fascinated by and worshipful of an end thing born out of the rationalist-empiricist-pragmatic mind, a thing I have already designated the Idol, through which finite mind would lift itself out of creation. I mean the machine. The machine is the closest creature yet to an embodiment of the gnostic dream of Being transformed by the *ratio*. The machine, in and of itself, need not contend with problems of ontology and teleology. It is symbolic, then, of mind's escape of the antecedent, though at the popular level of this intellectual infatuation there is the delighted curiosity about the advance of one machine above all others, a delight that symptomatically elevates the NEW at the economic level, leading to our throwaway world. Ours must be the instant ontology of obsolescence. But there is an "original sin" revealed in that popular worship: the elevation of the NEW inescapably implies both the *old* and the yet *newer*. The religion of the machine is thus tainted by the worldliness of reality.

At a remove from the popular mind's fascination with the machine, at a metaphysical level of the *ratio's* dealing with being, the machine is an image of, an idol of, the gnostic *ratio* at its strictest. That is, the machine is man as man would be if the *ratio* alone constituted man. The machine's ontology and teleology are the same, from the point of view of the machine itself—which is the point of view the gnostic *ratio* pursues for itself. One sees such a desire surfacing, sometimes in comic aspect, the comedy itself a refutation of the end desired. I recall a colleague's impetuous remark, after a painful visit to the dentist: if God had had his wits about him, he would have designed teeth like phonograph needles, easily replaced when worn. Thus are we reminded by the reality of being itself of inescapable reality: the machine as creature and man as creature are separate orders of existences, however much one might confuse the distinctions by the fancy of metaphor.

The machine has as a part of its nature, as distinct from man's, a fulfillment of Descartes's wishful desire: it is born grown. One replaces it with an advanced species; it does not itself change. Still we hold fitfully to the dream desire, symbolized verbally as a perpetual-motion machine. Such a creature would necessarily gather being to itself in perpetuity. At our moment of history we seem to think ourselves very near a realization of such a machine, one that must at last transcend its own body. The computer, in the popular and in the professional view of it, is very nearly a machine beyond embodiment. That is one reason we become so sardonic in our attitude toward this dreamed man-as-god when we experience delay in the affairs of untransformed man himself. The computer is at times "down" as opposed to "up." The metaphorical symbols (*down* and *up*) are no accidental choices here. When the computer is "up" it has seemingly transcendent powers. When "down," it is inert prime matter, dead body. Such a climate of thought about the computer's being is reflected also in the mystique of its "silicone" element, the seat of its "soul," though this element (which within the reality of physical nature is a "compound") is a concession necessary to prior existence, anchoring even the computer in the antecedent. Nevertheless, one can believe himself as near to prime matter on a timeless stage as is empirically convenient. And from that nadir of being we may leap, miracle of miracles, beyond matter. Since thought itself is a transcendent, we may teach the machine to think. Already, as in my own institution, we have begun formal graduate programs in "artificial intelligence," programs that we declare an attempt "to program computers to think." (As we might have anticipated, the Japanese are already well advanced in the pursuit of this transformation.)

But always comes an intrusion upon such moments of our seeming transcendence of reality: the insinuation of the precedent which forces our own thought toward reconsideration of causes, raising as always the specter of first cause. It is the inexorcisable problem, whether one is attempting a Lockean declaration of political contract out of Lockean epistemology or a Darwinian declaration of evolution or the creation of a thinking machine that "really" thinks. The problem cannot be exorcised because any attempt to do so is necessarily initiated on the authority of a *present* initiating mind. By that mind's very presentness, it already demonstrates the antecedent. (Consider, for instance, the irony in the assumption of a primal purity of mind in this present moment as that primal mind attempts to image being as being was a million years ago.) With the computer, as *we* reflect on the *machine*, a second is added, as Plato or Aristotle or Saint Augustine or Saint Thomas would remind us. Thus the purity of the machine in its ontological-teleological simplicity is violated by that second, our own mind. For only the machine, in and of itself, may be said to be free of that given of our being, "personality," though we observe a sentiment in us whereby we personify our favorite machine as companion or adversary. Only the machine, from its own perspective (which we may enter only imaginatively), can be absolutely indifferent, disinterested in its origins or ends or in being itself.

Meanwhile, as always, we find ourselves caught in the mystery of the life of being itself, which the machine in and of itself may in no wise share. Thus it can be at best only a most pale and unpersuasive image of life. It is arresting demonstration of Plato's "shadow of a shadow." Which is to say that, through the strictures imposed upon being by the gnosticized *ratio*, that "scientific" mind (the machine) replaces Plato's mimetic poet as the distorter of reality, the traumatic consequences of which we must increasingly deal with in the body of community. For our world puts the machine at the center in ordering the *polis*. Community as body is thus revealed as deconstructed and restructured (since the Renaissance) as the machine called society, the symbiotic relation of which to the computer is conspicuous. The collapse of our mind's significant participation in the being called reality—at the political, social, economic, philosophical, theological levels of community mind—is the price we have paid. The price is signaled by such insistent symptoms of collapse as the destruction of the family or that haunting sense of individual alienation in which the deposed self violently reaches toward being for some accommodation to being. Indeed, much of our world's excessive violence, I contend, is this blinded attempt of existential mind to reestablish a relation to the antecedent, so that *this present* self may be accommodated to the antecedent. Without that attempt, there cannot even be any belief in the existence of the alienated self, that self which has been deconstructed by the gnostic *ratio*. But it has not been so absolutely decon-structed that it does not still bear the vestigial antecedent. The alienated self is the botched Frankenstein monster created by the fanatically gnostic *ratio*. In this light, perhaps violence is something hopeful in itself. And, as Eliot's old man says in "Ash-Wednesday," we might even rejoice in it, "having to construct something / Upon which to rejoice."

Afterword
Looking Before and After

Personality is that little private area of selfhood in which the person is at once conscious of his relationship to the transcendental and the living community.

A creature designed to look before and after finds that to do the latter has gone out of fashion and that to do the former is becoming impossible.

—Richard Weaver, *Ideas Have Consequences* (1948)

When *Modern Age* was very young (the winter of 1958–1959), Richard Weaver (who was a founding editor) wrote in its pages about his resolute struggle "Up from Liberalism." He was looking back on twenty-five years of his own intellectual history, as I have been doing in recovering these essays of mine. He recalls that in the autumn of 1939 he found himself driving west across Texas prairie toward a teaching post "in a large technical college," returning to a position that had become increasingly intolerable to him: "It came to me like a revelation that I did not *have* to go back to this job. . . . and that I did not *have* to go on professing the clichés of liberalism, which were becoming meaningless to me." It is one of the signs of the newfound freedom of spirit he was discovering that he did finish his contract at the outpost of technology and liberalism in the Texas prairie, though he stopped professing liberal clichés; his sense of responsibility to that new freedom would not allow him to chuck the job for which he had contracted without due notice in order to go home to the North Carolina mountains. (A different sense of freedom from Weaver's was to sweep the academic world in the years just ahead. "Freedom" in the realm of idea, divorced from responsibility, was to be used to justify "ripping off" that conveniently vague monster, "The System," whether *freedom* was twisted to mean abandoning a personal commitment or perverting a public trust.) In due time Weaver began a recovery of mind, an education denied him by the institutions he had attended, the result of which reeducation was his posthumous *The Southern Tradition at Bay*. (A memoir in *Modern Age* in the spring of 1987, by an undergraduate friend at the University of Kentucky, gives an account of Weaver as "liberal" thirty years before the essay.)

In "Up from Liberalism" Weaver very nearly touches upon the private, as opposed to the personal; upon an open moment of soul-searching as he recounts his journey to a position whose conclusions are at last firmly personal. The distinction between *private* and *personal* is not easily made in our world, though one may immediately recognize a difference between the ghosted Hollywood memoir on the best-seller list and Weaver's essay. As a people (a community of persons) the Greeks understood the distinction well at one period; they ceased to do so as their civilization decayed. One could, I believe, trace the symptoms of that decay from the plays of Aeschylus through Euripides and discover valuable lessons for our own age.

It will have to be, increasingly, a private attempt to do so. That is, in the academic current of the moment, a student is swept along by the latest fad in "thinkers" and except by fortunate accident is not likely to encounter and consider with his teachers and peers either Aeschylus or Euripides, or most of the great minds in the Western intellectual tradition. Those minds will continue for a while, a fading influence on our thought, a residual and vague presence at best. But the deliberate deconstruction of mind, justified by vague social concerns if justified at all, or by exigencies of production that demand stylized production of specialized minds, is so largely institutional policy now that it will dominate for some time yet. Recently at Stanford University, for instance, faculty and students in concert—by all accounts a minority of the affected—engineered a violent rejection of Western culture from their undergraduate study. The term *violent* applies, not only to argument as noise to drown out counterargument, but to actual threats of physical violence of such a sufficient likelihood apparently as to intimidate the administrative authority of that institution. The result has been to replace Homer and Dante in the undergraduate Western culture course with the latest radical thinkers on pop social concerns, those whom the particular instructor happens to be "into" at the moment. A scattering of the older minds are still named, but with texts unspecified, so that there can be no assurance that two students from Stanford, certified as Bachelors of Arts, will have read the same works.

What happened at Stanford has been happening, usually with less spectacle and so with less media notice, throughout the American academy, in witness of which is the surprising attention paid to Allan Bloom's scathing indictment of higher education, *The Closing of the American Mind* (1987). Secretary of Education William Bennett visited Stanford to defend Western civilization, a strange necessity but clearly a necessity. At Stanford on April 18, 1988, he gave a clear and effective defense, at the level of vital intellect, of "Why the West?" (published in *National Review*, May 27, 1988), and he has been increasingly under attack by vested interests of the academy since. Professor Sidney Hook analyzes the consequences of the Stanford event in *Measure* (April 1988) as an "Educational Disaster at Stanford University." But such is the impetus of intellectual decline in the academy that I do not believe their cogent arguments, nor Bloom's, will have the effect we should desire. At most I fear the effect will be that the entrenched deconstructors of mind will be more cautious about stirring a public interest in what is happening to our young minds, "our hope of the future," as they will be told by some visiting name on their graduation day. Too much public interest might prove dangerous, for common sense is still potentially viable in the public mind. It would be very dangerous to stir it too much.

The present educational establishment would have to be "born again" intellectually if we were to recover mind in its proper relation to the realities of the world. That is not a prospect which would lead Jimmy the Greek to give encouraging odds. Certainly the signs of a return to clear-mindedness about the common good are not propitious in the academy. For such has been the accelerating trend of public education, higher and lower, that touchstones to the common good, bequeathed us by Western civilization, are ghostly at best in our curricula. A more certain knowledge of our cultural heritage is needed than we possess as a society, even to reenlist common sense in its defense.

But for our present purposes, perhaps we may still recall the personal witness Sophocles's Oedipus bears in addressing the citizens of Thebes, in sharp contrast to the moment of private agony when he recognizes and accepts his failure as king (however much "fated" that failure). The playwright knew it would be a spiritual violation of the audience itself to present the open spectacle of Oedipus' blinding himself at that moment. For our part, we have become inured to the public display of the properly private, to obscenities treated with sentimentality. A mother crouches grieving near a twisted bike, clutching her dead child on a public street; a picture of her affronts us from the front page of our evening paper. A television reporter thrusts his microphone at the mother of an Atlanta black child whose body has just been discovered in underbrush and asks in tenderized tones how she feels on hearing the news; the camera zooms in on her tearful face while block letters give her name. The extreme naturalism of fact and image is assumed sufficient justification for such violence as if an extreme naturalism were the whole of reality and thus sufficient justification for transgressions upon human nature. Thus the victim is further victimized, though that victim will know instinctively that he is violated. Idle curiosity and a fascination with the sensational are thus pandered to at the expense of the unfortunate. Such violations of persons as we have illustrated are a consequence of what Weaver calls "the repudiation of sentiment for immediacy."

Moments of revelation touch us at the deepest, most private seat of our being, whether they are visions such as the mystic guardedly reports or invasions such as affront us daily in the press and on television. And thus affected, we bear ourselves as changed in the community of persons, either enlarged or reduced in our capacities as humans. But it is a dangerous intrusion to open the private to sentimental curiosity. Nor is the object of that curiosity, the distraught mother, the only victim. The intrusion erodes the curious person from within. The manipulators of power recognize the advantage of such erosion, as the history of the public trials in the Soviet Union between the two world wars will remind us. Public drama of this nature intends to drug community, not purge it, the litany of confessions dulling a person's response into bland conformity. Our current inclination in the same direction is signaled by the increasing pressure to televise courtroom trials, thus providing a new species of docudrama which purports to make us better citizens. When the private becomes steady fare like Saturday cartoons for the children, when person is reduced to individual in public spectacle, justice as a virtue will suffer the same fate that violence as a reality does when the cartoon character, smashed by a stone or riddled by bullets, appears undiminished in the next frame. The individual of today's show returns on trial tomorrow in a new frame of references to the idea of justice, an idea increasingly removed from concrete reality as the televised individual is removed from his personhood. Ideas will seem inconsequential to reality when they will have become in fact subversive of reality.

Richard Weaver, recognizing the complex relation of the personal and private and the danger to public health when the distinction is lost, revisits his own moment of revelation in "Up from Liberalism," but with a proper discretion. He does so to explain his new conviction that "somehow our education will have to recover the lost vision of the person as a creature of both intellect and will." For it is the person of intellect and will who must establish a public presence in any community that is truly free. Such distinctions are well-nigh lost beyond recovery when the private is deliberately turned into public spectacle, into such obscenities as I have mentioned as our daily fare. We find a range of violations, from intrusions upon obscure citizens in their moments of private grief to elaborate "happenings" calculated to affront community by personal self-destructions in X-rated movies and plays. The pietistic defenses of the media for presenting this range of violations, always in the name of freedom, are so shrill that the tone of that defense ought to alert us. And we were alerted by *Ideas Have Consequences* to "the extremes of passion and suffering . . . served up to enliven the breakfast table or to lighten the boredom of an evening at home. The area of privacy has been abandoned because the definition of person has been lost; there is no longer a standard by which to judge what belongs to the individual man. Behind the offense lies the repudiation of sentiment in favor of immediacy."

Weaver saw our world fragmenting in consequence of the manipulations of personal freedom, the person thus forced or tricked into abandoning community responsibility, till he is left at last merely an individual summed by statistics, whether through Nielsen ratings or five-year plans. In the isolation of his individuality, he becomes easy victim of ideology, from the right or left. For, while the person alone may be sustained in solitude by his sense of encompassing community, the individual discovers not solitude but merely loneliness. He is the more easily driven since his community hunger is reduced to herd instinct, to ideological shelters out of the terrors of alienation, little noticing the keepers who drive him to the pen. Through the fifties and sixties and seventies there occurs an acceleration of the individual's concern for what was camouflaged to resemble personal well-being by ideologues but which turned out to be a discomforting randomness in nature and community. Violating the springs of their own selfhood, of the person, individuals struggled to put on "life-styles" bought of the nearest purveyor in the exhilaration of a panic vision. Bought from cut-rate haberdashers who clip and stitch the latest ideas, insisting them the only suitable cover for one's personal and private intellectual nakedness.

What cause has legitimate call upon us as persons? What idea is capable of restoring us to our personhood? In a confused moment of history, Weaver steadies us. He knew, early enough to help us, that violence of language and to language speaks a person or a people dislocated from the surest grounds of ideas, from an old faith in being that is necessary to community vision and vitality. It is the loss of that ground that he explores in *Ideas Have Consequences*, especially as that loss is reflected in our shifting from a primary concern with *being* to the chimera of a *becoming* divorced from reality. The limits of one's becoming, he reminds us, are already in our limited being; our potential is implicit. But when our language shows us committed to "life-styles" (as if one might out of desire alone purchase a cloak of being, the new purchase detachable at will), we are already well on the way to self and community destructions, destructions that are dangerous at every level of our encounter with reality.

My appreciation of Richard Weaver's contribution to conserving thought is not of his originality, of course. (Originality is an idea that we easily transform into a personal idol.) Weaver's concern with "the person as a creature of both intellect and will" finds its roots in ancient minds; it is a concern common to many of those whom I have chosen as fathers, some of whom I have intended to celebrate in these pages. He and they intend to recall us to common principles of mind as mind engages the world with deliberate will. What he and Flannery O'Connor and Eric Voegelin and the Fugitive-Agrarians speak for in common is a sacrificial openness, a suspension of that self-interest that cultures our pride as a raw egg cultures the hidden violence of bacteria. This openness of mind to reality we sometimes call love (a root meaning in *philosophy*). Its general presence among men in community we speak of as piety, and it includes a discriminating as well as a sacrificial openness—a balance of will and intellect that allows and governs sentiment, lest sentiment decay into sentimentality. Within the common bond of such piety, one recognizes originality when it occurs as a gift of grace, welcomed and valued, but not idolized either for itself or in that medium to community, the person, through whom it is given in the common good. (With rare exception, genius shines through humility.)

In our company of like-minded wayfarers, one is thankful that the personal limits of our several callings complement each other. Some, failing to recognize that blessing, might find Richard Weaver alone somewhat thin. The leaven in his logic is wit and irony. In him one might miss the deeper resonances of a poet's words, or that humor one finds in Weaver's fellow Southerners William Faulkner or Flannery O'Connor. But by such variety of persons the largeness of humanity is enriched; by discriminating piety we share in a largesse of humanity beyond our personal limits. Richard Weaver in our pilgrim company bears himself with the steady resoluteness of the prophet, showing with devastating incisiveness where and how we have lost the vision of the person as creature, as Faulkner dramatizes it with poignant humor. Weaver's manner as prophet is very much the one we know in those persons who are our companions of mind descended to us through the Old Testament.

The poet's way and the rhetor's way are not the same. The poet has a different freedom—to range among human sentiments acting out a movement of soul in words; the rhetor's is to examine and maintain the intellect's responsibility to words as words touch reality. A rhetor like Weaver tests the poet's imaginative visions with and against the limits of mind, lest soul be seduced by masked illusion—especially through the nominalistic temptation to the poet as he loses his ground in reality. (*The Ethics of Rhetoric* is concerned with a false poetry, with constructions of words that do not establish a true relation of mind to reality.) The tensions between poet and rhetor since Plato reveal their symbiotic dependence, despite their popularized wars. Thus T. S. Eliot speaks for both poet and rhetor when he says of a common concern, having practiced both callings himself: "Speech impelled us / To purify the dialect of the Tribe / And urge the mind to aftersight and foresight." Mind thus engaged becomes one in a community of minds no longer restricted to a time or a place, becomes member in that body of a timeless community whether it find itself in a London publishing house or a Chicago university. Still, home "is where one starts from," as Eliot reminds us in a serenity of conviction. We return to that home at the end of all our exploring and at last "know the place for the first time," grace permitting. Russell Kirk tells us, soon after Richard Weaver's death, that Weaver expected to go back home to Weaverville, there to spend his full years "writing and meditating in the place where his ancestors had lived and died." But that would have to be after his battles in the outer jungles of modernism, and he never came to that earned retreat.

There appeared in the *Southern Partisan* in fall 1981 a memorial Weaver gave of his Uncle Doug, dead at ninety-seven. "The Pattern of Life" is poignant, hovering very near the private, as was proper enough since it was a eulogy within the bosom of the family, given at a reunion at Weaverville in August 1954. Uncle

Doug's life was one denied Weaver himself, not because he died young but because of the responsibility he felt to stay abroad. He chose to wage words with and for those of us who have lost the good of the intellect, have lost the old vision of order made possible through will and intellect joined in a service to the fullness of person and thereby to the good of community. "What an extraordinary thing it is in this age," he says in the eulogy to Uncle Doug, "and what a fine thing in any age for a man to sit on his porch and watch the shade tree he planted with his own hands grow for sixty years! . . . In a world where so much is superficial, aimless, and even hysterical, he kept a grasp upon those values which are neither old-fashioned nor new-fashioned, but are central, permanent, and certain in their reward." And what a valuable gift is left us, we say in turn, in *Ideas Have Consequences*, *The Ethics of Rhetoric*, *Visions of Order*, and *The Southern Tradition at Bay*. What a lasting help toward our recovering abiding values. Weaver's words clear away wild random inclinations of the will and intellect so that we may the more certainly watch the steady presence of the permanent at the center of any home we return to, eyes opened. A shade in a weary land of words.

And so this tribute to Weaver and Brooks and O'Connor and Solzhenitsyn and Voegelin and all the others I have been privileged to praise in words through these pages. Now is a moment of winter sun. I sit on my front porch in Crawford and look at trees I did not plant, able to value the planting and accept my continuing responsibility to the life dormant in them. Able to do so in part because of these and other companionable minds who are with me in very real ways in this very real place. They remind me that my intellectual and spiritual state is affected by my consent to their wisdom, though I am responsible not to accept as wise all that they may have bequeathed me. But such is the clarity of their vision of man and his nature that they insist I must choose to will, in either accepting or rejecting. I know from them that my willing is consequential to my being.

In neither realm, spiritual or intellectual, can I plead the determinist's escape. We are deeply affected by ideas only through our ratification of them by intellect and will—*deeply* meaning to the good of our being. Recognizing the point, we join them in the struggle to recover the piety Weaver discusses in closing his argument about the consequences of ideas, "the belief that personality, like the earth we tread on, is something given us." He adds, "The plea for piety asks only that we admit the right to self-ordering of the substance of other beings." Sitting on my front porch in Crawford, in the middle of a winter day, I recognize in those words a depth beyond the easy shibboleths of *freedom* and *personality* that assail us from every quarter from the parasites of being. The oaks look dead now, and certainly they appear threatened by heavy tangles of ivy and knots of mistletoe. But that is only an illusion in a leafless season, as we each realize when we are moved to aftersight and foresight.

Index

Academic poetry, 3, 6
Acton, Lord, 123
Adams, Henry, 48, 49, 50, 144
Adams, John, 67, 77, 89, 95, 100
Advertising, 113, 121, 147, 163
Aeschylus, 88, 102, 233
Agrarianism, 107, 121–22, 147, 148, 149–50, 153, 155–58, 160–66, 168, 171, 236
Aiken, Conrad, 63, 75
Alger, Horatio, 67
Allen, Robert, 98–99, 100
Anabaptist, 132
Anarchism, 112, 115, 132
Anaximander, 180, 181, 184
Anderson, Bernhard, 179, 185–86
Andrewes, Lancelot, 76
Anselm, Saint, 211–12, 216, 225
Aquinas, Thomas: on accidents of the local, 41–42; Aristotle and, 196; on art, 29, 34, 49, 50, 51, 203, 205, 212, 213; on being versus doing, 110; on hunger for possibilities, 13; on limits of knowledge, 192; on mind and machine, 230; O'Connor's interest in, 29, 31, 32, 34, 51, 201, 206, 210; on Paradise, 94; Pound and, 77; principle of proper proportionality, 223; on reason and understanding, 26, 129, 149, 206, 218, 219–20, 224; Sartre and, 36; on society, 111; on spiritual development, 17, 224, 225; on truth, 210–11, 214; Voegelin's interest in, 201, 216, 219–20, 224, 225

Ardrey, Robert, 106
Arendt, Hannah, 21–23
Aristophanes, 127
Aristotle: on art, 11, 29, 31, 50, 213; on being versus doing, 110; Dante and, 196; on *intellectus* and *ratio*, 129, 218; on nature of humans, 119, 218, 230; Plato and, 206; Pound and, 174; on social order, 111, 198; on spectacle, 103; on spiritual development, 17, 184; Voegelin and, 184
Arnaut, Daniel, 68
Aufricht, Hans, 179
Augustine, Saint, 132, 178, 192, 206, 211, 216, 225, 230
Avarice, 71–72
Aycock, Charles Brantley, 116

Babbitt, Irving, 48, 137
Bacon, Francis, 36, 134, 203, 226, 227
Baez, Joan, 148
Barfield, Owen, 192
Barry, Iris, 99
Baudelaire, Charles, 48
Beardsley, Aubrey, 98
Beat poetry, 3
Bennett, William, 233
Berns, Walter, 24–25
Berryman, John, 44, 46, 47, 49, 51
Bertrand de Born, 68
Biddle, Francis, 64
Bilbo, Senator, 166
Blackmur, R. P., 47, 48
Black supremacy, 123

Bledsoe, Albert Taylor, 115, 117
Bloom, Allan, 233, 234
Blunt, Wilfrid Scawen, 96–97
Brooks, Cleanth: as Faulkner critic, 39, 40–42; importance of, 51; influence on Weaver, 20; New Criticism and, 41, 44, 46; as Southerner, 41, 43–44
—works: *Toward Yoknapatawpha*, 39; *Understanding Fiction*, 51; *Understanding Poetry*, 42, 49–50; *William Faulkner: First Encounters*, 39, 40–42; *Yoknapatawpha Country, The*, 39
Brown, H. Rap, 63
Browning, Robert, 77, 87, 91, 92
Buckley, William F., 135, 136

Caldwell, Erskine, 152
Campbell, Donald, 24
Camus, Albert, 178
Capote, Truman, 14
Carson, Rachel, 106, 125
Carter, Jimmy, 132, 165, 170
Cavalcanti, Guido, 68
Cazmian, Louis, 49–50
Ceremony: definition of ceremonial awareness, 3; definition of, 5; families and, 7–8; festivals, 161–62; importance of, 4–6, 166; poetry and, 3–4; reduction of mystery from, 161–62; ritual compared with, 6–7; technology compared with, 6–7
Chamberlain, John, 116
Chaucer, Geoffrey, 1, 14, 16, 37, 74–75, 127, 196
Chesterton, G. K., 16, 96, 100
Christianity, 4, 48, 62–63, 70, 94, 95, 96, 102, 177–78, 179–81, 184, 186–87, 192, 193, 200, 201–2
Churchill, Winston, 70, 143
Cicero, 110
Cleaver, Eldridge, 63, 114
Clichés, 22, 25, 26, 37, 209
Coffin, William S., Jr., 141
Cohn, Norman, 132, 178
Coleridge, Samuel Taylor, 196–97, 207
Comedy. *See* Humor
Communism, 109, 160, 169–70
Community: disintegration of, 130; educated people's role in, 135; families and, 7–8; Frost and, 58; in *I'll Take My Stand*, 154–55; importance of past to, 166; and individuality, 235–36; as machine called society, 230; as mass murder, 20; mystery and, 154, 161; O'Connor's vision of, 32–33; Plato's views of, 199; Saint Paul's view of, 133, 135, 167, 186; spiritual nature of, 16; Voegelin's views of, 173, 176–77, 183, 186, 187; Weaver's view of, 111, 112, 236
Computers, 147, 229–30
Comte, Auguste, 15, 177, 228
Confucius, 4, 67, 69, 70, 72, 77, 84, 85, 95, 96, 100, 104, 105, 112, 174, 198
Conrad, Joseph, 91, 112
Corrington, John William, 181
Country music, 150–51
Cousins, Norman, 135, 143
Cowley, Abraham, 36
Cronkite, Walter, 142, 153, 169–70, 171

Dabney, Robert Lewis, 115–19, 126

Dadaism, 35, 36, 222
Dante Alighieri: beginning of
    wisdom, 103; Christianity and,
    62; compared with O'Connor, 30;
    compared with Pound, 89, 90, 94;
    compared with Solzhenitsyn, 139;
    as influence on Pound, 68, 77;
    intellect of, 88; knowledge and,
    99; language of, 2, 127; meaning
    of myth, 134; Minos in, 63; on
    money, 72, 73; and nature, 67;
    personal evil and, 71–72; Platon-
    ism of, 196; social order in, 111;
    spirituality in, 17
—works: *Divine Comedy*, 2, 4, 12,
    38
Darwinism, 217, 230
Davidson, Donald, 50, 107, 139, 149,
    150, 152, 238
Deconstruction, 44, 204, 220–23
Descartes, René, 36, 203, 211, 218,
    220, 226, 227, 228, 229
Dixon, Thomas, 118–19
Donne, John, 17, 35, 36, 37, 41, 61
Door, Julia C. R., 76
Dostoevsky, Feodor, 91, 133, 137,
    143
Douglas, C. H., 72, 77, 96
Douglas, William O., 122
Douglass, Bruce, 179, 180, 184
Dryden, John, 149
Dylan, Bob, 107, 114

Economic theories, of Pound, 71–73,
    77, 97
Edwards, Jonathan, 96, 143
Egalitarianism, 112, 124, 143
Eichmann, Adolf, 20, 21–22, 23, 25,
    26
Eliade, Mircea, 17, 134, 196
Eliot, Charles W., 131, 134–35, 137,

138, 142, 143, 144, 157, 158,
    160–61
Eliot, T. S.: beginning of wisdom,
    103; ceremonial nature of lan-
    guage, 5; Christianity of, 48,
    62–63, 70, 94, 95; classical versus
    romantic mind, 99, 108; concern
    for failure in poetry, 206–7, 208;
    concerns of poet and rhetor, 237;
    on despair and collapse of piety, 8;
    editor of Pound's essays, 78; on
    future, 127; on history, 11; influ-
    ences on, 47–48, 76, 85, 87; on
    language, 53; on lost causes, 103;
    major themes of, 104; on Milton,
    42; nature and, 105; personal evil
    and, 71–72; poetry of, 77; on
    Pound, 63, 72, 74, 93, 94, 95–96;
    Pound's message to, 86–87; recov-
    ery of myth, 196; renewal of, 51;
    separation of thought and feeling,
    149; view of universities, 104
—works: "Ash-Wednesday," 47, 48,
    231; *Four Quartets*, 47, 106, 175,
    207; "Gerontion," 48; "Little Gid-
    ding," 4, 185, 212; "Lovesong of
    J. Alfred Prufrock, The," 37, 75,
    122; "Sweeney Erect," 135; *Waste
    Land, The*, 26, 49, 91, 93, 185
Elizabethans, 36–37
Ellul, Jacques, 6
Emerson, Ralph Waldo, 88, 107,
    124, 125, 133–35, 143, 144, 159,
    181
Environmental issues, 125–26, 171
Epstein, Sir Jacob, 81
Euripides, 5, 108, 233
Evil: anger toward those who commit
    evil deeds, 24–25; Arendt's con-
    cept of, 21–23, 25; attraction to,
    25–26; cost of, 13; Eliot's views

of, 96; figures associated with, 20, 21–22; Original Sin and, 21, 24; potential of, 20–21; Pound's views of, 72; pride and, 72; Solzhenitsyn's views of, 168–69; Southern views of, 19–20, 169; tolerance toward, 23–24; usury and avarice, 71–72; Voegelin's views of, 179–80, 185–86; Weaver's view of, 112

Existentialism, 32, 108

Family, 7–8, 167–68
Faulkner, William: Brooks as critic of, 39; community in, 16; compared with James Joyce, 10; complexities of, 42–43; contributions of, 237; on critics, 42; depths of reality in, 15; evil in, 21; family of, 66; as God-haunted writer, 14; humor of, 237; importance of, 51; influences on, 43; ironies of history in, 44; self-made man and, 67; view of characters, 10; view of tradition and family, 67
—works: *Absalom, Absalom!*, 18, 152; *As I Lay Dying*, 41, 44; "Delta Autumn," 18; *Go Down, Moses*, 18, 152; *Hamlet, The*, 44, 152; *Sound and the Fury, The*, 43; "Spotted Horses," 10; *Unvanquished*, 153
Fides, 223–25
Fitzgerald, F. Scott, 14
Fitzgerald, Robert, 47
Fitzgerald, Sally, 28
Flaubert, Gustave, 14, 77, 93
Fonda, Jane, 148
Forrest, Nathan Bedford, 108
Francis, Saint, 101
Fredrickson, George M., 106

Freeman, Orville, 122
Freud, Sigmund, 50
Frost, Robert: ambition of, 56–57; community and, 58; compared with Poe, 52–54, 55, 56, 58, 60, 61; compared with Pound, 88; games in poetry of, 55, 58–60; Pound's encouragement of, 75; struggle between heart and mind in, 59–61; traditional forms of, 54; as wily Odysseus, 54–55, 60
—works: "Acquainted with the Night," 60; "After Apple-Picking," 55, 57, 58–59; "Birches," 56, 57, 58; "Boundless Moment, A," 57; "Death of the Hired Man, The," 59; "Desert Places," 60; "Design," 60; "For Once, Then, Something," 55, 57, 60; "Home Burial," 55, 59; "Mending Wall," 57–58; "New Hampshire," 55; "On the Heart's Beginning to Cloud the Mind," 59; "Road Not Taken, The," 56; "Runaway, The," 59; "Stopping by Woods on a Snowy Evening," 59–60; "Two Looks at Two," 59
Fugitive-Agrarians, 147, 148, 152, 153, 236

Gable, Sister Mariella, 34
Galbraith, John Kenneth, 122
Garson, Barbara, 64n
Genet, Jean, 108
Germino, Dante, 182
Gesell, Silvio, 72, 77, 96
Gilson, Étienne, 32, 45, 51, 209, 218, 221
Ginsberg, Allen, 3, 47, 71, 94
Ginzburg, Alexander, 140, 142, 170
Gnosticism, 139, 143, 144, 159–60,

162–63, 166, 168, 170, 177, 182, 183, 189, 197, 202, 207
Gogol, Nikolai, 133, 143
Goldwater, Barry, 117
Gonne, Maude, 77
Gordon, Caroline, 45, 51
Gorgias, 203–4
Gorky, Maxim, 143
Grady, Henry, 155, 156
Graff, Gerald, 14
Graham, Billy, 169
Grau, Shirley Ann, 14
Graves, Robert, 63
Green, Julian, 45, 178
Gromyko, Andrei, 142
Grotesques, 26, 134, 151, 152, 153, 154

Hallowell, John, 176, 182
Hardy, Thomas, 112
Harvard University. See Eliot, Charles W.
Havard, William C., 155, 176, 179, 182
Hawthorne, Nathaniel, 14, 26, 53, 54, 64, 67, 70, 107, 112
Hegel, Georg Wilhelm Friedrich, 154, 214, 218, 228
Heidegger, Martin, 179, 182, 185, 191, 220
Hellman, Lillian, 141, 142
Hemingway, Ernest, 14, 91, 136
Heraclitus, 26, 71, 129, 150
Higher education. See Universities
Hiss, Alger, 86
Historiography, 132
Hitler, Adolf, 21, 124, 141
Hobbes, Thomas, 226–27
Hoffer, Eric, 106
Holocaust, 20, 21–22, 64

Homer, 3, 4, 7, 17, 68, 69, 77, 93, 108, 134, 181–82
Hood, Sidney, 233
Hopkins, Gerard Manley, 34
Horace, 77
Housman, A. E., 78–79
Humanism, 141, 148, 160, 161, 162
Human rights, 133
Humor, 9–10, 36–38, 108, 169–70, 209, 237
Husserl, Edmund, 138, 179, 182, 224

I'll Take My Stand, 17, 19, 107, 122, 148, 150, 151, 154–55, 156, 158
Imagism, 80, 81, 82, 85
Individual sovereignty, 117–18, 128, 129, 131, 132, 135, 137–38, 144
Industrialism, 155, 156–59, 160, 162, 163
Intellectus, 26, 129, 149, 150, 151, 164, 206, 219, 223–25
Irony, 9–10, 37, 51, 58, 106, 163, 168, 170, 175, 237
Irvine, Reed, 169, 170

Jacobs, Jane, 121–22
James, Henry, 14, 64, 67–68, 70, 81, 112, 143
James, William, 96
Jarrell, Randall, 47, 49
Jefferson, Thomas, 67, 70, 73, 77, 95, 100, 117, 124, 143
Jensen, Arthur, 138
Joachim of Floris, 128, 228
Johnson, Samuel, 36
Jones, Jim, 20, 21, 23, 26, 131, 132, 133
Jones, Madison, 14
Jonestown massacre, 20, 128, 131, 132, 133

Jonson, Ben, 2, 36
Joyce, James, 9, 10, 35, 37, 38, 43,
    75, 112, 215, 216, 217

Kant, Immanuel, 129, 214, 218
Keats, John, 57, 196, 197, 206
Kelsen, Hans, 182
Kennedy, John F., 52, 141, 156
Kephart, Horace, 152
Kerouac, Jack, 6
Khrushchev, Nikita, 155, 170
Kight, Morris, 107
Kirk, Russell, 178, 237
Kobysh, Vitali, 169–70
Koestler, Arthur, 142
Kung, Hans, 70

Lapp, Ralph E., 106
Lawrence, D. H., 75, 85, 91, 112
Leibniz, Gottfried, 219–20
Lenin, Vladimir, 110, 154
Lévy, Bernard-Henri, 140
Lewis, C. S., 9, 39, 167
Lewis, Sinclair, 163
Lincoln, Abraham, 117
Literalism, 107, 108
Locke, John, 119, 134, 226, 227–28,
    230
Lowell, Amy, 81, 82
Lowell, Robert, 44, 46–49, 51
Lytle, Andrew, 14, 108, 152, 155

McCarthy, Joseph, 64
McCullers, Carson, 14
Macdonald, Dwight, 64n
McGill, Ralph, 156
Machiavelli, Niccolò, 16, 23, 112,
    128
McKnight, Stephen A., 172, 179
Mailer, Norman, 121
Malatesta, Sigismondo, 67, 91, 93

Manichaeanism, 28, 112
Manson, Charles, 21, 23, 26, 132
Marcuse, Herbert, 108, 111, 112,
    115, 156
Maritain, Jacques, 29, 45, 47, 49, 51
Marx, Karl, 72, 154, 157, 159, 160,
    177, 189
Marxism, 141, 142, 159
Masters, Edgar Lee, 56, 75
Materialism, 107, 112, 114, 121,
    147, 160, 169
Mencius, 174, 175
Mencken, H. L., 71, 74
Metaphysical poetry, 36
Millenarianism, 132
Miller, Christine, 128, 131
Milton, John, 31, 35, 38, 41, 42, 77,
    82, 88, 103, 149, 163, 171, 207–8
Mitchell, Margaret, 11
Modernism, 132, 144, 147, 148,
    157, 168, 171, 172, 178, 237
Modern Manichaeanism, 28–29
Molnar, Thomas, 140
Monetary theories, of Pound, 71–73,
    77, 97
Monroe, Harriet, 74, 75
Montgomery, Marion: works,
    Fugitive, 146, 147, 148; "Pro-
    phetic Poet and the Popular Spirit
    of the Age, The," 153–54
Moynihan, Daniel, 120
Mussolini, Benito, 70, 73, 85, 95, 96,
    100

Nader, Ralph, 132
Nashville Agrarians, 150, 156,
    164–65
Nashville Fugitives, 5
Nationalism, 130
Natural-rights doctrine, 168
Naturalism, 14, 15, 16–17, 234

New Criticism, 41, 42, 44, 46–47, 48, 49, 51
New Humanism, 148, 154, 160
New Left, 108, 116, 118, 119–20, 121–22, 127, 150
News media, 234–35
Nicodemis, 4
Niemeyer, Gerhart, 17, 129, 138, 178, 182, 228
Nietzsche, Friedrich, 172, 179, 189
Nixon, Richard, 141
Nominalism, 16, 20, 128
Norman, Charles, 72
Nouveaux Philosophes, 140
Nunn, Sam, 170
Nuremberg trials, 63, 64, 86

Occam, William of, 20, 128
O'Connor, Flannery: Agrarian arguments in, 168; artist's role as viewed by, 29, 31–32, 38; Catholicism of, 14, 30, 31, 34–35, 38, 44–46; community in, 16; compared with Voegelin, 200–207, 210, 216; contributions of, 51, 236, 237, 238; craftsmanship of, 29–30, 154, 203; definition of art by, 29, 31–32; depths of reality in, 15; on destructive separations, 160; on deterioration of U.S., 139; on evil, 13; grotesque characters in, 154; illness of, 33; and life's relation to art, 49; as Lowell's friend, 47; on middleness of reality, 13; modern Manichaeanism and, 28–29; New Criticism and, 51; as "realist of distances," 28, 29, 32, 202; reason and, 34; reviewer for Georgia Bulletin, 44–46, 200–201, 210, 218; on Southern writers, 152, 153; on Southerners

as storytellers, 151; on talents as gift, 32–33; as Thomist, 16, 29, 31, 32, 34, 51, 201, 206, 210, 212; vision of community, 32–33; on Voegelin, 200–201, 210, 218
—works: "Good Country People," 14, 26–27, 36; "Good Man Is Hard to Find, A," 23, 25, 26, 146, 152; Habit of Being, The, 28, 47; "Life You Save May Be Your Own, The," 156, 159, 163; Mystery and Manners, 28, 29, 30; Presence of Grace, 44–46; Violent Bear It Away, The, 13, 23–24, 46; Wise Blood, 11–12, 46, 152, 154, 171, 209
Optimists, 160
Original Sin, 21, 24, 72, 95, 149, 150, 184, 225
Ovid, 67, 68, 77, 93

Paideuma, 174
Paul, Saint, 4, 8, 32, 51, 77, 133–34, 167, 180, 181, 186–87, 191, 225, 226, 227
Perloff, Marjorie, 46, 49
Petronius, 7, 127
Philosophes, 16, 140
Philosophy, 175–78, 185–86, 214
Pieper, Josef, 129, 156, 162
Piety, 3, 33, 108, 120, 124, 152, 173, 185, 201, 236, 238
Pisistratus, 1
Plato, 224–25, 227, 230, 237; disparagement of body, 176; on the fool, 208–9; Idea as transcendent, 56; on intellectus and ratio, 129, 218, 224–25; Locke and, 227; on metaxy, 143, 172; on mind and machine, 230; on myth, 134, 190; on One and Many, 119; opposi-

tion to Sophists, 217; on poets, 55, 177, 194–200, 203, 211, 215–16, 237; Pound and, 174, 197–199; Voegelin's interest in, 172, 177, 178, 184, 185–87, 190, 194–96, 199–200, 201, 206, 207, 208–9, 215–16, 217, 224–25

Plutarch, 2

Poe, Edgar Allan, 52–54, 55, 56, 58, 60, 61, 81, 87, 152

Poet: Eliot's view of, 237; Plato's view of, 55, 177, 194–200, 203, 211, 215–16, 237; Pound's view of, 67, 68, 77, 84–86, 90–91, 197–199; role of, 237; Voegelin's view of, 194–96, 199, 200, 205, 206–7, 209–10, 213–16

Pope, Alexander, 37

Populism, 164–65

Porta, Giambattista della, 124–25

Pound, Ezra: anthologist aspect of, 92–94, 105; arrogance of, 85–86, 90–93; bohemianism of, 86; charges of treason, 64, 68, 75–76, 85, 92, 101; Christianity and, 62, 96, 102; compared with Voegelin, 174–75; condemnation of Franklin Roosevelt, 64, 68, 73; death as theme in, 70–71; declaration of insanity of, 63, 74, 83–84, 86; defenders of, 63; degeneration of America, 64; economic theories of, 68, 71–73, 77, 97; editor of Exile, 76; Eliot's views of, 63, 72, 74, 93, 94, 95–96; encouragement of other artists, 75; on evil, 72; family of, 65–66; as fanatic, 74–75, 77, 84–85; geographic place and, 1, 112; as God's fool, 64–65; images of spider and web, 94–96; importance of language for, 5–6; in-

carceration of, 63–64, 97, 98–99, 100; influences on, 65, 67, 68, 77–78, 87, 100, 197; interest in capital of art in America, 72–73; on language's relation to the mind, 82–84, 93; Mussolini and, 70, 73, 85, 96, 101; perfectibility and, 62–63, 67, 112; poetry of, 77–85, 86–93, 189; on poet's role, 67, 68, 77, 84–86, 90–91, 197–199; pragmatism of, 70; public image of, 63, 85–86, 100; and publicly supported academy of artists, 69; recognition of own failure, 71, 94; relation of order to beauty, 174–75; respect of nature, 66–67; on tradition and family, 67–68, 69–70; as troubadour, 68; on universities, 104, 174

—works: ABC of Reading, 77–78, 90; "Aube of the West: Venetian June," 90; "Ballad of the Goodly Fere, The," 89; Cantos, 65, 68, 71, 72, 73, 82, 85, 88, 89–90, 93, 94, 95, 97, 104, 174, 175; Chinese Cantos, 93; "Credo," 81; "Envoi," 81; Fifth Decad, 97; Gaudier-Brzeska, 82; Guide to Kulchur, 78, 198; "Historian," 89; "Homage to Sextus Propertius," 68; Hugh Selwyn Mauberley, 81; "Indiscretions, or Une Revue de Deux Mondes," 65; introduction to Confucius to Cummings, 99; Jefferson and/or Mussolini, 73, 198; "Lake Isle," 78–79; Literary Essays of Ezra Pound, The, 78; Lume Spento, A, 90; "Masks," 88–89; "Mesmerism," 87; "Monumentum Aere," 92; "Mr. Housman at Little Bethel," 78; "Mr. Housman's Message," 78; "Mr. Shakespeare's Message," 79–80; "Pact," 87; *Patria Mia*, 68–70, 71, 74, 77, 95; "Pax Saturni," 92; *Personae*, 80, 87, 94, 96; *Pisan Cantos*, 66, 78, 87, 98, 198; "Plotinus," 87; *Poetry*, 78; "Portrait d'une Femme," 80; "Retrospect, A," 78; "River-Merchant's Wife, The," 80, 89; "Seafarer, The," 79, 89; "Sestina: Altaforte," 80; *Sordello*, 87; *Spirit of Romance, The*, 78, 89; "Virginal, A," 79

Pound, Homer Loomis, 65
Pound, Thaddeus Coleman, 65–66
Pragmatism, 107
Primitivism, 17
Privacy, 233, 234–35
Progressivism, 116, 124
Protest movement, 107, 112, 114–15, 116, 118, 119–20, 127, 139, 149, 150, 156–57
Provincialism, 1–4, 17, 49, 126, 138, 139, 153, 154, 157, 166, 170
Psychology, 14–15, 23–24, 144
Puritanism, 64, 70, 107, 227

Quintilian, 56

Racism, 116, 165
Rankin, Jeanette, 114, 115
Ransom, John Crowe, 46, 47, 48, 49
Ratio, 26, 129, 149, 150, 151, 159, 162, 164, 206, 218, 223–25, 228–29, 230, 231
Reason, 26, 122–23, 129, 149, 150
Reed, John Shelton, 155
Regionalism, 1–4, 140, 153–54, 157, 166, 170
Rexroth, Kenneth, 6
Ribicoff, Abraham, 122

Rituals, 6–7
Robertson, Ben, 152, 167
Robinson, E. A., 2–3, 55, 56, 197
Rodham, Hillary, 118
Roethke, Theodore, 47
Roosevelt, Franklin, 64, 68, 70, 73, 143, 160
Roosevelt, Theodore, 134
Rothschilds, 72, 73
Rusk, Dean, 141

Sacks, Oliver, 43
Sakharov, Andrei, 170
Sandburg, Carl, 57, 75, 88
Santayana, George, 48, 50, 137, 144
Sappho, 77
Sartre, Jean-Paul, 32, 36, 56, 107, 108, 179
Schwartz, Delmore, 47
Science, 123–26, 130, 137, 151, 163
Science fiction, 34, 36
Scientism, 157
Shakespeare, William, 2, 35, 40, 56, 79, 119
Shaw, George Bernard, 211
Shcharansky, Anatoly, 140, 142
Shelley, Percy Bysshe, 196, 197–98, 199, 200
Sheridan, Philip Henry, 108
Sherman, William Tecumseh, 108
Shockley, William, 138
Sidney, Sir Philip, 78, 195, 196
Slavery, 123, 165
Socialism, 121, 141, 160
Sociology, 14–15, 23–24
Socrates, 56, 72, 84, 195, 200, 201, 208, 226
Solzhenitsyn, Alexander: contributions of, 238; on disintegration of West, 139, 164, 168–69; distinction between Russian spirit and

communist ideology, 170; exile
of, 136, 142, 146–47, 153; Harvard commencement address, 128,
131, 133, 135–37, 139–40, 141,
142–44, 147, 148, 158, 159, 160,
169; on individual sovereignty,
135; as literary figure, 142–43,
148; men of the soil versus people
of the air, 153; portrait of Ivan
Denisovich, 136, 140, 153; portrait of old Russian intelligentsia,
136, 137–38; repression of, 170;
as Southerner, 153; on spiritual
development, 139, 140–44, 149,
164, 168–69; welcome in U.S.,
136, 142
—works: *From under the Rubble*, 19,
136, 137, 148; "Smatterers, The,"
19, 136, 137, 140, 153
Sophists, 201, 216
Sophocles, 2, 4, 88, 90, 99, 234
South: bardic mind of, 122–23,
151–52; Civil War and, 155;
importance of family in, 150,
167–68; literature of, 152–53;
militarism of, 109; politics of,
116–17, 165–66; suspicion of traveling salesman, 163; values of,
109–10, 114, 116, 118–19, 150,
151, 155–56; view of evil, 113;
view of nature, 151, 155–56; view
of reason and understanding,
150–51; science and technology,
123–26, 151
Spellman, Francis Cardinal, 31
Spengler, Oswald, 217
Spenser, Edmund, 196
Stalin, Joseph, 1, 21, 140, 141, 142,
154, 158
Stassinopoulo, Arianna, 140
Steinbeck, John, 115

Stendhal, 99
Stephens, Alexander, 115, 117, 119
Stevens, Wallace, 57, 58, 197
Stock, Noel, 93, 94, 96
Stoicism, 48, 144
Strauss, Leo, 106, 128, 129, 132
Suetonius, 119
Sunday, Billy, 96
Surrealism, 35
Swift, Jonathan, 37, 38
Swinburne, Algernon, 77, 87

Talmadge, Gene, 166
Talmadge, Herman, 166
Tate, Allen, 1, 2, 17, 47, 48, 49, 63,
139, 153
—works: "New Provincialism, The,"
1, 19, 49, 126, 138, 139, 140;
"Ode to the Confederate Dead,"
50, 91, 152; "Robert Frost as
Metaphysical Poet," 56, 57–58
Tate, Caroline, 48
Technology, 6–7, 112, 118, 123–26,
147, 155, 229–30
Teilhard de Chardin, Pierre, 187,
190, 191
Tennessee Valley Authority, 122, 125
Tennyson, Alfred Lord, 79, 88
Thomas Aquinas. *See* Aquinas,
Thomas
Thoreau, Henry David, 107, 155–56
Thucydides, 5, 7
Tiger, Lionel, 106
Tolkien, J. R. R., 33
Tolstoy, Leo, 133, 143
Toynbee, Arnold, 193, 217, 218
Tragedy, 108
Transcendentalism, 107, 124
Turgenev, Ivan, 143

Understanding, 26, 149, 150

Universities: academic "establishment," 120; administrative promotion of athletes, 130–31; and
education of elite, 134–35, 137;
facts and statistics and, 129–30;
graduate versus undergraduate
teaching, 39–40; humanistic concern in, 131; intellectual decline in,
233–34; modernism and, 157;
Pound's views on, 174; publishing
and, 44; research in, 130; specialization in, 40, 41, 44, 135;
supply and demand in, 120; undergraduate education at Stanford
University, 233–34; Voegelin's
analysis of, 138–39, 174; Weaver's
view of, 104
Untermeyer, Louis, 57
Usury, 71–72, 77

Van Buren, Martin, 93
Vanderbilt Fugitives, 77
Vidal, Gore, 106, 115, 123
Villon, François, 67, 91
Virgil, 74, 88, 99, 186, 223
Voegelin, Eric: on antecedent as antidote to negative theology, 225–31;
Christianity of, 177–81, 184, 192,
200, 201, 202, 225; on community of mature men, 173, 176–77,
183, 186, 187, 189; compared
with O'Connor, 200–207, 210,
216; compared with Weaver, 106;
contributions of, 172–73, 211–12,
236, 238; on Deconstruction,
220–23; deconstruction of human
life, 154; on deformation of reality, 142; early interest in neo-
Kantian positivism, 182, 184;
Eliot and, 175; on *fides, intellectus, ratio,* 223–25; on the fool,

194, 200, 207–12, 215; Harvard
address on "Immortality," 138; on
In-Between, 143, 148, 172, 176,
184, 205, 212, 215; on intellectual
climate of U.S., 138–39; on limits
of logic to the visionary, 215–16;
on modernism, 132–33; on mystery, 177, 184; on myth and
countermyth, 184–85, 216–18; on
new gnosticism, 51; O'Connor's
reviews of, 45, 200–201, 210,
218; on philosophers' common
ground, 219–20; on philosopher's
role, 175–78, 185–86, 193; on
piety, 185; on poet's openness to
being, 210–15; on poet's role,
194–96, 199, 200, 205, 206–7,
209–10, 213–16; on provincialism, 17; on reconstruction of
reality to fit millennial dreams,
20–21; on secular gnosticism, 159;
on signs in relation to reality, 25,
176, 184, 194, 196, 215, 218–19;
suspicion of man's desire for rest,
178–79, 181–84; theory of consciousness, 185–93
—works: *Anamnesis,* 181, 182,
188–89, 190, 221; "Concrete Consciousness, The," 188–89;
Ecumenic Age, The, 174, 181,
182, 183, 184, 186–87, 190, 191;
Enlightenment to Revolution, 129;
*From Enlightenment to Revolu-
tion,* 188; "History and Gnosis,"
180; "Immortality: Experience
and Symbol," 180; *Israel and Revelation,* 218; *Order and History,*
173, 174, 179, 182, 187, 201,
204; *Plato and Aristotle,* 185, 195,
201, 224, 225; "Quod Deus dicitur," 194, 200, 201, 208–9, 214,

217, 222, 223–25; *Science, Politics, Gnosticism*, 129; *World of the Polis*, 210
Voltaire, François, 128, 140
Vorticism, 80

Wallace, George, 121
Warren, Robert Penn, 20, 42, 49–50, 51, 104, 152, 160, 167
Watson, Tom, 121, 166
Weaver, Richard: Agrarian arguments in, 168; being versus doing, 107–8, 110; contributions of, 127, 237, 238; on deterioration of U.S., 139; editor of *Modern Age*, 232; education of, 103–4, 232; membership in American Socialist party, 103; mind as agent of being, 105–6; nature of order in, 110–11; organic metaphor for continuity of society, 105; particularism of, 104; on patriotism, 121; on provincialism, 17; reading of first-hand accounts of Southerners, 104–5; reviews of works, 115–16; sense of geographic place, 111–12; sense of history in, 119; on sentimentality and brutality, 20; Southern bardic mind and, 122–23

—works: "Aspects of the Southern Philosophy," 108, 109–10, 114; *Ethics of Rhetoric, The*, 237, 238; *Ideas Have Consequences*, 20, 103, 107, 126, 128, 129, 156, 232, 235, 236, 238; "Pattern of Life, The," 237–38; *Southern Tradition at Bay, The*, 20, 104, 108, 123, 126, 127, 151, 232, 238; "Up from Liberalism," 232–33, 235; *Visions of Order*, 238
Welty, Eudora, 162
Weyl, Nathaniel, 86
Wheeler, Joe, 118
Whitman, Walt, 47, 54, 57–58, 68, 87–88, 94, 95, 105
Williams, William Carlos, 52, 53–54, 56, 61, 66, 77, 85, 95, 105
Wilson, Woodrow, 118
Wit, 9–10, 36–38, 51
Wittgenstein, Ludwig, 214
Woodward, C. Vann, 155
Wordsworth, William, 37, 57, 84, 90, 97, 103, 129, 150, 196, 225

Yeats, William Butler, 3–4, 5, 42, 75, 78, 79, 85, 94, 105
Yerby, Frank, 11
Young, Stark, 17, 116